Episodes

in a

Cultural

Revolution

FOR LILY - THANK FOR
ALL YOUR HELP!

♡ lin

lin gentry

Fulton Books
Meadville, PA

Published by Fulton Books 2022

ISBN 978-1-63985-588-9 (paperback)
ISBN 978-1-63985-589-6 (digital)

Printed in the United States of America

For my beautiful goddaughters Paige and Drew Bonwood, who are my heart and my inspiration. This is my legacy dedicated to them.

Acknowledgments

Christine Bahr
Margo Dean
Jean Gregory
Marilynn Hall
Patricia McBroom
John McCutchen
Melinda Maxwell-Smith
Gail Onion
Kim Rowley
Kimber Selvidge
Bill Wittmer

I took my power in my hand and
went against the world.

—Emily Dickinson

Prologue

I was born in 1946. By the time the 1950s began, I already sensed the repressive attitudes influencing my life. No longer okay to go shirtless, I was painfully aware that the male of the species was much freer to act as they wished.

From kindergarten onward, it was obvious that I was challenged socially, and teachers even wrote to my parents of their concern that I sat alone and seemed unable or unwilling to mingle or play with others. My parents scoffed.

But the gender roles were already laid out, and I felt I fit in with neither the boys nor the girls. Uncomfortable with curly locks and frilly frocks, I coveted the male privileges already evident.

Precocious in studies and large for my age, the system seemed hard-pressed to ascertain where I belonged, so they skipped me to a higher grade, exacerbating my inability to fit in.

I idolized my dad who symbolized the power and personal freedom of men while my mother seemed passive and depressed, modeling the plight of the feminine. I eschewed Mother's role and spent the 1950s earnestly wishing magically to turn male with every succeeding year's birthday candles. Prepuberty dashed my hopes with the appearance of tiny breasts.

Though still quite young as the 1960s dawned, I became sexually active in an age where birth control was as yet inaccessible and my sexual desires were compellingly strong. I fretted about unwanted pregnancy yet seemed always to escape the consequences of young sex, again contributing to my fears that I was not quite normal.

Off to college at a mere sixteen years old, I discovered the freedoms to dress as I liked, choose whether to attend classes or not, and indulge in excessive drinking which provided a balm for my social inadequacies. After two years in a sleepy college hamlet, I began ferrying students to the Bay Area on weekends and became immersed in the progressive unrest of Berkeley post-Free Speech Movement. It was comforting to find other misfits, and it seemed an obvious choice to drop out of college and join those who would come to be called hippies.

The counterculture was vibrant, and it was hoped that the Vietnam War and the system which created it could somehow be overturned with love. The Summer of Love celebrated drugs, sex, and rock and roll while the military draft birthed all manner of protest, from picket lines at the induction center to emigrations to Canada.

As we moved toward the seventies, having ended the war and passed the Civil Rights Act, my rebellious nature steered me toward nontraditional job choices which frequently meant bashing barriers and entering more and more male-dominated terrain. Due to societal norms that still required a woman to wear a dress in any sort of remunerative employment, I instead targeted jobs which would either put me in a uniform or allow me to wear jeans.

The list of jobs spanned clerking at the post office, taking tolls on the Bay Bridge and to the city of Oakland, first as a meter maid, then municipal gardener, and, finally, as the first woman firefighter in the Oakland Fire Department.

Continuing in the childhood vein, in each position I was the outlier—only the third woman to take toll (aside from women who filled in during World War II and then were handily laid off when servicemen came home), the second woman to be a city gardener—and then the pinnacle of personal challenges came with the fire department. The year was 1980.

I hope my story resonates with those who metaphorically defied No Trespassing signs, entered worlds they were told they couldn't inhabit, cultures where they were unwanted, and took on challenges where they were assured they could never prevail.

Enjoy the journey.

Above all, be the heroine
in your life, not the victim.

—Nora Ephron

Episodes in a Cultural Revolution

Hoppy was always my main man. Hopalong Cassidy was the scion of the Wild West and early broadcast television. Along with my dad, he was my model of daring, adventure, and virility.

I was completely decked out with Hoppy drag—hat, boots, pearl-handled six-shooters, even fringed gloves and chaps. I practically slept in that outfit.

One of the most treasured photos I have of my childhood is me in my Hoppy costume (less the chaps), with hands on my gun butts and a Band-Aid on my knee. The Band-Aid wouldn't have shown, but with my mother's insistence in once again trying to force me into a dress, she had won the round on the day of this snapshot. In the picture, I looked ready to take on any bad guy you could serve up.

I supposed if my family was really paying attention or concerned about my development, they might have noticed that Hoppy was teaching me what I needed to know to be an honorable man. This was perhaps counterproductive if they were truly invested in churning out a young woman in the 1950s.

The clash between my fantasy life as a boy and the girl in the ubiquitous skirt for school set up a deep schism. And bridging this gap has been the focus of the bulk of an adult life spent healing childhood issues.

Hoppy wasn't the only costume. Today, rabidly pacifist and detesting the current war-mongering administration, I reflect on the little girl dressed as a soldier, climbing through the trenches which were later to become the infrastructure of a freeway interchange. Whatever part of my allowance wasn't squandered at the local record store on the emerging and exciting rock and roll of the time was spent in the adjacent storefront—an Army-Navy surplus store.

When entirely put together, my soldier ensemble included shoulder patches, ammo belts, cartridge cases, even a gas mask. Before donning our helmets and heading to the trenches, the neighborhood boys and I would even soak rags in ketchup and wrap our limbs in faux bloody bandages. What a fright we were to our mothers!

But the irreconcilable part continued to be the wardrobe struggle in school each day. God, how I hated being commanded to put on the dreaded dress! It was contrary to everything I was about in my mind. On the home front, all my peers and playmates were the neighborhood boys; the girls wanted to do stupid things like dress up dolls and play house.

When I got home from school each day, it was like a scene from *Superman*, another favorite TV hero, stepping into a phone booth and ripping off his street clothes to assume his accustomed identity. I couldn't wait to tear off that dress and get back in my jeans! Everything about the school outfit made a liar out of me and my true identity as a boy. Every birthday until I sprouted breasts, my wish upon the candles was that I would awake in the morning and be male.

Breasts pretty much ruined that dream, and I think at that point I liked my birthday just a little less.

I remember a babysitter we had, a mere neighbor girl, who refused to take me along on an outing to the movies to see *20,000 Leagues Under the Sea* unless I put on a dress. I held out but so did she, and to this day, I've never seen the film. Who did she think she was to try and exert such parental controls?

And anyone you ask who knew me at the time would tell you that the very term *parental controls* was an oxymoron. There was very little in my life that had the stamp of parental direction.

Ask Mrs. Murray, who twice busted me for my fascination with risky elevations. When I was just two, she called in a panic to tell Mom I was atop my dad's fifty-foot ham radio tower. The tale is legendary in the family mythology. Mother came out into the yard to retrieve me from the tower, and as she began to climb, she reported I growled out, "I can get down by myself!" I did.

Next morning, when I ventured into the yard for a repeat of my aerial feat, the bottom rungs of the tower ladder had been removed by my dad to prevent any recurrence. I stormed into the house and demanded, summoning as much authority in my voice as possible at two, "Who took *my* steps?"

Six years later, the very same nosy (I suppose well-meaning) neighbor called again, this time to rat me out for being atop a pile driver adjacent to the ongoing freeway construction. Same old story, only this time I was put on KP to do dishes for the next six months.

But for the most part, I flew under the radar, disappearing for entire days until time to return to the supper table. If my father was traveling on business (a frequent occurrence), even that family ritual was barely observed. I remember hanging out in the garage of an elderly neighbor while he tinkered at his workbench. When he attempted to shake his *shadow* by inquiring, "Don't you need to get home to dinner?" I informed him that when my dad was out of town, we didn't eat dinner. My mother would have blanched if she'd heard this. Then again, it would be more characteristic for her sadly to wag her head and shrug her shoulders.

Our neighborhood was idyllic, filled with fruit trees, open land, and vacant lots where our mock Army battles were waged and pasture areas with the occasional docile horse. Another tale my mother relished in telling was of me, way too small to be missing for several hours, finally discovered inside the barbed-wire fence of a field, reaching up on tippy-toes to pet the muzzle of a quite-large horse. A nervous woman, a stranger to my mother, was wringing her hands and fretting aloud, "That's a mean horse. Someone should get her out of there."

In memory, this is one of the few times my mom was paying enough attention to actually come looking for me. I have other memories, like the time in Eulie Forbragg's swimming pool. I couldn't yet swim but was bouncing around in the shallow end. Mom was talking to a friend, her back to me, and in water just around her chest. That would be water that's over my head. As I approached in an effort to get her attention, I started to lose contact with the bottom surface. While I watched her back, my mother was oblivious as I began struggling to get my breath above the surface.

Who knows the reality of such memories. I continue to hold a grudge for my mother almost letting me drown. If it weren't for her friend finally noticing me bobbing up and down like a soggy cork, again, who knows? But the feeling I carried in my heart was simply that no one was watching.

Travels with Dad

We had a lot of time together, my dad and me. For the first several years, I traveled with him on his business trips. I have some cute snapshots of me in my Hoppy studded jacket, little cardboard suitcase in hand, wearing my other favorite chapeau—a Daniel Boone coonskin cap. In this picture, I'm leaning against our '54 Olds just before departure on a road trip.

He was busy building a communications empire, starting with Elko, Nevada. He drove from Walnut Creek to Elko approximately three times a week. For this journey of several hundred miles, I was frequently along.

I was game for anything. Dad and I traveled up mountains on packhorses to visit microwave installation sites in the Ruby range of eastern Nevada. We were led by a real-live cowboy, the owner of the pack string, and dined along the way with Basque sheepherders encamped on the slopes who served us stew cooked over their campfire. Fairly romantic stuff for a six-year-old. Then again, my dad was a fairly romantic character.

We would also venture out on his business trips via private aircraft. I remember one particularly frightening morning as we prepared to depart for New York from Buchanan Field, the small municipal airport not far from our home.

The plane belonged to a local millionaire, back in a time when there didn't seem to be that many. Stanley Dollar (ironically enough) had huge land holdings in Contra Costa County. In later years, pieces were sold off to contain development of my first high school, lots of subdivisions, and even the Rossmoor Leisure World senior community, one of the first of its kind.

But this particular morning at Buchanan, it was too densely foggy to take off, so we all were busy waiting. The men (I seemed always to be in the company of a cluster of men) wandered off into a hangar to chat, leaving me on the plane. I'm not sure they even realized it, but it appeared I also was locked *in* the plane.

I was too young to realize that they weren't going anywhere without me if, in fact, they went in the plane. I think my fear, at six or seven years old, was that the trip would be cancelled and no one would think to look for me.

The bane of the middle child, I suppose. It appeared to me that no one ever quite noticed whether I was along or not. The proverbial invisible presence. This has been a theme throughout—I still have attacks of it.

Similarly, I was left for a seeming eternity one birthday while dining at a local restaurant. On my birthday, I was allowed to select where we would dine, and this year, it was the Villa de la Paix in Oakland. All the way in Oakland—a major excursion. Being the independent little cuss that I was, I wanted no assistance for a trip to the rest room. Well, the door to the stall got jammed with me inside, and it seemed I was stuck in there for hours before I finally wrested my way out. Returning to the table, after what must have been at least fifteen minutes, it seemed that no one had even missed me. But I had survived a fairly significant (child's portion) panic attack.

These misadventures contributed to a Lone Wolf sensibility. I got in jams, got out, survived, but always felt that the battle was known only to me.

Traveling with Dad was never an issue with the school system. Things were different in those days. When approached about the trip to New York, my teachers felt I was getting more enriching experiences and opportunities than if I was sitting in the classroom. Apparently, there hadn't developed yet the concern with the funds per day per butt at a desk.

There was no resistance from school.

And I loved the time with my father. I was his sidekick; he, in turn, loved having me along. I was, as he said, a real trooper. I never complained and was as little bother as could be. Not an unusual skills set for a child who feels invisible and fortunate just to be included.

My little brother was still an infant at this time. Later, his presence would operate as an end to my monopoly of Dad. No big surprise that when Bruce supplanted me as the travel buddy, it set up decades of resentment. The vestiges are still operative in our relationship.

Early Education

But to return for a moment to life at elementary school.

School was a love-hate relationship for me. Never a smooth journey, the odyssey began with starting kindergarten at four years old. This used to happen to a child depending on where their birthday fell in a calendar year. Mine fell so that I started early as they called it.

As I mentioned, the schism of dresses for school versus pants at home was torture for me. So at the tender age of four, in a foreign costume and environment, I found kindergarten impossible to navigate. Letters were written home about my inability to socialize. They reported that I sat in the corner of the schoolyard by myself, speaking with no one. The letters were shrugged off.

I have reflected over the years how today, in a middle-class home, that would be enough to precipitate family therapy. But not in the '50s and not in my home.

I could already minimally read when I began kindergarten. My love of words and the printed page blossomed early, no doubt from watching my mother lost in a book for a large percentage of each day.

I would come home from the school bus and bring to Mother portions of words I'd committed to memory, to ask her what they were and their meaning. But the ability to read came early and was the refuge for me that many found in the same pages. The children's classics: *Black Beauty*, *Little Women*, *Robinson Crusoe*. Good companions.

Early in the school years, I had joined a number of book clubs and received books in the mail, alongside the ones my mom had ordered for herself. I consumed them with gusto. And then I read hers. I don't think she knew that part.

One of my outstanding memories was sneaking her copy of *Not as a Stranger* by Morton Thompson. It gave me the first sexual stirrings I recall. A book about young medical student interns with actual sex scenes. I couldn't have been more than eight, but the impression was made—Mom's books had cool stuff between their covers.

The Thompson book was contained in a collection. They were called the *Reader's Digest Condensed Books*. I still think about finding a copy of the unabridged novel and assessing just how powerful the reading material was for a young mind.

This not too far afield from the adult content in the movies I attended twice a week. They were my other comfort and escape in a difficult landscape. Again, solitary.

Our one little movie house changed films twice a week, on Wednesdays and Sundays. So I would walk downtown on Saturday afternoon to check out the end run of one and again to the Sunday matinee to see the new film. No one was monitoring the content, and the ratings system was still decades away.

I chuckle to remember going to see the Stanley Kubrick film *Man with a Golden Arm* where Frank Sinatra portrayed jazz legend Gene Krupa. Of course, now I realize that the script was about this great drummer's heroin addiction. But in the hip patois, they kept referring to the *monkey on his back*. I returned home to tell my mother that I just didn't get it. I never could find the monkey.

Again, if she had any adverse reaction, I wasn't aware of it.

My love of the movies spawned another recurring theme. Together with the aversion to dresses, I began an attachment to uniforms beyond the neighborhood battlefield.

When an opportunity to sign up for traffic patrol at school presented itself, I learned that it also rewarded volunteerism with free movie passes. I was there, eagerly signing up.

We were presented with some ratty moth-eaten little red sweaters steeped in the ominous aroma of years of repeated wearings, sans any break for cleaning, and this quite-cool bandolier-style canvas belt, around the waist and across the chest, with an actual *badge* that we wore on the breast. Incredibly romantic for a young uniform freak in the making.

We would go to the supply closet, put on our outfits, select a bright-red STOP sign on a pole, and head out to be the guardians of crosswalks surrounding the school. I was in my element. Even though it was cloaked in a skirt, I had the accoutrements of authority and power. It worked for me!

In the movie house, I could be whoever I wanted. Dressed in my blue jeans and pale blue French-cuff shirt, in the dark and alone, the world became as I preferred it. The final crossover into passing as a boy was to slick back the bangs of my short hairdo, and on occasion, I would stuff a rolled-up pair of socks into my jeans to make me appear more like a boy. In this mode, I was even known to pick up the occasional girl, sitting with my arm around her, for the duration of the film. We never even kissed, but the entire ritual was thrilling for me. I truly was passing as a boy!

Not that my efforts were contained to the dark halls of cinema. On more than one occasion, out in the world with my father, folks would say, "Hello, Sonny." I would beam with pride for a brief instant until my dad would correct them with a chilly tone, "That's my *daughter*." The once-happy moment quickly evaporated.

My repeated birthday wish to change genders persisted. Later, lovingly and laughingly, I referred to myself as a cross-dressing toddler.

Mom's Job

Other than school and holiday gatherings, I was essentially given the freedom to live as a boy. My posse was the neighborhood boys, with war games and sports, evil pranks, and sneaking out in the middle of the night on warm summer sojourns.

The few girls on our suburban block held no interest for me. They wanted to dress up in their mothers' clothes, play tea party, and dress their dolls. I eschewed all such activities with a horror. Sissy pursuits for sure. In retrospect I think the source of my aversion was such a complete lack of female modeling with which I could identify. The girls were practicing the rituals awaiting them as wives and mothers of the '50s; I just couldn't see myself in that role.

From the youngest times, I sensed the lack of respect my mother suffered at the hands of the family. For this, I give credit to my dad. He was openly critical of her, in front of us, when we were alone with him. He trivialized the challenges of her days as a homemaker with remarks like, "I wonder what the crisis is *today?*" as we were heading home after a day of me working in his shop, assembling electronic components.

I knew one thing with utter clarity: hers was not a job I wanted when I grew up.

In contrast, my dad was dashing and charismatic. By the time I was two, he had entered the entrepreneurial world, beginning the construction of what would later become a communications empire and the inception of cable television. He traveled extensively while forging business alliances and developing cable installations in various communities throughout the western US. I frequently joined him. This life looked infinitely more interesting. Why would I want to be tied to a house and children, routinely ignored and disrespected?

Additionally, my father presented the double-edged sword of telling me I could be whatever I set my mind to—a rather radical notion for a girl in the mid-fifties. On the one hand, it was tremendously supportive, giving me great freedom of choice. The other side of the coin was the permission to reject what was expected from a girl of the time.

I noticed also, though not registering it at the time, that my mother was largely a depressed person—not something much talked about at mid-century. She was a stay-at-home mom, except for brief spells when she would do temporary clerical work in my dad's business—preparing the payroll, answering phones, and otherwise utilizing the skills she acquired in a fifteen-week secretarial course after high school. My dad's educational background was similar: an electronics course of equal duration. I would later become, like many of my generation, the first member of the family actually to attend college.

They were both native Californians, and both attended Berkeley High School, graduating in 1935. They met on the ferryboat crossing the Bay en route to their various jobs in San Francisco. My dad used the oldest pickup line in the books, "Haven't I seen you somewhere before?" after having noticed her on the ferry and doing some research in their high school yearbook.

After a reasonable courtship of two years, they married at twenty-two. If Mom had been paying attention to red flags as I do now, she would have seen the seeds of a bond which offered emotional abandonment and physical separation.

At the engagement party her parents threw in their honor at the elegant Claremont Hotel, one would have noticed that instead of the actual groom-to-be, he was represented at the table with a photographic portrait occupying a place setting. She met up with him in Miami where they had a civil ceremony before flying to Rio where they would live during their first year of marriage.

Dad worked for Pan Am Airlines as a radioman in an era when transoceanic flights did not operate at night and the journey to Brazil took a matter of days. Mom was alone on their first New Year's Eve and whiled away her days on the Copacabana Beach while Dad was somewhere in the skies. It sounds idyllic, and it seemed to work, but from the beginning, her marriage was pretty lonely. They stayed in Brazil until she was pregnant with my older brother, returning home so he would be born on American soil.

For the next few years, they resided in Southern California, my brother being delivered in Glendale. By the time I was born, six years later, they had relocated to the San Francisco Bay Area and had bought their first home in the Berkeley hills, where I was conceived. It's amazing to think that a home there was $5,000 in 1945.

By the time of my arrival, we were ensconced as suburbanites in an early prototype of the ranch-style home development, having moved to a small town fashioned out of fields and orchards—Walnut Creek.

This was a pastoral community, with horse paddocks and vacant lots providing the neighborhood playgrounds. The front yard of our home, having been carved from an orchard, had three symmetrically placed pear trees in the lawn. In the early days, my mom would preserve those pears: bell jars with red food coloring and cinnamon sticks, green ones with mint leaves and equally toxic coloration.

Our lot seemed huge at a quarter acre. We had other fruit trees: an apricot and a plum. The arbor my dad built was draped in Thompson seedless grapes, and blackberry vines formed a bramble in a corner near the incinerator. We also cultivated two large raised beds, one with a profusion of flowers and the other producing vegetables for the family table. The remainder of the ample backyard was an expansive lawn area—a nice place for us to grow and play.

Mom was a consummate homemaker, and I feel her influence in my own nest building today. But when she wasn't baking or cleaning or preparing supper, she was content to sit in the sun, smoke cigarettes, and read novels. I continued on my solitary journey: growing up as a boy only to be thwarted by adolescence.

Granny and Papa's on Allendale Avenue

I found solace and acceptance at my grandparents' home in Oakland. Oddly enough, the little house they occupied off High Street is a mere half mile from where I have now lived the last forty years. I stopped by one day when I saw an elderly woman tending the roses in the front yard. Margaret Bender is the same woman they sold their home to forty-two years before.

My memories of this house are warm and comforting. I would spend overnight visits there, with the immigrant parents of my mother. Their English was broken, their values were solid, they paid cash for everything, including their house. Papa was a machinist, a tool and diemaker who owned his own shop. My granny didn't drive, stayed at home, and was available to babysit.

Papa was from Germany and Granny from Holland. They both immigrated to the US in 1915 and met at the Pan American Exposition on Treasure Island in the San Francisco Bay. They married the following year and were delivered a daughter, Elsa, my mother, the year after that.

I loved spending time with them. Granny taught me card games, my favorite being canasta. We would dunk oatmeal cookies in tea with milk while we played to an unthinkable five thousand points. For a break in that routine, we would walk up to the hobby shop on High Street and buy plastic models of planes and cars that I would later assemble.

When Papa was home, I had free rein in his workshop, a charming out building with drill presses, table saws, and expansive benches bordered by an orderly assortment of hand tools. It still astonishes me to think that, though I was six or seven years old, he was allowing me to play with power tools, with the exception of the saws. He taught me safety in handling and caring for his implements. My favorite product was always a rubber-band gun.

Trouble at School: From Kindergarten to the Boys' Bathroom

For a number of reasons, not the least of which was the dress code, school was never something I enjoyed. I was good at the work, solitary at recess, and generally steeped in ennui. In addition, I stood larger and taller than most of my contemporaries.

The boys, normally my peers at home, ignored girls at this age. It was second grade, and it seemed that boys and girls just didn't mix at school. This felt a hurtful injustice.

Since I began kindergarten at four, I must have been about seven when my mother got a phone call one morning while I was getting dressed. On her end, it was a lot of "Mm-hmm" and "I see." She had a perplexed look on her face as she hung up the receiver and turned to me.

"Today, when you get to school, you're to collect your crayons and go to Mrs. Eckhardt's class." This didn't bode well; she was the evil third-grade teacher who had not, long before, held back or flunked my older brother. It would appear that I was being jettisoned into the third grade.

It was spring, with mere weeks left in the school year. According to the current plan, I was to spend a total of six weeks in the third grade, have the usual summer vacation, and return in the fall as a fourth-grade student.

Conflicting feelings ping-ponged about in my head. Wow, so much was covered in the third grade! So far in school, we had yet to touch cursive writing, math tasks like borrowing and carrying, multiplication tables, and even the beginnings of division. I was at once nervous and exhilarated to take on new and exciting material.

Add to this prospect the familial difficulties of pitting me against my brother, Bob, who had been held back. Even the same teacher though her individual influence had everything to do with his situation but very little impact on mine—*if* I did well in the next six weeks.

My father made no effort to disguise his disappointment in Bob's scholastics. He drubbed him, referred to him as bonehead, and generally never missed an opportunity to remind him of his lack of achievement. I felt bad for Bob, but I had a job to do as the prodigy.

At school, the advancement created new difficulties for my already-failing social skills. I was even told at one point that they skipped me because I was larger than my classmates and the considered opinion of school administrators was that I would fit in better with an older class.

Well, I might finally have been matched in size, but my social development had been sorely lacking all along. If I didn't fit in before, it was only exacerbated in the new milieu. I formed no bonds, had no friends, and was routinely ignored by the boys who were my posse at home.

From the perspective of fifty years later, it's no surprise that my next battle plan for survival was to begin acting out at school and home. I freely stole from local retail establishments, my favorites being office and art supplies. No reason I can think of, just lots of pretty colors.

In the neighborhood, the focus became acts of daring, stealing materials from the freeway construction site, attempting to start heavy equipment (which required no ignition key), and pilfering lumber with which to build my annual forts. I still chuckle at the image of struggling with an entire sheet of 4'×8'×3/4" plywood on my little red wagon, but I got it home and put it to good use. In typical fashion, my folks never inquired where I got it.

School supplies were also ripe for the plucking. I came home one day totally weighed down with contraband. When my mother asked about it, I simply told her they were giving supplies away because it was the last day of school. Again, no questions.

An overcompensating mentality began, where I was compulsive in accepting any form of a dare. No mystery that the challenges were posed by the boys. In the fifth grade, I remember being dared to enter the boys' bathroom during recess. Marching through the double swinging doors with a swagger, I thought, *No sweat.* But attempting to come out after establishing my derring-do, the boys had blocked the doors and left no exit. When the doors finally freed, Mrs. Griffin, the fifth-grade teacher on yard duty, was there to greet me. Of course, the boys had beaten a hasty retreat.

To her inquiry of why I went in the boys' room, I was only able to offer, "They dared me." "Well, *young ladies* don't accept dares" was her contribution. Now I was truly screwed. Who wanted to be a *young lady*? Not me! This was not a compelling argument for conformity.

Part and parcel with the feats of boldness was the need to develop a tough outer shell. I was a young badass in development. Nothing could move me to tears since the time some years previous when my parents sent me off to the movies, only to return home to find they had taken my dog Dusty to the veterinarian and had her put to sleep.

I've never heard any justification for this action, just that Dusty was old and would lie in our flower beds. Whatever my parents' reasons, I couldn't forgive their underhandedness. Upon receiving the news, I went to the crawl space under the house and burst into tears. I vowed they would never again see me display emotion or know how much they could affect me. I sincerely don't think I shed another tear for the ensuing thirty years.

Puberty Rears Its Ugly Head

School continued to be lonely and yield no companions, save one friendship with a classmate named Ricky. At the time, I was too young to appreciate our differences, Ricky being from the only African American family in Walnut Creek. Our availability to each other had everything to do with our shared outsider status. In other words, no one was talking to Ricky at school either. Years later, my mother remarked, "So she comes home with her first little boyfriend, and wouldn't you know, she picked the only little colored boy in town." I think it was the first awareness I had of race difference.

Ricky and I spent lots of time riding our bikes and forging memos from parents giving us permission to buy cigarettes. Typical of the fifties, I don't think a single shopkeeper believed the veracity of the notes yet nonetheless sold us our Winstons. We would sit in a large drainage pipe on Boulevard Way, feet propped on the opposite wall, while a small trickle of water passed below our legs. There we would smoke while we sang "The Sunny Side of the Street" and practiced spitting. The song we chose was in homage to the side of the pipe where we aimed our phlegmy trajectories.

The gang of neighbor boys continued to be my social focus near home, but the nature of the games was changing. Football was a favorite, but it took me some time to realize that I always had to play at the position of center while the opposing team would rush and grasp at the little swellings soon become my breasts. Lots of groping was going on, and I truly didn't understand.

Strip poker games were a favorite of the boys, and again, I was too naive to realize I was the only participant who ever lost more than a shirt or a pair of socks. One time, while playing poker at Danny's house, his mom busted in to catch us—Danny and Dickie and Dennis sitting around shirtless and me standing on the bed, completely unclothed, while the boys took turns tickling my private parts with some long feather. What to do—I was fresh out of clothing to take off. I vividly remember Danny's mother managing to convey the shame *I* should be feeling. I guess the boys were just being boys.

Though I didn't really have much sense of what the boys were up to, I had my own stirrings around sexuality. My first record player was one of the prototypical hi-fis—a console model with a cabinet lid that closed over the record player and upon which I could sit. My record collection was growing due to belonging to the Columbia Record Club, where I would receive albums in the mail. My choices from the catalog were consistently those albums with cover art depicting young lovers in romantic settings.

Even though my 45-rpm collection was becoming prodigious, with all the latest tunes and artists in the emerging genre of the new and radical rock and roll, the young lover albums were typically volumes of love songs from quite another era. It gave me an exceptional grounding in the ballads of the thirties and forties and a love of well-crafted melodies and emotion-laden lyrics.

It was the albums, including classical selections, which I would crank up full volume while sitting on the lid of my hi-fi, letting the beat and the music course up through my body. It amuses me to think, that well into later years, I actually believed I had never learned to pleasure myself.

My other favorite romantic sublimation was beginning the practice of kissing, but not on other humans. My usual targets were a large stuffed panda bear and the nook of my arm. I think there was probably some mounting of the poor patient bear as well.

I felt in control, in my personal world, of these first sexual stirrings. But with the boys, it was quite clear to me that I was being played for a fool and taken advantage of. Danny, however, did intrigue me. He was our resident bad boy, the one to be counted on to invent daring challenges and always be skirting the edges of delinquency. I remember being hauled out of his sleeping bag in the middle of one night when my father had discovered my absence from our own backyard and had come looking for me. I guess Danny was also the first place a parent would look when on the hunt for misbehavior.

I got taken home and beaten with a belt. Though sounding extreme, I remember my silent smirking that my dad was trying to whoop me through my jeans, and it didn't really hurt that much. I'm sure it did, but the discomfort was no match for my attitude of invincibility.

Danny and I were rolling around in his bag fully clothed, which was, no doubt, a relief to my dad. But this adventure put a bit of a crimp in the free rein to roam I had enjoyed while sleeping out in the yard for the entirety of each summer.

Night forays had long been a staple of the warm summer nights of our neighborhood. With friends a little older, those who hung out with my older brother, we would sneak out of our respective yards and rendezvous, prowling the neighborhoods quite some distance from our own. We sometimes hid near a dip in the road for long stretches, waiting for an approaching car, and when we saw one coming from a distance, one of us would lie in the road while another would flag the car to stop and help with some fictional emergency. As the car slowed, we would all jump up and beat a hasty retreat through the creek to darker territory. It was hilarious to us.

One of our adventures found us about a mile from home with some requisitioned blue poster paint. We had reconnoitered a lovely white split-rail fence and began the task of leaving our imprint with the paint.

Behind us, someone cleared his throat—some man out walking his dog at two in the morning! He queried, "Don't you think it's time you headed home?" We wasted no time, but as we began to quake, we were all too aware it was his intention to follow us to our parents where he would apprise them of our high jinx. Nearing a large field, we broke into a run and hid among some large pampas grass, discovering painfully its treacherous, slicing properties as the leaves shredded our arms and legs.

Our pursuer continued to search the field for us; we took the opportunity to break into a run, next tangling with a barbed-wire fence. More serious cuts and scrapes for those leading the retreat, but we did make it home without discovery.

I got away with a lot; hanging out with the friends of my older brother always provided opportunities to think outside the box appropriate for my tender age.

But as puberty descended, my brother's male friends posed new perils. They were beyond the innocent football grabbing, and when Bob's buddies began to drive, I found new vistas of mischief to navigate.

At twelve, I was riding with my brother's friend Eugene, a real creep in retrospect (what is one to make of a seventeen-year-old who wants to hang out with a twelve-year-old girl? These days, it could land him in legal hot water), and we were engaging the local gas station employees in a water balloon fight. While cruising at twenty-five miles per hour, one of them landed a perfect shot into the convertible, right into my face. It hurt like the dickens, but always the one with a brave countenance, I downplayed the damage. Lord knows I wouldn't have wanted to be excluded from future games!

While trying to scuttle through the kitchen avoiding detection, my right eye watering profusely and unable to pull focus, my mother stopped me and demanded to know what I was hiding. When we examined my eye in the mirror, the area of the iris, the normally brown color of my eye, was a deep red due to being filled up with blood. Trip to the doctor.

The diagnosis was a torn iris; the prescription was bed rest. As my mother assured the ophthalmologist she would keep me bedbound at home, the doctor just laughed. *Oh no, she's being admitted to the hospital. There's no way you can keep a twelve-year-old as confined as we can.*

To my utter humiliation, I was placed in the children's ward at Kaiser Hospital. Twelve was the cut-off age where a patient could be in either a ward or have a private room. My pleas for the more adult option fell on deaf ears. The difference in cost hadn't occurred to me, possibly because my parents never mentioned money in front of us kids.

But in with the babies I went, including one little stinker, about eight years old, who was hospitalized for a severe case of poison oak. When she learned how highly allergic I was, she would spend her out-of-bed time taunting me and threatening to wipe her oozing sores on my body. Not a pleasant experience. Meanwhile, I wasn't allowed to leave my bed even for trips to the bathroom.

However, the hospitalization didn't cure me from enjoying riding in the car with Eugene. On one of our afternoon tours, he pulled onto a dirt road that passed underneath a railroad trestle. There, I was properly felt up for the first time amid very mixed feelings of danger, repulsion, thrill, and sexual stirrings.

I hadn't been wearing a brassiere for very long, but Eugene wrested it free and fondled me. I was barely able to muster the courage to insist he stop when he started fishing around in my underpants. Reporting the crime to my older brother just brought anger at me and a warning to stay away from his friends.

Though we didn't really have junior high school where I grew up, by now, I was in the eighth grade. My choice to wear a brassiere was unpleasant to me, fueled by a seventh grader insulting me one day on the playground. "Do you wear a bra?" she snarled. When I replied in the negative, she retorted, "Well, you *should*!" Humiliated about my femaleness again, I figured it must be time to start wearing one.

Horrified at the prospect of going to a store with my mother and being fitted for a bra by some stranger, I asked Mom what I could do in the alternative. Her solution was to give me one of her old bras, which, of course, was a bit too ample in the cup. I soon found that filling up the empty space with small silk scarves both served the visual and also felt rather warm and cozy against my tender, incipient swellings. Again, the nightmare of entering the treacherous world of the developing female.

At the dinner table one evening, my father just looked across at me in disgust and said, "If you can't fill that thing up on your own, take it off!" This business of being a girl was just getting worse by the day.

An Eye for the Girls

As the boys around me began to take notice, I did as well. Other than a brief romantic alliance with a boy in my sixth-grade class named Bruce, boyfriends hadn't really occurred to me as a point of interest. And with Bruce, a friend of his just approached me one day on the schoolyard and asked, in his stead, if I would accept Bruce's ID bracelet and go steady with him. Sure. Why not? I had no idea what it meant. It did, however, mean that for that one September, I had someone with whom to go to the annual Walnut Festival, a carnival in town.

But the real target of my attention began to be the other girls in my class. I had virtually no friends at school of the same sex. Not until later, when I started forming romantic interests in girls, did I really develop any friendships.

Nancy was my first crush. I somewhere got the notion that her family was poor, I think, because Nancy's mother sewed her clothes for her. I began anonymously gifting her with things. Unfortunately, the most spectacular offering of all was my entire 45-rpm record collection, which would today be worth a fortune. Elvis, in monaural alone, would be valued in the thousands of dollars for the number of records I sent Nancy's way.

Nancy had a boyfriend—Jimmy. He was pretty cute, and I rather had a crush on him as well. My fantasies were fairly innocent. I would imagine Jimmy doing something to break Nancy's heart, then I would offer the comfort of my embrace to her. I had no concept of where this sort of thinking was heading and its implications for my future.

I still was only twelve and soon to enter high school. Thanks again to the misguided educators who jettisoned me precipitously through elementary school.

The Barren High School Landscape

When I entered my first high school, it was a brand-new facility and contained only a freshman class. It was an odd experience of isolation, just the one class, and the first time that kids from other neighboring schools were in the mix. So it wasn't the usual suspects, necessarily, but it also was only quite young high school kids, with no representatives from other grades to model behavior for us in this brave new world.

Our teachers all did duty teaching several classes as well. My favorite was Mrs. Cavagnaro—an Englishwoman with a bona fide accent and unshaved legs. Quite the novelty. She was my English teacher, my Latin teacher, and also my counselor. I adored her and excelled under her tutelage.

This new school was carved out of a marvelous old working cattle ranch which had sold off a small portion of their land holdings—the Dollar Ranch. Stanley Dollar was the man who owned the airplane I was once inadvertently locked in before our foggy departure for New York.

The best part of this pastoral setting were the cries of peacocks which still roamed near the Dollar ranch house. I vividly remember their calls while I couldn't wait for class to let out. The clear, piercing cries would stir me from nearly nodding off due to boredom. Skipping me in school had not solved the problem of making the unimaginative curriculum any more interesting.

Nancy was here at this school. And so was Jimmy. Still excluded, still on the outside, and now I was, for the first time, exposed to PE classes and the expectation of stripping down and showering among classmates. I was horrified! I was terrifically body shy, and absolutely no one ever saw me with my clothes off. This took some concerted machinations with the gym towels to fake running through the shower area and getting to my clothes before anyone else was finished and returning to the dressing area.

As under the social radar as I felt, I was mystified when someone taunted me with the name lesbian. I had to go into Mrs. Cavagnaro's empty classroom and look up the word in the dictionary. My gut wrenched as I read the definition and, at the same time, realized that it probably was apt. I was humiliated, afraid to go back out in the schoolyard; my wonderful teacher allowed me to hide out for a while and eat lunch in the deserted room for the next several days. My fantasies of Nancy took on a richer meaning.

Empire Building

My entry into high school was but one minor segment in major changes for the family. My father was entering with gusto what I like to call his empire-building phase.

From the time I was two, my dad had worked for himself. He was, though he blandly states that many others can claim the same distinction, one among many inventors of television. We bought our first set, he tells me, when the family moved to Del Hambre Circle, which was just before I was born.

The TV's place of prominence was in the garage, still some way from becoming a household fixture. We purchased our first Westinghouse ten-inch television, with its little round screen, in 1946, and all the neighbors would come over on Saturday night to sit in the garage watching *The Milton Berle Show*.

The extent of Dad's education beyond high school was a fifteen-week electronics course. From there, he began working for Westinghouse Electronics where he was in sales, as near as I can tell. But through his independent ways and visionary nature, the life of being someone else's lackey was not for him.

In the 1950s, my dad pioneered what was called CATV, an acronym for *community antenna television*. Dad would select a site, a hilltop overlooking a community which had no TV reception, lease an easement to erect an antenna on this high point, and build relay equipment which could provide the signal to homes which were individually connected by a cable link to the power poles where he ran the signal by permission of another easement. Yep, this was the beginning of cable TV.

His first system was in the town of Martinez. Old and quaint, a one-time railroad town and whaling port, Martinez had become the county seat of Contra Costa County. Sunken in a little dell between two ridges of hills, the good folk of Martinez couldn't receive a signal of any sort on their new-fangled television sets. By erecting an antenna and building microwave relay links from both the network stations in Sacramento and San Francisco, Dad was able to provide them with access to the new medium.

He had a great shop in Martinez—a front office area (where my mother sometimes worked as his secretary as well as the secretary-treasurer of his newly formed corporation), the executive office where he hung his metaphorical hat, a fabrication area with workbenches, and a large garage with some very cool trucks used for lugging around equipment and stringing cable on utility poles.

For a number of summers, I worked for my dad, helping to assemble electronic components as I had first done when he nurtured me through the construction of a Heathkit transistor radio. I loved that little blue radio, which I was proud to say I built all by myself.

But this work was more advanced—transistors, capacitors, resistors, learning how to read the markings on them and distinguishing one from the next. I learned to follow schematics and had a natural talent for the meticulousness and dexterity required for such assembly.

The other fascinating aspect of life at the shop were some of the personnel working in the business. Amid hushed and angry mutterings about one of his female assemblers and her quiet lunches in the car with Dad's office gal, I realized this woman, Bonnie, was the first woman-loving woman I knew. She sported jeans, which was almost unheard of for a '50s woman. Blond hair cropped short, loafers with actual pennies in the toe, Bonnie had a quite different energy that any woman I had been around. I think either Bonnie or the secretary were later dismissed, in the era when a boss didn't need any particularly good reason other than the presence of someone making him uncomfortable.

But Dad was definitely engaged in building an empire. The Martinez system begat a system in Elko, Nevada, with the construction of a microwave relay site on Spruce Mountain in the eastern portion of the state. In turn, the microwave dishes could capture signals from both Salt Lake City and Reno and eventually feed television to the entire state of Nevada.

The construction on Spruce Mountain was a minimalist building with climate control and racks of microwave equipment within. I joined Dad for several trips up Spruce in the winter, even making the journey by packhorses with an old wrangler named Bill Gobel, who provided the animals. I can't overstate the romance of these adventures: getting bogged down in snowdrifts, stopping to share meals with Basque shepherds on the lower slopes of the mountain, and all the while knowing (and occasionally hearing from my dad) what a great little trooper I was. I loved these trips.

As Dad's domain expanded into Colorado and Lake Tahoe, our economic status was also escalating. This was the late 1950s, and the postwar economic boom was in full momentum. We began to eat steak so many nights a week that the ungrateful spawn would whine, "What, steak *again*?" Convenience foods like TV dinners began to creep in the kitchen and Mom no longer put up jams and jellies or baked much. These were symbols of success.

With the new prosperity came the impetus to change neighborhoods and move up in the world. Dad had been contacted by a Dutch cousin of my mother who was a building contractor. Herman Tijsseling, the cousin, had bought some very elegant lots, all perched on a pair of hills in the neighboring town of Lafayette. Herman wanted my dad to lay the infrastructure for built-in cable TV in the development.

Dad was smitten with the highest lot on the hill. A prime spot with a 360° view of both Walnut Creek in one direction and the back side of the Oakland Hills to the west. A magnificent vista with Mt. Diablo in prominence was the breathtaking sight across the valley beyond our current home. He brought my mother up there one afternoon to show her this spectacular spot.

"What do you think? Isn't this lot something?" He gestured at the valley below.

"Yes, I suppose it's quite nice." Mom was never one to commit.

"But isn't this a place you could someday see yourself owning a home?" She knew him well enough to take his enthusiasm with caution.

"But, Bill, our house is almost paid for."

"But wouldn't you? Wouldn't it be something?" She finally deferred. "Good, because I bought the lot this afternoon!"

This was pretty typical of their dynamic: she holding back with fear and conservatism and he acting unilaterally in frustration with her circumspection.

The year was 1960, the beginning of some very important social climate changes. The construction on their dream home began, closely supervised by my father who visited the site almost every day. Both my parents were just forty-three. I was heading off to a new high school, the oldest school in the area, as soon as we took occupancy of our completed house on the hill.

At the same time, my older brother Bob had graduated from high school, a feat which his counselor pronounced was as much as could be expected of such a mediocre student. Poor Bob!

In his senior year, he had met a girl, and as was common in those days of no birth control pills and condoms sold only to twenty-one-year-olds, he got her pregnant and they married. She was just seventeen by a few weeks. Bob was nineteen. I often felt that his relationship with Susie had everything to do with finally finding someone close who was kind to him. His self-esteem had taken such a beating at the hands of the school system and my dad that it seemed the obvious choice to want to make a life with a warm heart.

Giant Culture Shift

Moving to Acalanes High brought an enormous cultural shift: upperclassmen, school traditions, athletic teams, and an even larger number of students around whom I felt uncomfortable. My isolation deepened.

Instead of my adored Mrs. Cavagnaro, I now had a real bear of a teacher for Latin—Mrs. Ochoa. She was considered by the students to be one of the harshest possible personalities teaching one of the most difficult subjects. It appeared that my sophomore laziness in Latin was about to be exposed. My studies had fallen behind in the old school, but now the grades caught up to reality and began to reflect my lack of diligence.

I'll never forget a lecture from my dad when my report card revealed I was earning a D grade from Mrs. Ochoa. It has stuck with me throughout the years. In trying to explain my poor marks by a declaration I was afraid of the tyrannical Latin teacher, he wasn't buying it. He growled, "You're not afraid of her. You're just like me, and I'm not afraid of *anybody!*"

My fear was genuine, but my father's assumption was nothing short of suffocating. I held that notion close to my heart for decades: I hadn't the right to be afraid in the world; it was my legacy to charge through life fearlessly.

The Latin grades barely improved after the lecture, but I was graced with a couple of wonderful literature teachers, eventually fueling a desire to major in the topic once away at college. Physical education continued to serve up a nightmare of sports for which I was uncoordinated and shower room scenes filled with dread.

In Concert

I entered Acalanes as a sophomore, and it was in this new school that I found first love. I'd met a neighbor boy from the hill, the son of a local veterinarian. Bob Underwood was a senior, and we began to hang out together.

Our awkward courtship was navigated amid the construction sites of half-completed custom homes on the hill where our two families were some of the first residents. We became inseparable: studying together, riding our revolutionary new ten-speed bikes, frolicking in my family's pool, and, of course, making out.

The most profound effect of this relationship was that, for the first time in my life, I actually felt connected to another human. This was very new territory, and it touched an achingly empty place in my heart. I was no longer braving the world on my own but had a cohort, someone who told me he cared, a person with whom to share an incipient worldview in its formative stages.

Since Bob was a senior, I was once again privy to the reading material of an older person: he was reading James Joyce's *Portrait of the Artist as a Young Man* and I was studying it alongside him. I was fourteen and Bob was three years older.

He was cute, he was funny, his family was close, unlike anything I'd experienced. The Underwoods would sit around their dinner table for a couple of hours chatting after the evening meal. I was accustomed to a family scene where we wolfed down our supper, rushing to be excused from the table. My dad departed right after the last bite to return to work in his shop.

I became a regular in the Underwood home and was a frequent guest at dinner.

Unlike my own family, Bob's parents were both college educated, and his father was the son of a presiding judge in San Francisco. A *woman* judge. This was fairly radical for 1960; I don't think we even appreciated just how unusual it was. The most major feminist movement since women had gotten the vote was still a decade ahead of us.

So the chat at their table was about affairs of some moment: the world situation and local politics. I recall that, during this time, Richard Nixon was campaigning to be governor of California. I was still under the pall of parental influence and considered myself politically conservative. It was 1962.

In the very near future, I would find less and less political and social agreement with my father in particular. It took the major portion of a decade of frustration and a flexing of new philosophical muscle before I realized he and I could *not* discuss politics. We still didn't even attempt it for the remainder of his ninety-three years.

All my bouts of sitting on the console stereo or smooching on my stuffed panda couldn't have prepared me for the explosive symphony of physical and emotional sensation that awoke when Bob and I got near each other. I began to get extremely curious about what sex entailed and how it might feel.

To his credit, Bob remained a gentleman as long as he could; I began to coax, cajole, and make attempts at seduction. We talked about it, discussing at length the risks as we knew them—only pregnancy came to mind. We were what many kids called engaged to be engaged, wherein we acknowledged we were too young to be exchanging rings but plenty old enough to want to offer up our young bodies in lust. It somehow legitimized our curiosity.

Eventually, my urgings won out over his more sensible and Victorian position. How long can a teenage boy hold out, anyway? The rite of consummation was on the plywood subflooring of a half-constructed model home. Our efforts at lovemaking were bumbling and less than romantic, but I had achieved a benchmark in my maturation.

Bob didn't seem plagued with guilt to any debilitating degree. Our focus became the discovery of new and inventive venues for our young lovemaking. On the very rare occasion, we got the opportunity to tryst in one of our own beds if the parents were out.

Social Intelligence

The relationship with Bob brought with it entry into worlds previously unknown to me. Through him and his family, I had my first encounter with the social graces—things like table manners and the consideration of others.

It sounds unfathomable in retrospect, but I really hadn't been taught even the most basic things about how to get along with others in the world. Over the years, when realizing these deficits, I felt like Ishi, the Aboriginal who was the celebrated 1960s anthropological find. I was a primitive just now entering a more civilized world.

On occasion, as a kid, a neighbor adult or some other outsider would inquire, "Where are your manners?" I had no answer for them and no parental model to fall back on. I would hear criticism when I didn't perform correctly but never got any social cues on the proper way to be. I'm sure it had an impact on my outsider status; party invitations never came my way nor did I ever form a group affiliation at school. I was painfully aware of my exclusion; my consolation was that it was nothing new.

My social milieu wasn't necessarily larger with Bob, but our alliance brought intimate input from someone who loved me enough to want to mold my behavior and have others see the goodness in me that he had discovered. His parents appreciated my intellect and served as social models. I loved the warmth of being among them and spent as much time in their home as I was allowed.

Bob and I looked toward a nonspecific future together—I began engaging in the heterosexual rituals of a girl planning to marry someday. I had a hope chest and filled it with household items from redeeming Blue Chip Stamps that came with retail purchases. I collected linens, salad servers, and cereal bowls. The chest itself was made of cedar and was a lovely piece of fragrant furniture that remained among my belongings way beyond any dreams of building a traditional home life.

In an effort to create an arsenal of skills for a future union, I took (the then mandatory) homemaking class and barely survived with a passing grade. Our first project was to sew an apron we would then wear for a year's worth of domestic endeavor. I hated sewing.

I did, however, manage to fabricate a lovely shirt for Bob, truly a labor of love, a Pendleton wool, long-sleeved creation of a rich blue-green plaid. The predominant memory is of pulling out, over and over, seams that were less than perfect and wrestling with the specialized stitching of buttonholes. Mother lauded my efforts, but the taste left in my mouth was the developing belief that love brought with it struggle for perfection and anxiety about performance.

Typical of any young person entering the wide world of sexual activity, Bob and I had no emotional grounding for the minefield we were entering. Birth control was not available, readily or otherwise. The birth control pill was yet to be developed and condoms were sold only to adults. Hell, we had only vaguely even heard of condoms.

The times were puritanical and repressive; enforcement of the mores of the day were left to the honor system. I just refused the convention and defied the honor system. I never felt bound by what was expected of good girls. So it became commonplace to worry about pregnancy.

I was graced with an exceedingly regular menstrual cycle and had, as my only resource, the so-called rhythm method of contraception. Certainly I was bright enough to count to twenty-eight.

But we had our scares. Or I should say, *I* did as I kept most of my anxieties about late periods to myself, not wanting to freak out my beloved. In those times when I was worried, I developed a habit of retreating to a favorite spot, high on a grassy hill overlooking the high school and doing some serious meditating that mostly took the form of making promises to a higher power that if I could just escape this one time unscathed, my behavior in the future would be exemplary. I called these sessions vigils and am not even sure where I learned the concept. Probably from literature, still my favorite place to hide from the doldrums of teenage existence. When I sat vigil, I was sometimes on the hillside well into dusk.

Even though I had the social protection afforded by a love relationship, I still had no friends, except Bob. After half a year of our association, he graduated and I was left on the social landscape once again alone.

I remember a dance in my junior year where Bob joined me—my grown-up, collegiate boyfriend. He had not gone away from home for his further education but was attending the local community (or at that time *junior*) college and living at home with his parents and younger brother. His father still wouldn't allow him to drive, which was a formidable humiliation for a young man who had graduated.

He attended the dance with me, and we wore matching bright orange shirts, the color of highway safety vests. I loved the color and thought it festive for the beachcomber theme of the evening. We also donned matching sailor hats. I think it was the first time I ever went to a dance with a date.

Bob was in a folk dancing troupe outside of school, most likely inspired by the fact that his parents were avid square dancers. The whole family loved to dance. We had a fine time on the dance floor, working up a giant sweat and twirling into a frenzy. I had the time of my life, feeling for a change that I was in some rendition of the social mainstream—previously a foreign country.

But the following Monday at school, I was to find, through the rumor mill and behind-my-back whispers, that again I had gone against the grain of social convention; our dancing was deemed shamefully uninhibited and our outfits inappropriately garish. Apparently, the social code was stringent in these matters, but without belonging to an *in* group, the cipher was unintelligible.

Relationship Mystique

Outside the high school culture, even just one-on-one with Bob, this was territory for which I had no navigational skills. The couple dynamic was something of an interruption to a previous free-rein narcissism; this was a new world where there was a larger focus than my own immediate needs and desires.

Within the context of this relationship, when there was criticism from my beloved or correction of my social shortcomings, it was harder to ignore than input from a parent, for instance. I *cared* what Bob thought; I wanted to please. I hungered for his approval in a way I had never acknowledged before. Lack of approval was so commonplace in my home that I didn't know to miss it.

So many worlds colliding: the social conventions of being a young woman, the effort to consider the feelings and boundaries of others, the newly emerging sexuality and its accompanying guilt and danger.

I followed the only model I had known to this point for womanhood—my mom. My efforts at the womanly arts were Herculean. I made a ritual pilgrimage to the beauty parlor every Friday afternoon to have my hair washed and set; I baked bread for Bob and his family at least once a week.

Beneath these attempts was a searing longing to fit in, to be worthy or, at the very least, lovable. Though fond memories of these two years with Bob are vague, I have more distinct recollections of when things began to go south. One difficult and painful memory is of a fight where, upon giving him a loaf of bread still warm from the oven, some unremarkable provocation caused him to fling it back in my face. We were nearing our end.

The Brink of Revolution

Returning to the life of the lone wolf in my senior year, I searched for new ways to identify a peer group. The eggheads, the other social misfits, had formed a coalition of sorts, gathering during their lunch period in an unused classroom to play bridge. I made an effort to join in and learned the basics of the rummy game.

Most of these students were in what today would be called the AP classes—advanced placement. We called them "honors" classes. Math, science, the Great Books…they shared the bond of an exalted academic milieu. Given my history of lax study habits and passing grades without much concerted effort, theirs was another inaccessible venue.

At best, I feel my presence in a foursome was tolerated, making do in a pinch. With my characteristically blasé attitude, I fell short of proper seriousness at the bridge table—apparently an unforgivable breach of convention. I didn't fit here either.

Somewhere along the line, I formed one friendship and cannot recall where Nancy and I made the mutual discovery of each other's intellect and sarcasm. We hit it off. Nancy was a year behind me in school, and though we didn't really hang out together on campus, her home was a mere block away. That was where we shared our frustrations with the status quo and the urge to be free of bothersome parents and boring peers. Nancy was the first real girl friend outside the childhood neighbors I grew up with.

It was the very beginnings of the British Invasion in rock and roll. Nancy was a brilliant artist and would craft charcoal renderings of the Rolling Stones, her favorite band. She was daring and rebellious, referring to her parents, Edgar and Mary, as Big E and the Spoiler. She made me laugh.

It was an awkward heart connection between two kids who didn't really know how to connect. We spent long hours in her room listening to music and fantasizing about our eventual escape to college and leaving the home hearth. A couple of times, we attempted a sleepover at my house, but eventually in the course of the night, Nancy would suffer from anxiety and need to phone her father for a ride home. How in God's name did we get so damaged at such a young age?

But Nancy loved the thrill of riding in my new little Austin-Healy sports car which I had been allowed to buy as a reward for acceptance to Chico State College. I used the $1,000 my grandfather had left me in his will, along with a balance my father provided.

The Healy provided a portal into a new universe of independence. I cultivated a passion for weekly sports car rallies and the continuous discovery of new back roads that wound through the remaining undeveloped pastoral landscape. Nancy would accompany as my navigator, clipboard in her lap, using the beam of a small flashlight to read the map and guide us through the rural countryside, making our way from one checkpoint to the next, with Lake Merritt in Oakland our ultimate destination.

This was a persona reeking of authenticity; it fit like a new skin. I was brimming with an exciting unfamiliar rush, nothing like rollers in my hair or ripping out less-than-artful seams in a garment; mastering the highways and byways was something I felt born to.

I had a friend now. I had a passion and someone to share it with. My heart swelled with freedom, mobility, and empowerment. It didn't take long before I eschewed the beauty parlor and began to frame a picture of a life that didn't require approval from kids I didn't like or respect.

My fantasy extended to a dream of sailing around the world by myself in a boat I would learn to skipper. I checked college catalogs as to which institutions had courses in celestial navigation that the stars might guide me in my journey; I wondered what was entailed in working as a lighthouse attendant, where I could live in solitude and prepare for my odyssey. My vision extended to learning to play the guitar and wearing my now-long hair up in a twist held in place with galvanized nails. I took up smoking a pipe.

It wasn't a studied effort at eccentricity but seemed to be springing quite naturally from a previously suffocated heart and imagination.

When Nancy and I weren't out exploring the countryside, she would regale me with tales of outings to San Francisco with her friend Bev from German class. They were both quite fluent with the difficult tongue and would go shopping in high-end stores, speaking only German between them, posing for the hired help as if they knew no English. We thought this uproarious in the retelling, the incredible awkwardness for the poor saleswomen. Much more clever and heady stuff than yakking about boys or sitting in a bridge foursome.

But one day, a casual and careless remark, now long forgotten, hurt me deeply. Nancy had a quick wit, a sharp tongue, and a real intuition for finding the soft underbelly of a feeling. I drove away from her home stunned and inconsolable, a serious dent in my trust in our friendship. I wasn't eager for a second helping.

I didn't travel far, down to the end of the block where one of the eggheads lived—Linda, a compatriot from Latin class.

Linda was a real brainiac, destined for a special premed program at Penn State University which would catapult her through medical school by the completion of her fifth year. She would be leaving just days after our high school graduation. Serious about her studies, Linda had never dated or hung out with the popular kids. She was another of the students who were just too intelligent to be deemed likable.

But at this juncture, me with wounded heart and she with an incipient case of spring fever, we were a perfect fit by the time I landed at her door fresh from the wounding at Nancy's. I was drawn to her incredibly virginal quality, literally sweet sixteen and never been kissed, and I think she found me a bit dangerous in a romantic sense. She came to love riding in my sports car, and her parents hated it. They saw me as dangerous as well, but not as some exotic pirate personality as did Linda. To her parents, I was a thorn in the side of the larger-than-life dreams for their daughter.

Linda was a straight A student, and though her grades never faltered, her parents sensed a lightness of heart, a casual attitude about school, that seemed out of character. Certainly this underachiever with the zippy little roadster could not bode well.

It's worth an aside to mention that any time throughout life that a parent would lodge a complaint with my folks, an assertion that I was a bad influence, my mother would acquiesce, wag her head sorrowfully, and say, "I know." Thanks, Mom. Here we were again. I was not well-liked by Linda's parents.

Again, it might have worked to my advantage if I had any sense of propriety, manners, or how to get along in the home of strangers. I did not. They were a proper bunch, her father an attorney, and I made a poor impression. But I really liked their daughter.

We studied our coursework in Latin and English literature together, even went to the local Presbyterian church together, just so I could be near her. On lazy spring afternoons, we would hike up to the same hill where I used to sit vigil while worrying about pregnancy. Lying on our backs, side by side, we would study the cloud formations and dream aloud of life beyond high school. I was terribly impressed with her special admission to Penn State and the fact that only three girls in the country had been selected for this program. I loved how smart she was.

I began to fantasize about getting physically close with Linda; thoughts of her made my heart race, and she filled my daydreams. I recalled reading a passage in the early pages of *Moby Dick* where Ishmael is seeking a bed for the night at an inn. The only available bunk requires that he pair up with the savage-like Queequeg, an exotic foreigner whose body was decorated with tattoos.

The sailor was frightened of this formidable behemoth, but it was, after all, the last bunk. During the night, Ishmael awakens to find the huge arm of Queequeg flung across his chest, pinning him down. When I read this, it gave me a distinctly sexual rush. Now that I was exploring these new feelings I had for Linda, I imagined replicating the scene: being in our spot on the hill, me with my pipe, lying down to study the clouds, only to roll over and casually drape my arm across her body.

A clumsy scenario but fueled with pure teenage passion, I bumbled through it and we made contact. It was on that hill that we shared our first kiss. Sensation exploded for me as it never had with Bob. Something important was happening here.

Boys Versus Girls

A childhood friend once asked me, "Why is it that you're so angry with men?" I had a quick and sharp retort at the time, stemming from issues of trust and betrayal, and she didn't push the issue. But it merits reexamination.

As I've stated, Dad was my model of all that was virile, exciting, strong, and courageous. Largely, I wanted to be like him, and there were a few instances of closeness that constitute the bulk of any warm memories I have of life as a little kid.

We would go trout fishing together, high in the mountain lakes of the Sierra Nevada, where I would squirm at putting a worm on a hook but loved sitting on the bank with a line dangling and the anticipation of an occasional nibble. Just me and my dad.

I didn't want anything to do with cleaning the fish, nor did I care to eat it. It was the being out of doors, no one but the two of us, making camp and enjoying the stars dotting the night sky that were the payoff for me. At night, as the fire was dying down and we prepared to crawl into our sleeping bags, Dad would dig a hole at the foot of my bag and place in it a couple of fair-sized rocks from the rim of the fire pit. Then he would gently scoop the surrounding earth into the hole to cover and insulate the hot rocks. The arrangement was quite effective in keeping my feet warm in the chilly nighttime temperatures. His caring for me was obvious and palpable; I went off to sleep feeling a warmth that extended way beyond my feet.

Or I remember a time, a little older, when we were traveling on one of his business trips and together we danced a waltz on the ballroom floor of the Ambassador Athletic Club, a grand old private residence club in Salt Lake City. I felt special; he was all mine in these moments. I remember wishing that folks no longer would mistake me for his son but instead think me his paramour. I was twelve at most.

Another trip found us in Syracuse, New York. I recall a business colleague of Dad's taking us to a jazz club where we heard the great Stanley Turrentine on saxophone though his eminence was still incipient in 1958.

These were the good parts—the travels, the partnership, the adventures of back roads, packhorses, and private airplanes. But soon my little brother Bruce would supplant me as the apple of Dad's eye, and I would be the one staying home while Bruce slipped into the shoes of fulfilling Dad's dream of developing a *real* son, an heir apparent to his business empire. As a girl, I just didn't fit the bill.

Brother Bob had already failed Dad's aspirations for him, with his habit of underachieving and his desire to marry young and start a family of his own. It's as if I was next in line for the throne, but still, there was the bothersome fact that I was female. Bruce represented the last great hope, the virtual basket for holding all Dad's eggs.

Near as I could tell, my dad had thrown me aside, abandoned me as his buddy and helpmate. Bruce was the new pal, and I was left home to witness the unappealing predicament of my mother: the plight of a mid-century housewife unraveling with her books, her cigarettes, her sunbathing, her Miltowns—and her utter aloneness.

The paradox of my coming of age with the accepted gender roles of the era could be construed by me as nothing less than unacceptable. It felt as if I was being dumped by my dad to drown in a culture where I just didn't have a place. Dad and Bruce were off now, into the skies, Dad having bought a single-engine Beechcraft Bonanza and arranging flying lessons for Bruce so as to become his copilot.

This perceived desertion compounded my already-confused feelings about who I was in relation to my dad. Decades later, I would recall in therapy sessions some of the blurred ego boundaries and inappropriate touching from my earliest years. As I said, I was experiencing a shift of desire from wanting to be his boy to desiring to be his woman, a primal conflict that served as the source material for an entire continuum of psychological angst relating to my development as a woman.

For the moment, it felt like abandonment, pure and simple. The first betrayal of many perpetrated by men in the ensuing years, but this was at the hands of the man whose love I wanted most.

The following years held forth an endless stream of use and abuse by men. Beginning with petty cruelties at the hands of Bob, a pattern began of briefly conjoining with boys and men, suffering through one-night stands or otherwise very brief liaisons and discarding the offenders before they could reject me. As the sexual freedom of the '60s unfolded, there were an appalling number of opportunities for sexual promiscuity with always the same end: I would make the decision that my partner was an unworthy opponent in what felt like a battle for selfhood and dignity.

A dynamic took form and dug in: men were not to be trusted and would predictably displease and dissatisfy. And somewhere through the gender confusions of my childhood, I gleaned the conviction that I was insufficient in my attractiveness as a female of the species.

In more introspective moments (and all throughout I had more than my share of those), it occurred to me that my body was the currency for obtaining love and caring, and typical of those experiencing childhood sexual abuse, if someone expressed any interest in me at all, their use of my body was the minimum payment due.

Jettisoned from the Closet

But I'm jumping ahead. For the moment, I was lost in the bliss of my first girlfriend and the love we shared; the romance we generated filled my heart in a way I didn't know possible. This was heaven. But school was out and Linda had left just three days after our graduation ceremony. I was going to miss her terribly. But my dad had devised a plan.

Linda was gone to her summer program at Penn State, and I was about to embark on a bicycle tour of Europe with the American Youth Hostel group. This was a graduation gift from my parents: a tour through western Europe of a couple of month's duration. We were to convene in and depart from New York City.

How perfect, I thought. Dad was going to fly me to New York in his plane, in conjunction with some business matters he had on the East Coast. At first he offered that we could stop in Pennsylvania and visit Linda if I wanted. I was ecstatic! Then it all came unglued.

As the plan for a collegiate visit gelled, Nancy had happened to mention something to one of Linda's younger siblings regarding my proposed visit to their sister at her campus. When news of this got to Linda's parents they were apoplectic. The sky fell in one day when I returned from a bike ride and my father called me to the patio with a grave tone in his voice.

Linda's father had contacted my folks to say that their daughter's personal journals, left behind when she went off to college, had been usurped by her parents and read. The entries were exceedingly intimate and brought to the fore questions of a sexual relationship between us. They contained declarations of love, romantic poetry, and all manner of incriminating material one could imagine.

Linda's father, being an attorney, flexed his metaphorical muscle with an ultimatum, informing my father that we could either cancel our plan to visit Pennsylvania or her parents would have me exposed as a lesbian. My father caught me utterly off guard with this information.

Dad's proposed solution, not being one to be bullied, was to meet with Linda's father for lunch, peruse the journals himself, and make his own determination of my alleged perversion. Depending on his conclusions about my relationship with Linda, he would either assent to cancel the trip to Pennsylvania or, in the alternative, sue her parents for defamation of character.

He wanted to know if the accusation was true. What a pickle.

To this day, I'm a bit amazed at how quickly I devised a strategy to save my skin and reputation, all under the guise of honor and chivalry. I told him that even though I was Linda's best friend, I had never been privileged to see her hallowed notebooks and didn't feel it right that these two grown men should be poring over her most personal content while having cocktails. I agreed to decline the side trip to Pennsylvania in exchange for keeping her innermost scribblings away from prying eyes. As for my reputation, I told him I didn't really care what her parents thought and didn't think he should validate their vicious gossip with his concern. In keeping with a time-honored Gentry sentiment: "Fuck 'em if they can't take a joke."

For the time this sufficed and in due course, Dad and I set off for New York City in his plane.

Though I was invited on a number of occasions to take the yoke and try piloting on for size, I was never comfortable with the small aircraft. Too cramped, no bathroom, long hours of sitting in the same position—even as a passenger, it wasn't a great fit for me. I found the piloting boring on some level; it was clear this wasn't going to be a passion we shared.

As we traveled eastward over the course of a few days, I silently devised a plan: once settled in my Manhattan hotel room, I would book a flight on a small shuttle and head for Pennsylvania to visit Linda before my departure for London. Meantime, Dad would be off on his eastern business chores, and we would be safe from parental censure.

Coeds on the Loose

Having bid farewell to Dad, I went straightaway to the desk to procure assistance in booking my reservation on a twelve-seat commuter plane to the airfield nearest Linda's campus. I was just sixteen and had never performed tasks like this for myself. The desk clerk was helpful; traveler's checks were the power to purchase I would use after the cab ride to the airport.

It's entertaining to think back these sixty years and reflect on a time of no credit cards (in the hands of kids), no cell phones, and needing the actual intervention of adults to accomplish what the average eight-year-old could pull off today.

Linda, having established a modicum of independence through her move to school, was able to guide me through the process during our phone conversations from my hotel. Within a day of my Dad's departure, I was on the way to see my girl.

Though I had visited the college campuses of institutions where I had applied for admission, I hadn't before visited the inner workings—the cafeteria, the activities center, and, of course, the *dorm*. This was a magical world, life centering around a bedroom free from parental prying eyes and bothersome little brothers. Just the roomie to circumvent, and that seemed relatively easy. At last we managed some alone time, albeit with that thrilling paranoia surrounding our illicit secret—our love for each other—and the imperative of remaining undiscovered.

The plan was for our time on campus to be relatively brief, then she would in turn book a flight, return with me to New York, and spend time free from even the roommate in our own private room. Breathtakingly erotic for a pair of sixteen-year-olds.

It was June in New York—sweaty, gritty, noisy, even in 1963. The rapid pulse and shimmering vibrancy of this high-density metropolis added its own contribution to the adrenaline rush of our time in the Big Apple.

We didn't sightsee, visit museums, or paint the town. Once in my room, it was sheer, melodramatic, heavenly, sheet-soaking lust. Our conversation was peppered with avowals of how much we had already missed each other and how lonely we would be in the summer ahead.

We thrilled at the adventure of interruption from the housekeeping staff, scrambling to wrap ourselves in sheets and blurt out directions not to be disturbed. Other than that, it was sheer paradise—until the room phone rang.

It was my father, who had decided on his return home from Syracuse to stop by and bid me farewell one more time. He wanted to take me to dinner; I declined, excusing myself with some tale of being exhausted. Well then, he wanted to know, could I just come down to the bar and have a parting cocktail with him. Again I begged off, all the time trying to disguise the quivering of my voice and the post-passion shortness of breath.

Though I felt guilty about the lies and about denying him, it was a clear choice to stay sequestered in the room with my beloved. Reluctantly, he settled for wishing me a pleasant adventure for the coming summer and left for the airfield while I returned to my girl and our last hours together.

Our time together was charged with sweetness and passion and over all too soon. The next morning, I was off to convene with my AYH group and depart for London by air; Linda returned to Pennsylvania on the commuter shuttle.

A New View of the World

When first meeting my fellow travelers, I had a crestfallen moment. It didn't take long to deduce that I had been placed with eleven other kids my chronological age, which meant that I was the only one in the group who had already graduated from high school. The majority of them were two years my junior. To my way of thinking, that left them insufferably immature and unworldly while *I* had just taken an unsupervised flight of adventure, on my own, in order to perpetrate a tryst of unparalleled deviance. How cool was I? How cool were they *not*?

Though we had chaperones on the tour, today the memory of them is vague. The only girl among us, I remember with some detail, was the daughter of a San Francisco businessman who had just opened an importing retail enterprise called Cost Plus, which soon became an institution and still thrives today, some forty-five years later. Her name was Debbie Bartlett.

We had shipped our own bicycles ahead from San Francisco and our first day in London was one of *Some Assembly Required*. Once we had the wheels back in place, the saddles mounted and the brakes in working order, we began our odyssey.

In the ensuing days, we wound out of London, south through Canterbury to Dover, where we were to take a ferry across the channel to Belgium.

It was a delightful ride, well within our capabilities, and each night we came to rest in a hostel where we would share a bunk room with girls from all over England and the continent. It was an exposure to diversity that was new for this girl from the suburbs of the Bay Area.

In Canterbury, we visited the cathedral, dripping with history going back to 597 AD and where Archbishop Thomas Becket was murdered in 1170. Also in this quaint town I purchased my first guitar from a charming older gentleman in a local pawnshop. I didn't yet know how to play, but I had a determination to flesh out that part of my exotic fantasy of the future I had planned.

Though I couldn't ride my bike with the guitar, I left the shop-keeper with the price of the guitar, plus some money, for shipping it home for me.

All residents of the hostels were to be out by 8:00 a.m. and the doors were locked behind us 'til day's end. I'll never forget the shock of a 6:00 a.m. wake-up call of blasting recorded bagpipes in one of the dorms as a sort of surreal reveille. Or the night a young British traveler, Helen, ensconced in a bottom bunk, called out in a quiet voice to her friend above as they drifted off with the colloquialism, "Rosemary, are you gone?" That still cracks me up.

But as we snaked our way along picturesque country roads toward eventual disembarkation at Dover, with its famous white cliffs, I missed Linda ever stronger with each passing day. It was some of my earliest indoctrination in the ways of obsession, and I was discovering I had an enormous talent for it.

I was also lavishing in a brand-new independence, only tangentially supervised and unfettered to explore some of the decadent entertainments of adulthood, like drinking alcoholic beverages.

Building an Avocation

Though I had already evidenced a propensity for and an attraction to drinking, in London, I was considered *legal* even though I'm sure the local permissions weren't set at sixteen.

Like many toddlers, early on, I had a liking for the taste of beer. Adults would think it rather adorable, when gathered for a neighborhood barbecue, to let me totter around and finish the dregs of a beer can or taste a cocktail and delight in my scrunched-up little face reacting to the exotic and vaporous flavors. (I still shudder to remember how the small assembly crowed with laughter when I once drained a can in which someone had extinguished a cigarette. Ugh!)

By six or seven years old, I had already had a parental limit set on my drinking—one beer a day, all my own, at least in the summer months. This was just another of those facts of my childhood that seemed perfectly normal until some therapist or peer later reacted in horror. But what was significant to me, when entering recovery from alcoholism in my thirties, was that even at that tender age, before approaching the bottom of a can, my obsessive thoughts were already focused on the next day's ration.

These habits continued through childhood. Occasionally, my parents would have gin fizzes on a Sunday morning as a special treat, and I was permitted to imbibe. I remember eliciting a snort of laughter from them when I said, "Those are too strong. I prefer martinis." When I said I didn't get the joke, I felt a rush of pride when informed that a martini was a much stronger drink than a fizz.

But I didn't seriously experiment with drinking until my senior year in high school. My first drunk was one night after a movie when a friend, Pat Spingola, stayed over for the night and we got into my parents' liquor cabinet. There was a half-filled bottle of gin with additional quarts of the same as backup. I had the brilliant idea that if we wished to remain undetected, we would need to nab a fresh bottle and finish the whole thing. It never would have occurred to me, then or now, to just drink a portion and pour the rest down the drain.

The only mixer available was ginger ale, and as my folks were in the other end of the house asleep, we also felt the need to make our drinks without the benefit of ice due to the noise the ice maker might make. So it was gin and ginger ale, warm and sickening, that comprised my first truly oblivious alcohol adventure.

We silently dipped in the pool (lucky we didn't drown we were getting so blitzed) while we put away the entire fifth of gin, eventually getting sick and vomiting all the way down the hall of the house en route to the bathroom. The retching and ruckus awakened my parents to whom I wobbly protested that I must have gotten sick from something I ate at the movies. Again, they took the flaccid excuse without comment though the whole house must have reeked of alcohol.

And it was alcohol's effect that caused me to be deprived of my beloved Austin Healey when I went off to college. It was shortly after graduation during a night of drinking in the hills overlooking the high school, and it left me altered enough to hit a curb when I pulled into a service station for gas—the station my older brother worked in. The misstep caused a puncture in the low-slung car's oil pan, and I was still operating on enough brainpower to know it wouldn't serve to keep driving. Seeking my brother's help, I instead exposed myself to discovery when he opened the trunk of the Healey and found the remains of a case of illegally acquired beer.

Going off to college without the benefit of my darling sports car was the punishment meted out when my brother ratted on me to my parents about the beer. This was one of the earlier instances of his adult posturing now that he had left the roost and lived on his own. The first, and most egregious, was when he tattled to my parents that I had become sexually active with neighbor Bob. He was quickly becoming someone I couldn't trust to keep my confidence. Probably, I never again confided in him.

My attraction to and exploits with alcohol were further facilitated by acceptance to Chico State College, which, at the time, was ranked by *Playboy* magazine as the third-ranked party school in the nation. That was where I was headed upon my return from the European tour.

The Work-Around

As our tour left Great Britain, we ferried across the English Channel to Belgium, spending our first night on the continent in the charming city of Bruges, one-time capital of Flanders. A beautiful and picturesque metropolis with snaking canals and stunning cathedrals, it was our first overnight before cycling off to Antwerp and Brussels.

Theoretically, I was shopping and sightseeing with the group whereas, in reality, I was joined by a couple other adventurous souls among us and exhilarating in the liberty to purchase and consume bottles of red wine, all the while unchaperoned. One of my favorite photos from the trip (one which understandably inflamed my father when seeing it upon my return) was of me clutching a bottle of burgundy to my chest and reclined in a cobblestoned gutter. I thought it was a hoot; my father peremptorily and ceremoniously flung it in the fire.

But throughout Belgium and upon entering Germany, wending our way from Cologne to Bonn and headed for Frankfurt, I was aching to be reunited with Linda. Though the sites were fascinating, educational, and colorful—the architecture of villages and the gorgeous stained glass of the churches—getting home to my beloved was taking form as a consuming passion.

The more I thought about it, the more I pined. The plan I was hatching was to phone my parents from Bonn, plead unendurable homesickness, and hopefully make an early exit from the tour and catch a jet back to New York where I could finagle another stop in Pennsylvania to visit Linda. I thought the stratagem flawless.

The call worked, tugging at the heartstrings of my folks back home. The part I hadn't planned on: my dad booked me a nonstop flight on the then-new over-the-Pole route from Frankfurt to San Francisco. So no tryst with Linda.

I returned home still heartsick and suffering the punishing recriminations of my mom and dad, disappointed in my early return, and putting me in indentured servitude at my dad's company for the remainder of the summer. They were understandably angry about the additional expense of changing my flight plans and determined to teach me a lesson in fiscal responsibility by exacting repayment.

I was now home, still blue, and suffering constant teasing about how I wimped out on my supposed fantasy vacation. Linda was still at Penn State, and I was in the suburbs awaiting my collegiate adventure in the fall.

The First (Seriously) Broken Heart

Toward the end of summer, as the weather started to turn in its mild Bay Area way, Linda was due home for her first visit. It was still problematic to connect with her through the veil of her parents' disapproval, but I was determined to find a way. Perhaps Nancy could help, or maybe Linda could use the family car to steal away. I waited impatiently, my stomach in knots.

Finally, the day arrived, and through information gleaned from mutual acquaintances, I knew Linda was home. I couldn't wait to call. The suspense, the longing, the wait to hear her voice were almost unbearable. No matter how sweet my imaginings, I suppose there's no way that the actuality of speaking with her could live up to my expectations. Worse than unmet expectations was the devastation of what was to come; what had such emotional power in its inception was predictably matched in the anguish brought by its end.

Linda's voice was distant—certainly a bad sign. Her tone non-committal—another scare. The delivered message was curt and precise. While in Pennsylvania for the summer, Linda had discovered boys, or more importantly, they had discovered her. When I had phoned her long-distance from Germany, she told of dates she'd gone on where it seemed boys were taking advantage of her: make-out sessions and attempts at vanquishing her virginity. That conversation was part of the urgency I felt to return home and reassert my devotion to her in person.

But once home, I found she was firmly ensconced in the heterosexual milieu. What she had to tell me was that our love was strictly childish experimentation and that what we had, she had now out-grown. She didn't even want to see me. I was reeling. Thank God I had already discovered the blissful oblivion available through alcohol.

Release from the Nest

I was delivered to collegiate life by my parents, moving all my needed personal possessions in Dad's station wagon: the clothes I wanted for my new life, especially jeans and sweatshirts; my baby blue Smith-Corona portable typewriter; toiletries and a hair dryer for my then shoulder-length hair; a clothes iron that enabled me to eventually take in ironing for extra cash. But when thinking back, it's what my loads didn't include that seems significant and telling of all that lay ahead to be discovered. The books I came to treasure, the poets I learned to enjoy, the direction of my musical interests—all that was still ahead of me, waiting to be plumbed.

It was a three-hour drive from my folks' home in Lafayette to Chico, and it was a hot and sultry fall afternoon when we made the trip. I couldn't have begun to imagine how different the climate of my new home would prove to be. Chico was blistering hot, sitting in the northern end of the Sacramento Valley, with an Indian summer that would last well into the first chilly days of mid-October. We were hot from the drive, cars not being routinely equipped with air-conditioning in 1963.

I had made my choice to attend Chico State from among three schools to which I had applied and been accepted. San Francisco State felt too close to home, as did San Jose. But above all, in perusing school catalogs, among the three, Chico was the only one that really *looked* like I felt a college campus should: ivy-covered walls on an impressive bell tower rising above the Spanish tiled roof of the old brick student activities center, lush lawns surrounding a quad with rose bushes in a formal arrangement, even a babbling brook running right through the middle of campus. At this time, the total student body of Chico State College was a mere 3,000 students. A small college by any measure.

Across the creek and over a quaint footbridge were more lawns, large enough to serve as playfields for students tossing about the odd disks that were the beginnings of the Frisbee craze. On each side of this green expansive carpet lay the dormitories: Shasta Hall for boys on the north border and Lassen Hall, the girls' dorm, on the southern edge.

I was moving into Lassen Hall—three stories high of brick construction, a large ugly rectangle reflecting none of the antique beauty of the activities center and the classroom buildings. The dorms suffered from being a newer construction, most likely a product of late 1950s architecture. (One of the poets I came to know when I later got into journalism referred to the dorms as resembling Kleenex boxes.)

The bricks helped a little in keeping the room temperatures down. My room was at the western end of the second floor, room 222, and I remember feeling it was a good omen—that two was a lucky number for me. Keeping in the superstitious vein, I appreciated that just as the room in which my mother stayed when I was born at Kaiser Hospital, this window was the second tier up, the second window from the right. Meant to be, I figured.

As the three of us busied ourselves trekking repeatedly up the flight of stairs to my new room, carrying boxes from the car, depositing them in the middle of the floor to be organized later, we began to feel the strain of the hot day and the pending separation. We started to get cranky and short with one another.

Now my dad can be a pretty abrasive guy, and I'm sure it's exacerbated by stress though, in those days, we didn't analyze such things or look for cause and effect. I was recently enamored with an emerging form of music, not the faux-folk offerings I'd been listening to, like The Kingston Trio and the Limeliters, but by a more authentic and earth-bound sound of Woody Guthrie and lately the young Joan Baez.

Well, my dad chose this day to openly criticize my taste (big surprise) by likening the vocal stylings of Baez to a squalling cat. As usual, knowing just how to push my buttons, he had been oblivious to how badly he hurt my feelings with his harsh opinions. I went into a sulk, the moving chore was coming to completion, and we all said goodbye with hard feelings and silence between us.

It was a difficult way to part, but later in the evening, and in the weeks to follow, I was glad for the rift and the distance it put between us. It gave me a layer of protection from what would be my first real case of homesickness.

Life in Lassen Hall

My move into the dorm had been earlier than the bulk of the students as I was scheduled to attend Frosh Camp, along with other freshmen. Here, we were to gain an orientation about campus life, class schedules, how to navigate the registration process, rushing fraternities and sororities—everything they could think of to help ease our transition. So by the time I arrived, I had been notified in advance of the name of my assigned roommate, Cindy, but she was yet to move in.

I settled in before heading off to camp, chosen my bed and side of the room, arranged my clothes in the closet and placed them in the drawers, and hung on the bulletin board a treasured ink drawing my uncle had done of the charming little Austin Healey I had to leave at home. The bottom of the drawing was inscribed, "To Lin from Unk."

Lin had been my family nickname since I was a little girl. I preferred it to my given name of Linda ever since fourth grade when I read in *My Weekly Reader* that in the year I was born, 1946, Linda was the most common given girls' name. I supposed it was due to the popularity of film star Linda Darnell, but at the time, I remember being gravely disappointed in the lack of imagination it showed on the part of my parents.

While I was still at camp, Cindy had moved into our room. Unlike me, she had received no word or info regarding the identity of her new roomie. She was a sophomore and already had a circle of friends in Lassen Hall from the previous year. Left to uncover my identity through detective work and reading the inscription on my uncle's drawing, she greeted me upon my return as Lin. Likewise, she began introducing me to girls she knew in the dorm as her roommate Lin. This was great! It felt comfortable and familiar and filled to some extent the void left by the distance I felt from my family.

The next days revealed a number of unanticipated wonders: meals could be gotten in the dining hall on a flexible schedule, we were free to smoke openly (a habit I had taken up seriously since graduation), and, most amazingly, we weren't required to attend class and *we could wear jeans* when we did! This was the first time in my life I was able to attend school without the nightmarish costumes dictated by gender role expectations. I thought I was in heaven!

My only previous experience with a similar freedom of dress was in the sixth grade when I was in a student play written by class-mate Rose Wills. The title of the play was *Turkey Pox*, and in it, I was cast as a young black boy; my costume was jeans, my beloved French cuff shirt, desert boots, and blackface. After the production was over, I was allowed to remain in my costume, sans the makeup, and it was the happiest day I could remember in school up until the college years.

Cindy was a friendly girl, seemed a bit sheltered, but was gen-erally a good student and good company. We were going to be a fine fit. The utterly unique aspect of dorm life for me was that of commu-nity. Our supervision came from a lovely RA, or resident assistant, named Roberta Logan. She was African American, and this, too, was new for me.

The only woman of color I had ever known was our house-keeper, Victoria, who came in once a week on the bus all the way from Oakland to clean, wash, and iron. She was one of those won-derful but rare presences who made me feel utterly loved. Victoria also taught me my love of ironing. I would awaken on Friday morn-ings to the squeaking sounds of the built-in ironing board. She chose to do this quietest task at her early 7:00 a.m. start so as not to disturb anyone still sleeping.

But I digress. Roberta set a few mild limits within a fairly strict overall structure to dorm life. In the early sixties, there were defi-nite curfews; after which, we would be locked out of the dorm. It was clear that an infraction had serious repercussions in the form of lost privileges. Doors locked at 10:00 p.m. during the school week and on the weekends at 1:00 a.m. The weekend lockout seemed a generous allowance; plenty of time, it proved, for me to get enough mischief under my belt. Down the hall, I discovered a new friend named Sue Remley. On a fall afternoon, I had heard a clear, high, melodic soprano drifting down the hall to the accompaniment of a lone acoustic guitar. I was certain it was a Joan Baez recording, but not one with which I was familiar. I was pretty sure I had them all at that point.

When I rushed down the hall to see who I might discover with a similar passion for folk music, I found Sue sitting on the edge of her bed, quietly strumming chords on her guitar, and singing a traditional folk ballad. This was the first time I had seen someone make music right before my eyes, with the exception of Stanley Turentine on the trip to Syracuse with my dad. Sue became an important person for me to befriend.

Like me, Sue was not a real mixer and had probably been a rather shy girl in high school. And at last, here was someone who knew how to play the guitar! Even better, she promised to teach me some fundamentals. I proved to be a quick study, mastering about ten chords, dabbling in minor keys (the best fit for the mournful songs that sounded so captivating in Sue's clear voice), and even learning some nontraditional tunings, my favorite being D modal.

Shortly into the semester, Sue came home to Lafayette for a weekend as my house guest, with our primary aim being to visit pawnshops in downtown Oakland and search out an inexpensive guitar for me to buy. It was a thrillingly novel experience for both of us; the shops clustered in the part of town near the county jail and the street crowd seeming a little rough to this pair of doe-eyed girls from the suburbs.

My dad was still giving me a ribbing about the guitar I had purchased from the kindly gentleman in Canterbury while on my bike trip. Dad relentlessly insinuated that I had been taken for a sucker, leaving this man with cash to cover the cost of shipping the guitar and confidently averred that I would see neither the money nor the instrument. Boy, did I ever gloat when, late in the summer, I received a lovely note from Canterbury, along with an international postal money order in the amount of all monies I had given him, both for the guitar and the shipping. It would be too costly, he regretfully informed me, to send the guitar along. According to his best research, the expense of shipping would far outweigh the value of the instrument itself.

The weekend mission with Sue was successful; I returned to school the proud owner of an acoustic, generic guitar, albeit one with a nice tone. She had given it a sample strumming in the store and approved of it as a starter instrument for her eager pupil.

Beyond her lovely voice, our shared tastes in music, and the valuable teaching Sue could impart, we didn't seem to have a great deal in common. Her valued distinction was that she was the first new friend I could call my own in Lassen Hall. But the truly influential individual who entered my world was my next-door neighbor in the dorm, a junior named Dianne.

Dianne seemed enigmatic and sophisticated; even more intriguing than her upperclassman status was the fact that she somehow had a double room to herself with no roommate in evidence. She was involved in campus life in ways that neither my roomie Cindy nor Sue were: Dianne belonged to a sorority and was also editor of the *Record*, the Chico State yearbook. I was captivated by her seeming maturity and worldliness.

Dianne convinced me to add the journalism class to my course load that would put me on the yearbook staff. I think staffers possibly weren't easy to come by, but she seemed sincerely interested in having me join their collective creative effort. As editor, Dianne was also the teacher of the three-unit course and had the responsibility of grading her staffers. She reported to a faculty advisor who supervised both the yearbook and the school newspaper.

I had chosen a fairly hefty course load for my first semester. I thought I wanted to be a lab technician by the end of college, never bothering to reflect that my high school education had been largely focused on liberal arts and very light on science and math. With five semester units of chemistry on my plate and no high school chemistry in my transcript, my courses were anchored in difficulty with just that one course. But I had elected to carry fifteen units, and now

Dianne was advocating that I add an additional three. I recall her saying, "Remember, the more you have to do, the more you will get done." The rationalization worked; I registered for her class.

Square Peg/Round Hole

I desperately wanted my collegiate experience to be a huge shift from the sort of isolation and ostracism that high school had represented. I wanted to fit in. Eccentricity wasn't the order of the day; rather, I was hoping to find a life where I could date, be asked to parties, find a group of friends with whom to hang out.

I tried rushing the sororities, putting on my best outfits, but utterly puzzled when it got to the part of rush week where the rushees visited the sorority house for a formal tea. These teas were an aspirant's opportunity to put a best foot forward and convince the sisterhood of the asset one could be. When I was told it was appropriate to wear white gloves to tea, I couldn't believe what I heard. I owned no gloves (and never had), gave a fleeting thought to borrowing some, but had serious reservations about how out of character I would feel in an environment where gloves were *de rigueur*.

I limped through the remainder of Greek Week half-heartedly, without white gloves and without much resolve to jump through the obligatory hoops in an effort to make a good impression. No stunning surprise that none of the five sororities on campus were interested in having me as a pledge.

Even Alpha Chi, the independent sorority to which Dianne belonged, showed no interest, and they were known as total party girls. On some level, it was just one more instance of how I didn't fit. Looking back, I can see that qualities for which pledges were being chosen were just not in my quiver of arrows: a call to service, a sense of community, trading hair and makeup tips—whatever. One more time, I failed at being a girl.

Greek Week ended and the experience was behind me. The rank taste of rejection and failure began to fade. I surmised that being a member of a clique, bonded in sisterhood for life to a group of young women, was not the direction my college lifestyle would take. By contrast, I was loving journalism, learning new skills like laying out and pasting up pages, mastering the foreign vocabulary of printers and photographers, and, not least of all, working closely with my editor. I was an eager apprentice, even garnering notice from Fred Clarvoe, our faculty advisor.

Acquiring skills such as the guitar and learning new fields like publishing were some of the first experiences where I gleaned valuable qualities about myself: focus, single-mindedness of purpose, diligence and hard work, a passion for the task at hand. Nothing before had interested me enough to give it such concentrated attention, and the approval and encouragement I felt from my various mentors was an entirely new thrill. I just worked harder and harder.

But lying by the side of this road were fifteen strongly academic units that got not much attention at all. Chemistry totally confounded me, so the obvious choice was to sleep in rather than attend lecture or lab. Biology was equally stultifying, but an English composition class was easy enough to sleepwalk through, and I can't even remember what else I was neglecting.

My first semester was drawing to a close, and I was settling in to campus life, if not settling down in the classroom. I was ever more aware of a burgeoning identity that had less and less in common with my suburban roots. During semester break, I elected not to return home and instead stayed in Lassen Hall with a mere skeleton crew of staff and a handful of students who lived too far away to make the journey home for just a few days. There was a ghostlike quality to the quiet halls replete of giggling girls or visitors in the lobby.

After a couple of days, I was in the lounge watching television when a story came on about a young girl and her mother murdered in Oakland. I was incredulous when they reported her name—Carolyn Martin.

Carolyn was a transfer sophomore to Lassen Hall, a charming and beautiful girl who had come to Chico after spending her first year at a community college in Oakland. She was vivacious, always smiling, and an easy fit with all the students she met, boys and girls alike. She had left a boyfriend at home, an Eric Somebody, who had not been happy about her moving far from him. He had visited her once or twice, and the general assessment was that he was having trouble accepting her desire to end their relationship.

I discovered that Carolyn's father was a physician and her mother a woman who had performed tireless public service. Mrs. Martin had been named Oakland Mother of the Year, and the mayor presided while a brass plaque had been set in concrete on the Mothers' Walk at the Oakland Morcom Rose Garden just the previous year. From television reports and clippings which my mother forwarded, I learned that the bodies of mother and daughter had been stumbled upon by Carolyn's younger sister when returning home from school. Before the end of the break, while the halls were still filled with hush, Dr. Martin quietly arrived to gather up Carolyn's belongings.

Soon, kids would return from the holiday, bringing boxes of homemade cookies, new outfits, and a solemn acknowledgment of our collective loss of Carolyn. In just two months, with the violent ends to the lives of President Kennedy and now Carolyn, there was a pall of uninvited and unwelcome maturity settling upon us all, a sense that life contained senseless acts and cruel surprises. (Eric, the beau, was questioned but never arrested and the crime remains unsolved some forty-five years later.)

Transitioning into Spring

Within a few days, the buzz of Carolyn's story had subsided and we turned our thoughts to registration for the coming semester and the issuance of report cards for the one just completed. The administration was transitioning their registration process to the newer computer model, the sort with stacks of punch cards and an admonition not to bend, fold, spindle, or mutilate. Grades were still being issued in a more traditional format: a typed-out form with letter grades entered upon it.

Though I expected grim news, the first semester's grades still managed to take my breath away; the large letters in red across my report card read ACADEMIC PROBATION, but the real stunner was my GPA of 0.8! I was pretty sure my parents were not going to be proud and equally confident that a career in the sciences was not on my horizon. The consolation prize was that Mr. Clarvoe and Dianne conferred, and on her recommendation and with his approval, I was made assistant editor of the *Record*. My neighbor and I continued to have reason to work together closely, often late into the night, in our journalism offices in the upper level of the student activities center.

Spending so much time in the activities center, I began to encounter other oddballs, folks unlike the kids in class, the dorm, or the dining hall. There was a staff writer for the paper, a young guy named John, who had already been in the military and was now attending college on the G.I. Bill. He was an aspiring poet and opened my world to realms like the Dadaist movement in art and e. e. cummings in literature, an appropriate accompaniment to my new discovery of playwrights such as Ionesco, Beckett, Pinter, and Albee.

John also taught me about photography and showed me around the journalism darkroom, instructing me in developing film, loading my own film, mixing photographic chemicals, and using the enlarger.

I took to it so readily that Mr. Clarvoe agreed to let me shoot the cover photo for the *Record* we were in the process of producing.

I was impassioned by the shot in my head, seen on countless evenings strolling around campus—the elegant profile of the towering Trinity Hall, our campus activities center, its belfry covered in ivy, backlit by a horizon of deep oranges (from burning off the rice fields in the valley to the west) while a veil of evening lavenders and deep purple descended, seeming to crush the fiery colors with their weight.

With Mr. Clarvoe's blessing, I was permitted to borrow the department's 4"×5"-view camera—the historical-looking sort, supported by a tripod and complete with black drape to enclose the photographer and shut out ambient light. It was a warm evening, and I think I accumulated forty-five mosquito bites before the shot was complete. The film plates had to be sent out to a professional lab as the shot was in color and our facilities were strictly for black-and-white photography. When the lab returned the transparencies, there was one small problem: I had shot the wrong side of Trinity Hall. In other words, the way I had composed the shot would have put the bell tower on the back cover of the yearbook! I considered this a disaster, but my mistake had cost the department too much in processing to allow for a second opportunity. We decided our readership would be none the wiser if we just reversed the image by flipping it over so the proper exposure made the front cover. But to the discerning eye, it is forever immortalized that the ivy covering the tower is actually on the wrong side.

This error was, in fact, prescient of a character trait still with me: a flair for focusing on the immediate goal to the exclusion of any ability to see the ensuing circumstances. But my vision was realized in capturing the shot, albeit the *wrong* shot, and my interest in photography continued. Of course, one of the most fruitful outcomes of this new passion was discovering yet another safe place Dianne and I could hang out—the darkroom.

Another fabulous character who blipped across my radar was a transplant from New York, Norma Kwestel, not a student but a young devotee of Georges Osawa, the originator of the macrobiotic diet. Norma had relocated to Chico to help found Chico-San, one of the earliest organic food producers. The collective had chosen Chico as fertile rice-growing country and hypothetically a safe distance from any perceived nuclear threat in our Cold War paranoid fantasies. From Norma, I learned about organic foods and tomes such as *We Are All Sanpaku*, sending my young, impressionable mind on yet another wild and fascinating junket, worlds away from (and much more relevant than) the need for white gloves.

The Rumblings of Revolt

I was intellectually stimulated in an entirely unfamiliar way. The air was electric in my new world: the expansion of my interests and opinions, worldview, and creativity seemed boundless in potential. This new milieu was unfolding so quickly, and I was barely through my first year in Chico.

Meanwhile, in the Bay Area, progressive thought was burgeoning. When I had come home for Thanksgiving break that fall, I was hearing on TV and radio about the riots at Sproul Plaza on the Cal Berkeley campus. In phone calls with high school classmates who attended Cal, I was filled in on the student unrest featured in the headlines: the Free Speech Movement. I didn't really get it but found the chaos and rebellion of bullhorns and overturned and ignited police vehicles exciting and stimulating.

Just as I didn't really get it when, just days before, the holiday break President Kennedy was assassinated. My family background had taught me nothing of empathy or a national consciousness. With the entire campus in a pall during the following week, a national shroud of grief paralyzing not only the campus but the country, I could heard my father protesting in his most booming Republican voice that we (the nation, according to him) were all sick of hearing about it. I think my mother felt it detracted from the joy of her forty-sixth birthday on the day after the tragedy.

Blindsided by Love

For my part, and for the moment, the only revolution I knew was happening in our sleepy Chico hamlet, where, as well as acquiring a new knowledge of journalism, I was honing my skills as a drinker. After all, my school had a party reputation to uphold, and keg functions were always available, with or without an actual invitation. Dianne knew some fun guys, her contemporaries in the men's independent fraternity Lambda Pi. Among them, I met a couple of particularly nice and better-than-average young men: Bill Clarke and Lani Waller.

Bill and Lani were roommates in off-campus housing, renting a basement apartment and holding the acquisition of an education second in importance to having a good time. I learned they were both fifth-year seniors. I hung out at their place frequently, and we listened to the new emerging music and shared a lot of beer. The guys were sweet and even seemed somewhat honorable, never trying to take sexual advantage and always available to be a good ear. I think their exceptional qualities had to do with their advanced age—they were both twenty-three while I was still seventeen.

As well as introducing me to her friends, my alliance with Dianne was having even deeper impact on my emerging self-awareness. Ever since high school gym classes, horrified to be seen naked by the other girls, I realized I had an inordinate body shyness that made it challenging even to go swimming with other kids and share a dressing room.

As we grew closer, I shared this vulnerability with Dianne, and she insisted we take on the task of getting me through this timidity. Having no roommate and therefore optimal privacy in the dorm, she convinced me to pose nude for her, and it would augment the figure drawing class she was taking.

It was a tremendous struggle at first, but I so trusted her and she went out of her way to make me feel safe. The door was kept locked, and at first she would draw me, lying on my side on the bed, my back to her, the better to hide my face. Eventually my shyness faded, with the end result that we had grown closer in a way that is only accomplished by sharing deep fears and insecurities, coming through it to find comfort and acceptance.

I began work on a volume of poetry for her, writing a new short poem every night before turning out the light. In a small six-ring red booklet, I neatly penned my thoughts and confidences and expressed my gratitude for our friendship.

The creativity began to pour out of me: pen and ink drawings, attempts at song lyrics, and a return to painting with oils which I had begun in high school. I felt so alive though very little of my collegiate experience was taking place in the traditional classroom setting.

A few months into the first semester, in mid-December, Dianne came home with me for the weekend to my parents' house. Not atypically, we found upon arrival that my parents were out for the evening and we had the house to ourselves. What else to do but invade the liquor cabinet and explore what brand of trouble we could find? I remember it was Friday the thirteenth of December 1963. I'd say it was a day that would live in infamy, but someone already beat me to it. I still hold any Friday the thirteenth to be my lucky day.

Once we'd gotten pretty high, we started making phone calls to various friends. She wanted to talk with her high school boyfriend John, who was currently a senior at St. Mary's College, then all male and in a town neighboring Lafayette.

We were pretty drunk by this time and after chatting with him in the silly manner that springs from a young inebriated woman, all giggles and flirtation, Dianne wanted John to talk to me and handed me the phone. I had never met him, but she had spoken of me often, and I think it was his mission to get some background information about her new friend. Di went to get us another drink.

I remember lying on my back on the couch in my parents' den, chatting with John, when she came back in the room with our cocktails. As I was preparing to hand over the phone, she totally shocked me by zeroing in and planting a warm, wet kiss directly on my mouth. I was stunned but also terribly pleased; as she drew away from me to take the receiver, her face was painted with a luscious mischief. She was quite tickled with herself.

I, in turn, couldn't wait to end this stupid phone call and explore what other make-out prospects might be on the agenda. Soon John had said his good nights, and we found it fortuitously near an acceptable bedtime. With tension and apprehension that was almost palpable, we headed for my bedroom.

Other than my adventure with Linda in the skinny little hotel bed in New York City, this was a first-time luxury—in a double bed with a warm, naked woman who seemed to want me. I was a bit at a loss as to how to proceed but was fairly sure I could trust my instincts. My parents were kind enough to have not yet returned.

The making out was sweet and tasty in spite of the flavor of gin. We were loosened up enough to enjoy a lush level of foreplay: long, lingering kisses; succulent, soft lips; tender nibbles flirting the edges of seductive pain. We were worked up to the point where I wondered if I had permission to take the lovemaking to a deeper level. I began to explore the warmth between her thighs, the humid, pulsing come-hither pull, when I thought I heard her hoarsely say, "Don't start that."

The rapid-fire succession of ugly thoughts in my mind ran the gamut from shame and humiliation to rejection and embarrassment. I was speechless but deferred to her wishes. We hugged a bit more and rolled over ostensibly to sleep. For my part, only the alcohol finally brought unconsciousness. I couldn't stop agonizing about the terrible misread I must have made about Dianne's affections.

We awoke the next morning with the sort of hangover that was becoming increasingly more familiar and that only the very young can survive. I don't really recall much of the rest of the weekend but was still moping internally for the love of this woman I had come to feel so deeply about. It wasn't until our drive back to Chico on

Sunday afternoon that we had an opportunity to discuss what had happened during our lovemaking.

It seemed that I had not so much misread as misheard. What she actually said to me in the heat of passion, Dianne revealed, was, "Don't stop there." Oh my god! I could have been blissfully exploring every inch of her but instead fell off to sleep feeling like a bad lover and a worse friend.

Clearing the air about our thwarted passion brought such relief as well as the realization that, indeed, she wanted me and I, in turn, desired her. Without mentioning it, I'm sure she was as acutely anticipatory as I about dorm room 224, Dianne's room, the room with unfettered privacy. We knew we were heading into something great.

I want to say a word here about lesbian culture, of which I knew nothing at the time and, in fact, did my lion's share of helping to develop. Today, we joke about "What does the lesbian bring on the second date? A U-Haul." Of course, this to mean that after the briefest of liaisons, two women are ready to build a nest together and fashion some manner of marriage.

In 1963, I can say with confidence that I was the only lesbian I knew, with the exception of the mannish electronics workers my father had employed in his shop; the extremely butch women who slicked back their short hair and had real pennies in their loafers, collars turned up on their jackets, and hands stuffed in the pockets of their jeans. Here I was, with my long hair that I no longer coiffed and my coed effect, strumming a guitar and composing poetry. The word *beatnik* hadn't even reached the media and was equally unknown to us. People who thought me unusual would remark on the casual style of my hair, long and straight, sporting bangs, and say, "You look just like Mary in Peter, Paul, and Mary. Only she's blond and, um, actually you look nothing alike."

So if a lesbian was, in fact, how I defined myself, I knew I was a *new* breed of woman-loving woman. I was making it up as I went along, as were Linda and Dianne in their turn. These were both women whom I brought out by that meaning that I'm happy to take responsibility for being the one with clever notions and an illicit agenda. The instigator, as it were. The proverbial bad influence as I had always been known.

Lesbians were out there in the world of literature in novels like Radclyffe Hall's *The Well of Loneliness* or plays like *The Children's Hour* by Lillian Hellman, published in the 1920s and '30s, respectively. But I hadn't heard of them. Good thing, for when I did get around to reading them, I joined other young, confused, and horrified lesbians in their pain of reading such dismal and doomed portraits of the poor unfortunate women who chose the path of illicit love. If you're not familiar with this literary genre, I can assure you, most of the protagonists die, either by their own hand or some obvious, tragic act of God's hand.

This said to underscore the fact that once Dianne and I had reached an understanding (that we shared deep caring for one another and mutual sexual desire), the die was cast and we were a couple. Simple as that. In years to come, that was a pattern that strongly took hold, almost out of necessity, given the scarcity of potential partners in the still-repressive social climate of the early sixties.

Nothing was clearly defined. Dianne still dated various frat boys of the Lambda Pi, still strung along John Flynn finishing his education at St. Mary's, but at night, when we were locked safely away in the dorm or in the private niche we carved out as our executive office from the larger area of the yearbook workroom, she was all mine.

Nor did I perceive of myself as exclusively being with women. I had sex partners, in fact way too many sex partners, of both genders for the ensuing fifteen years. But I was clearly emerging as a character in some culture of *other*. Not so much a culture of lesbianism but the merest zygote of what would come to be called the counterculture.

Counterculture Calls

This otherness of mine was trying to emerge in a social and political climate where Barry Goldwater was campaigning for president and Chico was a stronghold of the budding John Birch Society. I even recall tales of one of our professors being dismissed for radical thinking and whose wife, a junior high teacher in the neighboring town of (ironically named) Paradise, had discovered her classroom was bugged with listening devices. No surprise that the couple found their way to the radicalism emerging in Berkeley.

Dianne was an education major, the last class where it was possible to matriculate without declaring some separate major and minor and then seeking a credential. She intended to work with elementary school children and it was obvious she would be great with them. In fact, it was during this early time in our relationship that she introduced me to *Winnie the Pooh*, tousling my hair and declaring I reminded her of Tigger. Nor had I ever heard of *The Jabberwocky*. I guess, as a child, I'd been too preoccupied with the racy and adult novels I pilfered from my mother.

With Dianne being in the education department and given the repressive moral code of the day, we had to be especially careful to keep our love clandestine. Were we found out, it would be the end of any hope she had of teaching. Sad to say that it is only in the last ten years or so that teachers in more enlightened regions can be openly gay without parental spasms about recruiting their children or corrupting their morals. We hid our love. That was a given.

We would venture out into the forest while she collected butterflies for her elementary school science class, but even the cover of nature couldn't dispel our fear of possible discovery. Swimming in Big Chico Creek, we maintained the façade of the company of men while we frolicked in the rushing waters to avoid the scorching spring temperatures.

Dianne introduced me to Bidwell Park, 2,500 acres of stately oaks and grasslands donated to the city of Chico by Annie Bidwell in 1905. The expansive park was even used to portray Sherwood Forest in the 1922 film *Robin Hood* starring Douglas Fairbanks but now provided a wealth of recreational potential for the students from town, largely in the form of its suitability for keg parties and its numerous swimming holes.

Our opportunities for closeness were guarded and scarce; they remained largely in the dorm or our office. I remember a day she called me in a panic, sounding truly terrified, her voice quaking with emotion, "I can't talk to you over the phone. Meet me in the little bleachers down by the side of the creek" (the one that ran through our campus).

I raced to make the assignation, heart pounding in my breast, and couldn't imagine what would make her sound so frightened. She had been to our office and found that the lock on the door had been changed. We were certain we'd been detected and that this was just a prelude to severe consequences yet to come from the administration. As well as the fear of discovery, we were dashed to think that our private place had been invaded, perhaps even searched, and racked our memories to think what might possibly be uncovered that could incriminate us. For the moment, we couldn't even gain access to see if anything might have been riffled through.

The next day, a casual note from Mr. Clarvoe explained that all the locks in the activities center had been changed to operate with one master key. A simple and harmless explanation, but the intense fear we had experienced remained hard to shake.

The second semester of my freshman year brought a refreshing shift out of the sciences and into the humanities, still a relatively new term. Literature became my major, with a minor in psychology. Classes and instructors got infinitely more interesting and thought provoking. I was smitten with the poets of the Romantic period: Yeats, Keats, Milton, and especially Samuel Coleridge. I lapped it up as my instructor opened discussion of Coleridge's "Christabel" having a lesbian subplot and tried to conceal my especial interest by not asking more questions than others in the class.

In US History, I heard the first unsanitized views of our government and its leaders—information about presidents and their mistresses, liaisons with slave women and children spawned, dirty deals where we had robbed indigenous peoples of their land and their rights.

Psychology, though an introductory class, nourished that part of my young mind that had always been introspective, seeking to understand my inner workings and motivations. I began to analyze my family dynamics in a more informed manner and learned to scrutinize my own motives and hidden agendas in dealings with others. I especially related to passages and chapters I read about the formation of self-image and gained insight into my fiercely asocial childhood.

I didn't feel less lost but thought at least someone was writing about my predicament, if only from a clinical point of view. I began the long road to finding my way out from under academic probation. I got more rigorous about attending classes, stuck with subjects I could find interesting, and made an honest effort to complete assignments and stay awake in class. Concurrently, I conscientiously toiled at living the life of a young party school coed and learned to navigate prodigious hangovers.

Dianne had been approached about taking a job as housemother at one of the small student rooming houses a couple of blocks from campus. We feared how the short distance might separate us, but she opted for the job to help defray housing expenses and provide some financial relief for her parents.

There she had a large room to herself and thirteen young girls to shepherd in the two-story Victorian. We had a slightly greater modicum of privacy than in Lassen Hall and also had some fun times hanging out with the girls, watching our afternoon soaps *As the World Turns* and *The Secret Storm*, and thrilling over the new crazy-looking band from the UK, the Beatles. I still marvel to think we were shocked at the length of their hair in 1964.

Dianne and I savored our love, worked hard on the *Record*, and drank a lot of beer on hot spring evenings while fighting off the

B-52-sized Chico mosquitoes. Those hot, starry nights in the sleepy little valley town were exquisite in their own way, with wild violets growing out of cracks in the sidewalks and a plethora of unidentifiable floral fragrances free-floating everywhere. Soon the yearbook would be put to bed (sent off to the printers), and we would need to confront the pending separation that summer would bring.

Home for the Summer

I spent that summer under my parents' roof, attending school at Diablo Valley, the local junior college. Still working diligently to elevate my grade point average, I enrolled in two classes I felt I could perform well in: sociology (which I had already dropped once in my spring semester) and Spanish, which, like other languages, came easily to me.

It was a restless situation, living at home, while I was obviously morphing into someone who no longer readily fit into the republican, conservative atmosphere of Lafayette. Things were changing radically just the other side of the hills in Berkeley. The previous spring, Sue Remley had come home with me so we could attend a concert by Joan Baez at Wheeler Hall on the Berkeley campus.

Baez was twenty-two at the time, and the material she sang was a powerful experience for me, steeped in protest songs and inter-tune patter about how she was withholding that portion of her income taxes which fed the defense budget. I was hugely impressed when she said she didn't care if they put her in jail and that she wasn't really refusing to pay, just demanding that the tax collector come collect her money rather than making the government's job easier by passively mailing it in.

This was in protest to the simmering situation in Vietnam though I don't think I'd even heard of the Vietnam War before this. The lesson was about making one's voice heard and was my first inkling of anything approaching grassroots politics.

Concurrently, I was starting to see a lot of my friend Liz Busch who lived in the neighborhood. Another oddball, she was one of those eggheads who didn't really socialize at school, but we had come to know each other on the fringes.

Liz's dad, Oscar, taught mathematics at our high school, and her mother was an enigmatic character with only one leg; the prosthesis she wore was actually a wooden peg, like you would imagine on a seafaring pirate.

The family had a total of four children: Julie, the eldest, had already left the nest. Nick, a rollicking, rock-climbing, guitar-strumming character, was Bob Underwood's class and had graduated ahead of us. Liz's younger brother, Greg, was a couple of years behind us in school. Nick, with his beard and guitar, held quite a bit of fascination for me, and he would regale us with tales of joining his high school friend Jeff Shurtleff, now at Stanford, on the streets of San Francisco, serenading strangers and collecting donations which they then forwarded to Meals for Millions.

Jeff was equally spellbinding, singing for us new protest tunes he was learning in the freethinking atmosphere of the Stanford campus. I remember him teaching me the chords to play the tune "Masters of War," written by Bob Dylan and not yet recorded. According to Jeff, who personally knew Joan Baez, Dylan had taught the tune to his friend Joan, who, in turn, taught it to Skinny, as Jeff was called by his friends.

Skinny also brought home to Lafayette stories of his adventures, getting high on morning glory seeds which he claimed had an hallucinogenic effect. "Only the varieties *Pearly Gates* and *Heavenly Blue* will work," he warned us. I couldn't wait to try it out and quickly procured them from the local nursery. But it would still be some months before I actually made an effort to transform the hard little nuggets into something digestible. He also told of experiments happening in the low mountains that lay between Stanford and the sea, the hills of San Mateo County which would later become famed for characters like Ken Kesey and his Merry Pranksters, and a guy named Owsley. They were exploring a new substance called LSD, learned about from Timothy Leary and Richard Alpert, then both professors at Harvard University. How could this be a bad thing if such educated cats were fooling around with it?

I spent the summer enjoying the freedom of my beloved little Austin-Healey, going to sports car rallies, attending my classes, and hanging out with the intellectually stimulating crowd at the Busch's.

At home, I was practicing obstreperousness, making every effort to let my parents know I was developing into a person who didn't share their politics or worldview. It took perhaps the next five years to realize there was no talking political differences with my father, and my mother was her usual passive, deferring self with no thoughts she could call her own. I lined the upper border of the walls of my room with album covers, affixed with staples, of the musical artists who were important to me. When I felt the need to be particularly irritating, I would put on albums such as Theodore Bikel singing Yiddish folk songs and then join in singing along with the libretto on the album cover. It made my dad crazy!

I also started spending evenings venturing into Berkeley and Oakland, passing through the Caldecott Tunnel to the instant refreshing of the cool marine layer and more urban thought. I met some young guys attending summer school at Cal and began to hang out at their apartment and was delighted that they also sang and played guitar.

The kid named Carl convinced me, after several beers, that I really should explore further my singing and praised the impassioned place I could reach in my vocal range when fueled by alcohol. Carl exposed me to another sort of independent thinking; his dad, living in Southern California, was a part of the Anti-Digit-Dialing League, a group opposed to abandoning our traditional telephone exchanges for a world where everything was reduced to numbers—just one more affront to our individuality, they protested.

One night, when the conclusion of a sports car rally landed us at a pizza parlor called the Grand Prix on East 14th Street in Oakland, I got fairly gassed and, at the urging of my navigator, Carl, took the offer of a guitar from the performer of the evening and sang a couple of tunes. Audience response was keen and Edie, the owner of the joint, inquired whether I would like a regular gig singing at the Grand Prix. The terms were four-forty-minute sets for $25 and all the beer I could drink.

It sounded like a bargain to me as I knew I could drink enough beer to possibly put her out of business! Looking back, that was a huge amount of material she wanted for very little recompense; I think she could tell that I was underage and without much bargaining power. My false ID was created from some blank forms for federal government drivers' licenses I found in and took from a bureau drawer in my Uncle Ferd's house. Just as when buying cigarettes from the local merchant as a little kid, presenting barely believable notes from Mother, it seemed a proprietor just wanted to see *something* without much concern for its validity.

I truly enjoyed the singing and the attention it brought me. And the beer. Some evenings I played with so much zeal that I would look down to see the tops of the fingers of my right hand bleeding from the frenzy of my impassioned strumming. I would laugh and ask the bartender for a few Band-Aids.

In the club, I met another older gent, a surveyor originally from Nova Scotia, who struck up a conversation with me after I sang the song about the Springhill Mine disaster of 1959. We grew to be friends; he joined me as the occasional navigator on rallies and lived in an apartment above a storefront near the Grand Prix. Peter was twenty-four, not a citizen of this country, and provided a still-broader perspective of world affairs. (Some forty-five years later, Peter Dodge resurfaced by locating my dad via email. We still correspond.)

I felt substantially matured over the course of the summer. I was learning about the war, about the condition of workers, about bar culture, about my talents for singing and playing guitar. On the horizon was the fascination of an hallucinogenic era and an itch for the more metropolitan life.

I felt more distant than ever from my parents' life in the suburbs, and only the lure of seeing Dianne upon my return to campus kept me motivated to pack up my things and return to Chico in the fall. This time, I would have my little car supporting my independence and have my girl back under the same roof as she had accepted an RA's job in the new Craig Hall, a coed dorm at the western end of town.

Craig Hall and the Myth of the Coed Dorm

Craig Hall, the exciting newly constructed dormitory at 1400 W. Third Street in Chico, billed itself as being coeducational. Though the male students were no longer in a separate building, the men and women were separated by a lobby with lounge, reception area, and dining hall. At 10:00 p.m., the girls were still safely locked away from the boys. But those of us on the ground floor quickly discovered the ease of slipping the screens off windows to the outside and freedom.

Dianne was here, and due to her position as a resident advisor, she, once again, had private quarters where we could freely enjoy our love. Roberta Logan from Lassen Hall had also made the transition to the new building. She was my RA on 2 East while Dianne was the RA for 2 North. Our housemother was a chain-smoking crone named Doris Radin, widow of some famous cat named Paul Radin, a one-time Cal professor.

One of the other RAs had long been suspected by us as also being a lesbian. She was in a curriculum to be a professional Girl Scout of all things. Her name was Diane, her girlfriend's name was also Lynn, though each was spelled differently than our names. Both girls were deeply involved in a lifetime of scouting, both were on track to make the GSA their livelihood, and both Lynn and Diane were every bit as protective and paranoid of their love as we were. Di and I even caught them necking in a stairwell late one night, and boy, did they blanch! But we never spoke an acknowledgment of our outlaw status, and they remained extremely guarded around us.

Shortly after the beginning of classes, my mother called with some terrible news. She wanted to save me hearing it through media channels and felt it best to inform me personally that Liz Busch had died.

What Liz had confided to me during the summer was her sexual affair with her first cousin Max from Salt Lake City. She had been attending her first year of college at UC Davis, and the romance had culminated thereafter, apparently, years of flirting with each other. Max called himself a Jack Mormon, meaning though he was raised in the Mormon faith, he smoked and drank and generally behaved in ways not tolerated by the LDS establishment.

I turned to Liz's family to gain more information than I could glean from the news media, calling Georgia the minute my mother told me of her passing. The story unfolded thus: Liz had discovered she was pregnant upon returning to Davis for the beginning of our sophomore year. Max had come out from Utah to join her and find a solution to the problem.

The best anyone could figure, Liz and Max had obtained something from a drugstore they thought would cause the fetus to abort, and in her apartment at Davis, they administered the potion. Keep in mind, there was no avenue for a nineteen-year-old girl to obtain a legal abortion at this time. Something went wrong and Liz's heart stopped beating. We also didn't know any system of resuscitation in 1964 like CPR.

Max was frantic, pounding on Liz's chest and attempting to force air through her mouth. He hurriedly put in a call to their uncle, a physician also named Max, who lived and practiced in Sacramento some twenty minutes away. Uncle Max arrived on the scene in time to pronounce Liz dead, and that was the end of her young life.

After campus authorities had removed the body for future transport home and her uncle had signed a certificate of death, Max, under instructions from his uncle, was told to follow in his own car while they caravanned back to the elder Max's home in Sacramento. Somewhere in the course of the drive, young Max reversed direction, headed westward toward the Bay Area, hastily scribbled a request to be "buried next to my love, Liz," parked on, and leaped from the upped deck of the Oakland Bay Bridge into the dark waters below, washing up on the shores of Alameda some ten days later.

I asked my mother to save any newspaper clippings she could find, and I headed home to be near for the funeral arrangements.

I found the Busch household, understandably, a somber scene. Julie was home, as was Nick, also many relatives from Salt Lake I had never met. Max's body had still not been recovered when a service was held for Liz in nearby Pleasant Hill. I remember being stunned by how she looked in the coffin: fully made up, which was certainly not her way, and in some frock her mother had chosen. It was a bitter awakening to see that, in death, folks would make of us whomever they had wished us to be. After a subdued reception in the family's home, I drove back up to Chico to face the second week of classes and the work that had piled up while awaiting my return. I wrote home that I was anxious for classes to get underway to take my mind off all the terrible things.

I took comfort in Dianne, who steadied me as only a close friend, lover, and ally could. Apparently, my mother had reached out to her, asking her to keep an eye on me. I discovered this only after my mom's passing, in a letter she kept which Dianne had written—a progress report of sorts. Dated September 23, Di wrote,

> *I too was worried about Lin. But she is accepting Liz's death better now even though it's a hard thing to comprehend or justify. Lin realizes how much she will miss Liz and what a waste it is. It has helped her to talk about the fun they had and the long talks. Fortunately, classes have started and she is very busy with the yearbook. I think she will be an excellent editor and is very excited about the book. This and classes keep her mind off the tragedy, and she's thrown herself into the work, which is so good for her. She will miss Liz all her life, but she has learned to accept it. I'm so sorry for her, but being up here with so much to keep her busy is a great help. She said she was glad you told her—that she didn't have to find out from someone else.*

Something like this is so hard on Lin since she values her friendships very much. But she's a strong and sensitive person, so I think she will be able to adjust without hurting herself. You should be very proud of her. She's a good friend and a dedicated worker. I hope this has helped ease your mind even though I've found it difficult to help her justify her loss. Everyone here has tried.

Sincerely, Di

The semester got underway, the yearbook deadlines began marking off the weeks, and my sophomore year was careening forward.

The fall in Chico is a glorious time, with an Indian summer of sorts, daytime temperatures still in the eighties, lovely balmy evenings, and crisp overnights. Since my new dorm was a mile and a half from the center of campus, I was able to successfully advocate my need for a car and was allowed at last to bring the Healey to school. Dianne also had bought a car over the summer—a 1963 red Pontiac Le Mans.

Whereas the average coed returned with tales of their summer vacations, I came bearing the vinyl vocal renderings of Bob Dylan, Joan Baez, and the even more obscure Judy Henske, a Canadian with a low, husky voice and a haunting folk repertoire with numbers like "Baltimore Oriole," which I was learning to play and sing. For the more traditional tastes, the Motown Sound had made its way west from Detroit. Di and I would drive out to Bidwell Park, top removed from my little roadster, blaring the tunes of the Supremes singing "Baby, Where Did Our Love Go?"

A new cast of characters occupied Craig Hall's women's wing. My next-door neighbors were a charming pair: Susie Madley, a freshman from Orange County, and her roomie, Marie Lagorio, whose dad owned the largest commercial cherry orchard in the state down in Linden, lower in the Sacramento Valley.

Madley struck my fancy immediately. She shared my love of singing but, unlike me, didn't need to be fueled with a few beers before she would belt out tunes at the top of her lungs. She had sung in a barbershop quartet in high school and reminded me how I enjoyed that music when introduced to it by my first love, Bob. Madley was game to listen to the new music I had imported from my radicalized summer, acknowledging that she had never heard anything like it. (Madley would leave Chico a year later, transferring to Cal Berkeley, and amazed us all by getting a role in *Hair: A Rock Musical* when it opened in San Francisco.)

Marie was a sweet girl, a proper Catholic girl, and an easy person to befriend. Her gift to me was a trip home to her family's farm one weekend, where for the first time I saw migrant workers living in the Lagorio fields in cardboard shacks and abject poverty. Marie didn't prove to be memorable, but the image of those workers was, and remains, indelible.

I continued to work diligently to improve my grade point average. I was now editor in chief of the *Record*, and Clarvoe was hard-pressed to let me keep the job when he learned of my grades. But he knew me to be a hard worker and seemed to have faith in my ability to buckle down and get the job done.

My letters (first-class postage of 5¢) home were filled with youthful musings: intentions of carrying a triple major (English, Psychology, and Education) to better prepare for my scheme of a stint in the Peace Corps with Dianne once I graduated. I was trying hard to erase the embarrassment of my early academic record, and by the end of fall, I had acquired a 2.5 for the semester and a 2.1 GPA overall. I was finally off academic probation!

In the spring, I enrolled in Spanish, English Literature I and II, Music Appreciation, Swimming, and Badminton. Letters home spoke of aching muscles and falling into bed exhausted, but I was buoyed by my success and fueled by my dreams.

I also began to cultivate some strange study habits. Somewhere, I had learned of the incredible amounts of work that could be accomplished by taking diet pills, the sophisticated timed-release sort, not merely the familiar Benzedrine tablets. I obtained a prescription for them by telling the doctor I needed help with weight loss and began employing them regularly as study aids. My habit was to procrastinate on the larger portions of my homework assignments such as term papers, then pop a bunch of pills and stay up for two or three days straight, writing feverishly and passionately. And perhaps unintelligibly.

One such marathon bout of academic fervor was a paper I was ignited to write after reading J. D. Salinger's *Catcher in the Rye*. Like many my age who were on the cusp of embracing a cultural revolution, this small volume spoke directly to my heart about the schism between the values taught in childhood and the perceived hypocrisy of our parents' lives in light of those values. Holden Caulfield was obsessed with phonies, and I felt his pain. But the larger pain I related to was the subject of my paper: the adolescent negative self-image.

I wrote with a fire in my belly for two days and nights, still needing to request an extension on the paper's deadline; I was so fervid and impassioned that I just couldn't quit writing. Even then, the subtext didn't elude me. I was writing about myself, not Holden.

I continued to venture home on weekends and, while there, would spend most of my time visiting Berkeley. But I stayed around the house enough to discover the wonders that could be found in my mother's medicine chest. Mom had Percodan, an amazingly powerful painkiller, anecdotally described as synthetic morphine. Why she possessed a (seemingly endless) prescription for it was unknown. Also unknown were the numerous times I helped myself to a few of her stash.

The rift between me and my dad continued to widen in the political arena. I was quickly learning that trying to have a dialogue with him was an impossible situation. Like many Republicans, the only view of the world situation he could tolerate was his own. My frustration with his narrow-mindedness grew to the point where we barely had anything to talk about with each other. As my social consciousness grew, his world seemed ever to shrink. It would still be a few years before I could exercise the right to vote, but I knew we wouldn't be voting the same ticket.

During the spring, I decided I'd outgrown my pawnshop guitar and revisited my old pal Mr. Reilly at Reilly's Music Store in Walnut Creek. Gerry Reilly remembered me from my tiniest days, squandering my allowance on 45 rpm records in his shop. I selected a beautiful Martin guitar, the model 0016-C, the *C* being for *classical*, or nylon stringed. Because we had a history, Mr. Reilly extended the offer of a payment plan as I was unable to come up with the $280 in one payment.

My love of the guitar continued to draw folks to me with similar interests. One night, driving from my parents' house into Berkeley, a pair of fellows in an adjacent car hailed me as we drove through the Caldecott Tunnel. "Come join us," they hollered, so I followed them into central Berkeley where we stopped at a coffee house on Telegraph Avenue.

One of the pair was visiting the area from New York; he was here to study guitar in a master's class with Andrés Segovia, the famed classical guitarist and recording artist from Spain. I had forged another Berkeley connection, as well as meeting my first New York Jew. My world felt like it was expanding to the point of bursting at the seams.

Then I would return to the bucolic tranquility of Chico.

An Important Man
in My Life

During January of 1965, I had taken my roomie Kathy home for the weekend to Lafayette, and while there, we had ventured together into Berkeley to prowl around and then to Oakland that I might show her the Grand Prix where I had sung. Still underage, still sporting the same pathetic phony ID, we had no trouble being served beer with our pizza.

We met a guy, a cute guy, named Ron Franck. I guess I had given him my parents' number as my mom later wrote me that he had called. He had left his contact information with her and I was delighted. As I wrote to her, "Good, now I have an excuse to phone him, simply as a courtesy, of course." I told her, "Remember, he's the guy Kathy and I met the night we didn't return home until seven in the morning." I'm not sure what the three of us did all night, but my best memory is that we drove around the town in tandem, Kathy and I in the Healey and Ron in an equally cute Triumph TR-3, stopping at various spots like the expansive lawns at Lake Merritt in Oakland and also hitting the beach in Alameda, Ron's hometown just across the Estuary.

Ron and I kept in touch, and on my increasingly frequent visits to the Bay Area, we would hang out, drink, ride on his motorcycle, and generally enjoy the vibrant atmosphere of the emerging Berkeley counterculture.

I told Ron about Skinny's tales of getting high on morning glory seeds, so we went and bought some. Figuring out how to transform the rock-hard little seeds into some form that could be assimilated into the bloodstream was no easy trick. We ground them up in a pepper grinder and filled empty gel caps. We ground them over hamburger and then ate the meat. We put a wad of seeds in our cheek like chewing tobacco and waited for them to soften, which seemed to take forever.

At this point, I had gotten a job of sorts, tending bar and singing in a lesbian-owned dive on San Pablo Avenue called the Blind Lemon, named for the blues singer Blind Lemon Jefferson. I was coming down from Chico every weekend and not even bothering to check in with my parents. Pat Weaver, the owner, and her Canadian lover, Noël, slept in a small apartment in the rear of the building; I slept on their couch. I jokingly referred to them as my mother and father (Noël being the more butch, she was Dad) and delighted in not only finally meeting some other lesbians but also real live old-time, worldly, and experienced lesbians, not the newly emerging sort like myself.

I was a hit with the tourists and played it to the hilt, smoking a cigar while pouring drinks, talking foul-mouthed sass to flirtatious, fat strangers, and singing raucous blues during my breaks. Ronnie would hang out at the bar, sipping his draft beer which cost all of a quarter, and we would exchange winks while each sporting a lump of morning glory seeds in our cheek. When the bar closed, we would ride around most of the night in one car or another until I crept into the bar's apartment at dawn.

One night, around 3:00 a.m., we were tooling around out in Walnut Creek. I must have been staying at my folks' house that weekend. We had ground up the seeds and put them in gel caps, then each swallowed several of those. I had adopted a firm belief that none of these substances really affected me.

Ronnie had given me pot to try, and I felt nothing. I persisted in thinking I was unaffected when we were stopped by a police officer near the gate of Rossmoor Leisure World which was still under construction. At the entry of the development was an enormous sculptured likeness of a globe, and we were fascinated to just sit and stare at it. Nah, I wasn't high.

The officer wanted Ron's license, which he provided, then, turning the beam of his flashlight in my eyes, asked my name. When

I told him my last name was Gentry, he said, "Hey, I know your old man. He lives up on the hill, right?" That threw an unholy scare into me, but I didn't inquire what their connection might be.

He couldn't find any real reason to detain us, so he patronizingly cautioned that "one can't be too careful. There have been a lot of thefts around here." I almost lost it when Ronnie, staring down at his feet, responded in all seriousness, "I know. Someone stole my shoelaces." The irony was that they actually were missing.

My relationship with Ronnie became a sexual one but unique in contrast to what I had suffered through thus far with men—the groping, grasping, drunken fumblings of one-night stands and various free-love liaisons. Ronnie was tender and had an endearing way of letting me take control of the situation, waiting for me to approach him. It felt safe and I trusted him.

The Year Winds Up

I spent the spring semester balancing the responsibilities of school and the yearbook, my relationship with Dianne and my life in the dorm on the one hand, and my exotic life as a bartending, blues singing, freewheeling Berkeley denizen on the other. I planned to enroll in summer school at Cal and earnestly hoped I could convince my parents to subsidize an apartment there while I took university courses in Shakespeare and Psychology 1B.

With the end of the term would also come Di's graduation, and she would be off to the larger world of a teaching job near her family home in the suburbs of Sacramento. She had continued dating guys; on her arm in Chico was Stu McIlhenny, the heir to the Original Tabasco Sauce fortune and local fraternity boy, and the tried and true John Flynn was her escort when she was home on holidays. My heart was still in her thrall and she was a deeply loyal friend, but our romance was destined to die by attrition once June rolled around.

Another major loss toward the end of my sophomore year was the ruination of my little Austin-Healey. Driving one night from Berkeley to my parents' house in Lafayette, I noticed that the temperature gauge was running hot but figured that, once on the freeway, the rushing air would cool the engine. I made it almost the full distance to their hill, but then the car stalled at the bottom and wouldn't start again. I hiked up the enormity of their street and figured I would deal with the problem in the morning.

The prognosis wasn't good. The considered opinion of my dad and brother Bob, the Chevron mechanic, was that I had blown the head gasket, lost most of the motor oil, and cracked the engine block. The car was ruined. My father set a dubious example for me when he suggested a solution to our dilemma; he proposed putting some additive or other in the crankcase and slowly driving the Healey to a car dealership in a neighboring town. There they accepted my dear little roadster as a trade-in, seeming to think her engine in good running order.

Looking back, I'm a bit appalled at my dad's lack of integrity, but at the time, I thought him most clever. Dad always liked to think he was getting over on someone or some institution, and I still find examples of where that gene surfaces in my own character.

The little car that brought me so much pleasure and adventure—in which I had learned to drive and shift gears, to double-clutch and peel out, to navigate a rally course or just discover countless new panoramas—was leaving me forever. It had been a sweet ride. In her stead, I left the lot in a brand-new 1965 Ford Mustang, a car aficionados considered a classic from the very first model that rolled off the assembly line.

With the Mustang, I was able to develop a taxi service of sorts for the girls on campus. I had a reputation as the quickest (and wildest) ride home, a flat 2 hours and 15 minutes, from the door of Craig Hall to the Claremont Hotel in Berkeley, a distance of 130 miles. My passengers would split among them the cost of a full tank of gas; the trip would consume half of that. The remainder of the tank got me around town for the weekend, then on the return trip, we would repeat the gas ritual and what remained would last me the week in Chico.

No one could compete with my quick delivery. I traveled the levee roads where Highway Patrol were rarely seen, skirting through hamlets like Hamilton City, Ordbend, Bayliss, and Jacinto. I could stay on these back roads all the way to Dunnigan before I hooked up with any major highways. It was a scenic route, rarely another vehicle, and sometimes an adventurous crossing of the Sacramento River on a one-car cable ferry. But since I had twice suffered license suspensions for too many speeding tickets, the avoidance of the law was a far more compelling objective than an appreciation of the scenery.

The school year finished out in this fashion: the yearbook and heavy course load turned out successfully, grades continuing to improve and the book receiving wide praise (not the least from my mentor, Dianne, proud of her successful handover of her "baby"). The Berkeley siren song called to me throughout the spring, with many more of my weekends spent in bars and folk dives and a very few home visiting the folks. Ronnie and I remained close, and I slept less at the Blind Lemon and more at his place on Channing Way about a mile from the bar.

Dianne and I bid farewell, maintaining weak hopes that we would somehow stay in touch. I don't think either of us quite believed it.

A Summer of Epiphany

The summer of 1965 found me on the brink of a path that would forever determine the course of my young life. *Forever* being a pretty loaded word, but the adventures the period put on my plate had enormous impact and influence.

My parents had agreed to let me rent an apartment in Berkeley, and Ronnie found a wonderful little vacancy just down the street from him on Channing. It was a studio apartment with a lumpy, foldout couch for a bed and a kitchen with a two-burner stove where outstretched arms could reach every corner of utility space without moving one's feet from the center of the room. A tiny bathroom and small closet completed its features.

I was quite into signs and symbols and felt it had great import that my little studio was across the street from the playing field of Berkeley High, where my parents had both graduated in 1937. And the street address was the same as the year of their births: 1917. My first little home, all my own, at 1917 Channing Way.

Nest building had been a recurring theme for me throughout. Whether it was in the forts I constructed every summer on Del Hambre Circle, sleeping within and even cooking meals over a camp stove in a home of my own making, or instantly personalizing a dorm room, the urge had always been quite strong to create a sense of home and belonging anyplace I lay my head. Even as a little kid, I reflected I was attempting to replace some enormous missing ingredient in the shelter my parents provided. Over the next several years, even during a period in my Berkeley time, when I changed apartments every month (honest!), friends would remark how quickly I settled in and how homey my residences consistently felt. "*When* did you move in?" they would ask. When I would respond that it had been just a couple of days, they were astonished. "It looks like you've been here for *months*!"

It was a talent I took pride in, but Channing Way was the first real opportunity to put my personal stamp on a place and create what felt like a true home. I was ecstatic that my parents had given me this chance to stretch out a little and feel quite grown up. I registered for the summer classes at Cal and settled in to continue, I hoped, the diligent task of improving my grade point.

With Ronnie just up the street, we naturally saw a lot of each other and continued together to enjoy the vibrant energy of the campus town where so much was happening. One day, he approached me with a surprise: he had actually scored some LSD and wondered if I'd care to try it. I had lingering questions about my body's ability to respond to chemicals in a normal way, just as I felt that I had never actually gotten pregnant because perhaps I couldn't. There was always a nagging sense that nothing about me really functioned as it should.

I was game but fairly convinced that this, too (still thinking I hadn't gotten high on any of our morning glory seed adventures), would not really have the desired effect. After perhaps an hour passed, sitting on the floor in Ronnie's apartment, he asked if I felt anything. "Don't think so," I replied. "Well then, here, better have another hit. Then we'll know for sure." He was aware of my insecurities about having a proper response to the drugs. As much as anything, I hated to see him *waste* the precious stuff on me.

This was before acid came in pills or on little squares of blotter paper or in windowpane form. This was straight lysergic acid dropped on sugar cubes. I have to say it tasted a lot better than the caustic, acrid morning glory seeds we'd been chomping on!

Well, the second hit didn't go to waste. But I did. Very wasted. Hurrah! It worked. And we were quite loaded. Being the young fools we were, we got on Ron's motorcycle and headed up to the Berkeley Hills to view the summer-evening panorama of the Bay spread out below.

Up behind the Cal campus, winding past Memorial Stadium and the Hearst Greek Theater, the streets climb ever higher, making tight, twisting little turns barely navigable by a large passenger car. But on the motorcycle, we easily achieved the end of Panoramic Way, where the pavement terminates and a fire road begins. We left the macadam and continued to climb until we were as high above the town as we cared to go. It was time to stop and just soak in the view.

The city was sparkling below us and, of course, ultra vivid with the aid of the chemicals in our systems. All the lights of the houses, the bridges, and the freeways seemed to shimmer and blink at us. We parked the bike in the middle of the trail, took the blanket we had brought along, and nested up against a copse of eucalyptus trees to the north of where the bike sat.

I remember lying on my back, holding my hands at arms' length, with them backlighted by the night sky and falling in love with the shapes of my fingers. I was entranced with the intricacy of each digit, how deft and clever a creation they were, and imagined that by lacing together the fingers of my two hands that they were making love to one another. Ronnie was busy with some preoccupation of his own.

It could have been minutes; it might have been hours. One of the first impressions I had of this new experience was the utter insignificance of time. But at some point, we both got a terrible start when we heard the screech of a large cat. These hills are known to have the occasional sightings of mountain lions; sometimes they're even alleged to venture down into the yards of luxury homes high in the hills and knock over a garbage can or two while foraging for food.

No mistake, this was the harsh, grating yowl of a cat! Worse, we couldn't quite tell where the sound was coming from. To say the least, we felt incredibly vulnerable in our altered state and quickly whispered our way to a plan: perhaps we should creep back over to the bike and try turn on its headlight to scare the cat away. Or at least keep him some distance from us. I was shaking.

We hadn't heard the sound a second time when we had reached the bike, only to realize that we'd been so scared out of our wits that the key to the bike was still in Ron's helmet on the blanket we'd left some fifty feet away. We decided to stay in the middle of the road, away from the brush, and calmly walk down toward the paved neighborhoods until the light of dawn might give us a safe passage back to reclaim the motorcycle and the rest of our goods.

Being no reasonable judge of the passage of time, it didn't seem long before the town below began its waking process. I imagined that I could hear a quiet roar of collective toilets flushing and showers starting up. A little later a slightly more full-bodied thunder could be assumed to represent all the automobiles pulling out of driveways and garages and heading for the streets and highways and all the busy places the citizenry at large were headed. We finally deemed it safe to trudge back up the hill to where the motorcycle awaited.

It seemed so melodramatic in the moment but actually still does today; as we approached our little encampment, coming up on the bike, we could detect three distinctly different sizes of cats' paw prints in the surrounding area. We had enjoyed the good grace it seemed the gods bestowed on us as young drug freaks—a glow of protection and safekeeping that continued and flourished into the sensation and belief that we were truly harbingers of a new and wonderful world. We were the beginnings of the flower children, Ronnie and me and others like us.

The Avenue

Berkeley that summer was like nirvana. The center of my activity was Telegraph Avenue, or the Ave., between Sather Gate of the UC campus and Dwight Way. With its coffeehouses and bookstores, especially used bookstores, the Ave. was a hub of vital energy, a mix of students and kids just hanging out, intellectuals engaged in socialist discourse, and pensive sorts playing chess in the sidewalk café of the Forum.

We played and sang music on the street, much as I had heard described by Skinny and Nick, only the pennies thrown at us went to no worthier cause than a bottle of cheap red and enough change to score a joint or two. Conversation was lively and seemed to focus on not just dissent around the Vietnam War but government intrusion upon our lives of all sorts. The selective service draft was still operational for a few more years, and there were frequent demonstrations in downtown Oakland at the induction center which was commonly called the Draft Board. Young friends were scheming ways to accomplish a 4-F rating of medical unsuitability for military service or feverishly making plans to emigrate to Canada, a country not willing to extradite our draft dodgers for service in a war they felt illegal and imperialist.

Acid, or the possession thereof, was still legal as we young miscreants were a couple of steps ahead of the legislative process. This has pretty much been the history of recreational or designer drugs—they're created quicker than the law can assess and condemn them.

If one had enough LSD on them for a presumption of intent to distribute, then there was a problem. But I remember a day on the Avenue, if not this summer then the next, when we all were cognizant of a new statute going into effect which would make simple possession of the substance a crime. I was stoned and on the street, having already started my day with a hit of acid much as I would today have morning coffee or tea. A cohort wandered by who'd made it his mission to pass out free tabs (now tabs) of acid to any interested party. "No thanks, brother. Already high." "Have some more," he says. "Today it's still legal." What the heck, I graciously accepted the offering.

Somewhere in this mélange, a short, dark stranger entered my landscape. Wayne Johnson had seen me around, heard me play, and was making an introduction that I might join him and some friends to make music in a nearby flat. I gathered a couple of other friends, more pot and my guitar, and we went to the apartment of a Cal undergrad named Rachel. By now, I had traded in my classical Martin guitar for a larger steel-stringed model, a D-18, the *D* standing for *dreadnaught*. My old pal Gerry Reilly had brokered this deal as well, giving me a more than generous credit on the trade-in. The dreadnaught retailed for somewhere around $600, extravagant for the time, but the powerful sound of the steel strings was essential to the fingerpicking and modal tunings of my music.

Wayne was a character, an import from all over, and a smooth talker. He was fascinated with my contralto voice and powerful delivery and said he saw great things ahead for me as a singer. He definitely had my attention. He spun tales of his friends who lived in San Francisco and had a sound studio on Nob Hill: Peter and Judy Weston. According to Wayne, some of the singers we revered had been sheltered by Peter and Judy, given instruction on the intricacies of the recording arts, until deemed ready to make a demo tape to shop around to record labels.

This was an exciting new era in music. Most established record labels were frozen in the mold of pop tunes and the spawning of top-forty hits. Labels like Vanguard, on which Baez recorded, were still fairly in their infancy. Folk music was morphing into a more consumable product with a large, clamoring, incipient audience in the protest-minded youth of the day. Dylan tunes such as "Masters of War" and "God on Our Side" were staples of our street serenades. AOR programming formats, or album-oriented radio, was just beginning to come on the scene at local stations like KSAN, sadly to later become a country western station.

Wayne saw great things ahead for me and my voice and talked of taking me across the bay to see Peter and Judy. We did make it over there once, and I was impressed with all the sound equipment in the ground floor of their three-story Victorian home. That visit, Wayne assured me, was not a time to talk business or sing for the couple but merely to get to know one another and get me on their radar. It was awhile and quite a bit of adventure later when I realized what a bull-shitter Wayne truly was. But this was a pretty sweet fantasy.

Concurrently, a handful of wonderful rock bands were breaking on the scene, and local impresario Bill Graham had begun to produce concerts at the Fillmore Auditorium in San Francisco, at the corner of Fillmore and Geary Streets. For an admission of $2.50, one was free to wander the four corners of the huge auditorium or linger at stage's edge with your head mere inches from the PA system, a favorite of mine. These were the earliest public performances of some exceedingly fine, raw, revolutionary rock and roll—the likes of Jefferson Airplane, Quicksilver Messenger Service, the Grateful Dead, and Big Brother and the Holding Company. By the next summer, additional concert venues, equally accessible to the masses, would spring up with Chet Helms' Avalon Ballroom and occasional offerings at the local Longshoremen's Hall down by Fisherman's Wharf.

I was at Longshoreman's and on acid one night when I was heading for the restroom between sets and an amazing vocal blast from the stage stopped me dead in my tracks. I thought it was the voice of a guy, so powerful that I was stunned. I turned, trancelike, and wended my way back to the dance floor and edge of the stage to realize this was a tiny long-haired young woman emitting all that sound. "Who," I asked my pal, "is *that*?" It was Janis Joplin, and pouring out of her were the opening bars of "Down on Me." I had never witnessed or heard a powerhouse voice like this out of a woman; not even the raucous stylings of Judy Henske could touch it. I was utterly smitten with Janis. I wanted what she had; I wanted to be on the stage. Wayne was appearing to be a more attractive proposition with each performance I attended, albeit Janis had a band behind her and I did not. Wayne started having me jam with some local guitar players he knew, and drug hazed as we were, our rehearsal sessions were earnest.

Dad as a radio operator
for Pan Am Airlines

Mom at her engagement luncheon
at the Claremont Hotel

Mom and Dad during their first year of marriage in Rio De Janeiro

Departing for Elko with Dad   Trout fishing with Dad at June Lake

Carmel-by-the-Sea with Dad

Mom modeling a kelp
skirt in Carmel

Frolicking in the tub with neighbor
buddies Blythe and Kim Rowley

Styling my own kelp fashion

The full Hoppy Cassidy get-up

Easter at Granny and Papa's

Dodge Ridge with Mom, Bob, and
Bruce while Dad takes the shot

Dad with teen-aged
Brother Bob

©1980 San Francisco Chronicle
Skills drill on 100' aerial
during the academy

Satire of cheesy male firefighter
calendars produced each year (and
very popular with gay men)

Being interviewed by CBS's
Wendy Tokuda on graduation
day from the fire academy

Bodybuilding in the last
year of my fire career

Happiest times of the 50s

Happiest times of the 80s

Foreign Affairs

Wayne would float in and out of town, and Ronnie was still a constant in my summer. Classes continued: a very different affair on this large university campus, with huge classroom populations and actual instruction coming from graduate assistants. I remember feeling cheated that one might register thinking a renowned professor would be imparting his special knowledge when, in fact, it was just some kid (I felt) a mere few years older than me. That cynical chip on my shoulder that was the legacy of my dad was beginning to take form.

Ronnie and I had an amazing bonding experience during this time. It seemed that everywhere we traveled, we saw some species or another making love. Ladybugs, horses, no matter. I would shout, "Stop the car," and there was yet another mating ritual seemingly being performed for our sole benefit. In the wee hours of one morning, I recall driving in Oakland's Lakeside Park, around the shore of Lake Merritt, when we parked the car and glanced over to a large lawn area. Hundreds upon hundreds of ducks were engaged in mating! It was astonishing, the elaborate dance between the sexes, the males bobbing their heads up and down and the female's response as she stretched out her wings and waggled her head as if to say no just before a full-body shake that ruffled all her feathers. Eventually, and quite to our surprise, the male would pounce on her and the act would be consummated in a face-to-face posture. We were transfixed.

Classes drew to a close, but I still had my apartment rented through the month of September. Wayne reappeared one night, pretty drunk, and wanted to know if I'd like to drive down to Baja, Mexico. He wasn't seeking sex as, by his own admission, he thought he had the clap or gonorrhea. Upon the mention of México, I acerbically retorted, "I'm *not* going to marry you," to which his parrying response was "Nobody *asked* you to, bitch."

Charming young folks we perhaps weren't. Hopping into the Mustang with my guitar and very few possessions, we aimed the car southward, down the California coast through Big Sur and toward LA and the border.

We rarely did anything without the enhancement of drugs, alcohol, or both and entered into Baja sleep-deprived and stoned. Outside the borders of our homeland, we found prescription drugs readily available over the counter in any local farmácia and promptly scored some Dexedrine diet pills to compensate for the energy toll of the long drive. Next stop: a local tavern.

With copious tequila and very little coaxing, Wayne and the bar crowd convinced me to climb up on stage and join the house band in doing a cover of the Stones "I Can't Get No Satisfaction." Sloppy as I may have appeared, I was still a hit with this bunch. Before long, we left the saloon and found a justice of the peace where we did just what I swore I wouldn't—we got married. With the discrepancy in our builds, the justice got a kick out of me carrying Wayne across the threshold and out of the official's office. It was, by now, nearing dawn, but we drove the rugged sixty-eight miles from Tijuana to Ensenada and found a spot on a local beach to park the car and catch some shut-eye.

Morning light was accompanied by an enormous hangover headache and the first foggy recollections of the preceding night with its attendant regrets. My mind began to race, if you could call it that, with thoughts of how to rescind this match I had made. By Mexican law, I was underage to marry without parental permission; we had not consummated the union due to Wayne's gonorrhea. I was oper-ating with the diminished capacity of an inebriated state of mind. Once fully awake, we made one more stop to score at the farmácia and headed north to the border inspection.

Inspections were more lax then, and even if the car was perfunc-torily searched, placing contraband on our bodies was a safe bet to sail through the border and back onto domestic soil. Once back in Berkeley, the next task ahead was to somehow get out of this ridiculous marriage that never would have happened if I'd been in my right mind.

Wayne wandered off again, and my only recourse was to deal with the situation on my own. I knew I didn't want my parents to find out about my escapade as they were still giving me shit about precipitously leaving Europe and never missed an opportunity to portray me as impulsive and foolhardy. I was trying to construct some adult credentials here; going to Mommy and Daddy for a bail out didn't suit my ultimate goals.

I turned to Iris Cavagnaro, my old Latin teacher. She lived quite near the hub of activity in Berkeley, just west of the Avenue and one block south of Ashby. Her home at 3030 Deakin Street sat right behind our local co-op grocery store, one of the first of its kind, where all shoppers were members of the cooperative and received benefit of profit sharing. It was quite revolutionary for the time.

Iris's first suggestion was that I go to my parents for help as I'm sure her orientation as a school counselor left her duty bound to recommend. When I eschewed that course, she suggested in the alternative that I seek out free legal advice from Alameda County Legal Aid. This seemed the more adult choice. I secured an appointment time a few days hence; the small, cramped office in downtown Oakland was sweltering in the August afternoon.

A short, fat, bald-headed man, his forehead beaded in perspiration, greeted me and gestured me to take a seat in the wooden chair across his desk. His inquiry about my need for free services then progressed to my description of the elopement snafu and my need for his assistance. I'm sure it's of no shock to anyone truly disenfranchised within the system, but this middle-aged shark of a man sensed my powerlessness and my need for his help. I was appalled when the conversation turned to a verbal propositioning about the quid pro quo he would require for obtaining legal advice.

Still reeling from his suggestion of sexual favors in exchange for professional expertise, I was horrified when he slithered around the large oak desk and proceeded to try and feel me up. I ran from his office with nothing gained and my confidence in tatters. One more hash mark on the chalkboard of my increasing distrust of and distaste for men. I figured it was time to regroup and returned to Iris for further advice.

Iris's best offering was the reiteration that I take the problem of my Mexican marriage to my folks and to have them help me somehow quash it. Meanwhile, Wayne was somewhere other than Berkeley, and I didn't really care.

My parents greeted my dilemma with the same weary, exasperated disappointment that felt so familiar. My father knew a judge, Sam Hall, who sat in superior court for Contra Costa County, one of his old cronies from the Martinez cable-system days. I don't know any details, nor did I ever have to appear in court, but the marriage went away. I wonder even today if it was the record of this brief encounter ending in annulment that caused my later application to the Peace Corps to be rejected.

Still living in my apartment on Channing Way, Dad made a date to come in and take me to dinner one evening so he could ostensibly explore ways he might be of assistance to me. More likely, he wanted an opportunity to counsel me on what a mess I was making of my life.

We went to dinner at the Alta Mira Hotel in Sausalito, dining on the terrace, a beautiful spot with a spectacular view of the entire Bay to the east. He basically wanted to know, "What the hell is the *matter* with you?" I tried to explain about Wayne's interest in promoting my singing. Dad voiced his concern that nowhere in the plan did he hear any evidence of financial feasibility. My retort was that I felt an artist's life, by necessity, involved poverty and struggle.

He looked so disappointed in me that I could barely finish my meal. His approval was ever harder to attain; the more *I* grew, the further apart *we* grew. Perhaps a normal course for a fledgling trying to flee the nest, but I so hoped he could share some of my excitement or enthusiasm about a singing career. We wrapped up at the restaurant, paid the check, and headed back across the Richmond Bridge to my apartment.

I was proud to show Dad the home I had created for myself. I felt so terribly grown-up, and to prove it to him, I had even procured libations in anticipation of his visit. I always had red wine on hand for my own consumption but had purchased gin specifically to serve him on this occasion. We chatted and we drank, sitting on the lumpy sofa which doubled as my bed.

The drinks served to loosen us up, and it seemed we began to share in a way we hadn't for a long time. I spoke of my hopes and dreams, and it appeared he listened. The conversation gradually became more confidential, more intimate. I had wanted for some-time to try psychotherapy, still a rather new science to the middle class. In the 1960s it was not yet much of a consumer item but rather thought of as either for the elite or the insane. I knew better from my studies in psychology at school, but my father never missed an opportunity to impart that he thought it was all horseshit.

I figured out it was time to help him become a bit more informed about my life, if he really did want to know why I had chosen this path of rebellion and nonconformity. Hoping it would give me a sympathetic ear toward therapy, I plunged ahead. "Remember when Linda's dad accused me of being a lesbian? Well, it was true. And it still is. I'm *still* sleeping with women."

I have to say, as an aside, that the gay lifestyle just wasn't on the national radar at this time. It would be another five years before *Time* magazine would have a cover declaring The Year of the Homosexual. And in the intervening years, my mother was often relieved that my roommates were girls while other moms were having to live with the unutterable shame of their daughters shacking up with their boyfriends.

The other common thread in this twilight era was the frequently encountered attitude of men if I tried to voice my preference for female sex partners. Without exception, I mean without a *single* exception, their reply would be "Well, you just haven't been fucked by me." Irritating, yes. Tiresome, yes. Unimaginative, yes. Another hash mark in the box of how predictable and unsatisfactory men were persistently proving to be.

Well, this evening with my dad, he carried the standard like all the rest of them. My own father says to me, "Well, you just haven't had a good man." "I've had plenty of good men," I replied. "Perhaps, but you haven't had *me*." More than horrified, more than frightened,

I was so utterly disappointed and crestfallen. He was no better than any of the scumbags I might encounter on the Avenue or in the Blind Lemon. But it did create an opportunity for some frank discussion and some things I had wondered about for a number of years.

There had been a night when we were in Aspen skiing. Four of us were sharing a bunk room and we had chosen beds so that my dad was sleeping in the bunk below me. I had a miserable head cold and couldn't really get to sleep, so I bundled up and found my way to the lounge of our hotel where I called Di long-distance. This was while we were still together. But when I returned, stepping on the edge of his bed to get a leg up, my father reached out and grabbed my ankle and just held on. I was frightened; it felt predatory. I pulled my leg away and clambered up into my bed. We never spoke about it.

So this evening in my little apartment, I wanted to know. Wanted to know what that was about. I also had questions about his purported years-long affair with an old family friend. He responded that the rumors were true and that she was insatiable and drawn to his exceptional sexual prowess. This isn't the sort of stuff one wants to hear from their dad. At one point in the conversation, he validated my inquiry by saying, "You had your chance in Aspen." Truly creepy.

But part of me was captivated. Just what was he proposing? I asked. He put forward the idea that he and I should go away together for a few days, plainly with the intent of having a sexual liaison. My head was spinning and not just from the wine. With nothing really resolved, no plan struck, he left for home and I was left with some very confused feelings.

By the next morning, awakening with a bit of a watermelon for a brain but enough sense to know I was aggrieved, I determined, "That's it! This earns me therapy for sure!" I went directly to my mom to inform her of Dad's suggestive behavior the night before. "Your father told me about that," she said forlornly. "He claims you must have drugged his drink." I can't convey how thoroughly that broke my heart; I felt completely alone.

When I pleaded to speak with a therapist about it all, my mom conferred with her friend Betty, whose son Neil had passed through a terrible spell of acting out. There was a man, a psychologist, whom

Neil had seen and apparently had helped to get their son on a better track. My parents agreed to an appointment for me to visit his office in Walnut Creek.

Another very common albatross for any lesbian seeking dialogue with a man was the male's unending curiosity about the details of the sexual union between two women. Well, only minutes into our hour of consultation, this shrink met all my expectations; that's what he wanted to talk about. "Just what is it that two women do in bed together?" I couldn't believe it! I didn't care to have any more appointments with him. In fact, I was disgusted.

I took my tale of frustration once again to my mother. Our communication wasn't the best, but one thing we could manage was to get drunk together and then speak a bit more freely. Dad was still often absent in the evenings while busily building his company at the shop.

Mother told me of finding a suicide note atop of a box of my belongings while packing up to go to school. This was before departure to my first year at college. She had never spoken to me about it, nor did I even remember writing it. But apparently, it pertained to my broken heart over Linda and some dire feelings I was living through. Mom had been unsure if she was snooping or if I had left the note exposed to scrutiny as some cry for help. Good thing it wasn't the latter as she never did say anything at the time or question whether I was in pain.

But here we were again. The reality of my lesbianism was now fully acknowledged, and I was essentially out to my parents. No matter that I had men like Ronnie in my life, it was clear to me that women were my path, even if I had to kiss a lot of frogs in between girlfriends. So Mom and I are drinking in our manner of sharing and wondering how to assimilate this awkward issue with my dad.

Brilliant! We decided to take a road trip. Me and Mom in my Mustang, even bringing along my little calico cat Nepenthe. We would head to her friend Sara Jane's down in Los Angeles. Confident that Sara would babysit the kitten, we were then motoring down to Baja for a couple of days. I remember that Dylan had his first radio side, "Like a Rolling Stone," which was radical not only because it was Dylan on the airwaves but because the song was also much longer than an ordinary single, ringing in at 6:09. I still chuckle when I recall my mom crowing out, "How does it *feel?*" along with the car radio.

After an overnight and more drinks with Sara, we left Nepenthe in her care and pointed south toward the border. At least it wasn't the same coastal route that Wayne and I had taken mere weeks before. We drove the first night to Rosarito, the little beach town halfway between Tijuana and Ensenada. Finding a modest hotel, charming with its ceramic tiles, lush gardens, and native motif, we checked in and visited the restaurant where we continued consuming tequila while indulging in a bountiful meal of enchiladas, beans, and rice. After dinner, we headed for the bar.

It's as if the only thing we knew to do to avoid the metaphorical elephant in the living room that was my father was to just keep drinking and partying. No mistake, we were having a grand time; we just weren't confronting at all the family crisis.

I got Mom to shoot pool, something I'd become rather proficient in while at Chico, and she was a pretty good pupil until the booze and the chili peppers caught up with her. She excused herself and ran to our room. When I later checked on her, she was sick as a dog and wanted nothing more of the evening. Encouraging me to go ahead and have fun, I returned to the bar and the pool table, where I played strangers for $5 a game and, once again, made an avocation of fording off unwanted advances from men.

Next morning, both a little green around the gills, we piled in the Mustang and continued south to Ensenada. This was when the Dylan song really became our private joke. How did we feel? God-awful, that's how! Though our destination was a mere fifty-three miles from Rosarito Beach, it seemed like we'd been captive in the car all day. In fact, the condition of the highway, a term loosely applied, was so poor that those few miles did take *half* the day.

The scene in Ensenada was similar to the night before. Nice motel, decent restaurant, plentiful bar. Only this time our roles reversed a bit. For one thing, some man attached himself to us and butted into our dinner, ingratiating himself by buying us drinks. He was clearly interested in my mother. Tonight, I was the one who over-did it and spent the latter part of the evening in our room, mostly our *bathroom*, while my mom entertained this stranger in the bar.

The next day, as we headed back toward the States, Mom showed me a silver cigarette lighter the man had given her. Also a confession of sorts, she told me that he had offered to give her a sedative to slip me, a mickey he called it, so that it might knock me out and she could slip away to his room for sex. *Honest to God*, I wondered, *are all men totally disgusting?*

One more crazy moment graced our odyssey. I need to men-tion that my mom was quite tanned from years of lying out in the sun, either while reading or playing Scrabble with Lucille, and was wearing a sundress she had purchased in Hawaii the day we left Baja for home. When we got to the border check in Tijuana, the officer stopped us for the obligatory confirmation of our right to enter the United States. "Citizenship?" he asked of me curtly. Just as crisply, I replied, "US." Then when he looked across the front seat to ask my mother the question, she apparently hadn't really heard what he said. Instead of an answer, she smiled and nodded her head, looking quite like she hadn't understood a word he said. *Christ!* I thought. *He's going to think I'm importing an illegal alien!* The three of us had to have a bit of a conversation before the agent was convinced she was a citizen.

The Last Autumn in Chico

There were only a few weeks left before returning to school, and during those, I managed to avoid my dad, and he me. Going back to Chico, getting away from this mess I still couldn't sort out, felt the appropriate way.

Once back at Craig Hall, things were different in some important ways; Dianne was gone, off teaching in Sacramento, and I was being interviewed for a position as RA, or resident advisor, in the dorm. I didn't know the first thing about counseling others but was always ready to render my opinion or judgment. During the interview, Mrs. Radin, our housemother, voiced her concern that, based on the previous year, she rather considered me one of the dorm's problem drinkers. Illogically, I was wounded and felt her judgment preposterous even though I was frequently seen coming in before curfew with an empty pint mug in each hand.

Doris Radin was a character. She smoked at least three packs of cigarettes a day and had a formidable hacking cough that emanated from behind closed doors, setting on edge the teeth of all within earshot. She was the widow of a relatively famed anthropologist, Paul Radin, who had taught at Berkeley and Mills College, to name a few on a lengthy list of hallowed institutions. So ole Doris was different, well traveled, educated, had lived in liberal environments, and for those things, I appreciated her. For her creepy cough, stooped crone posture, long, rangy gray hair, and opinions about my drinking, I disdained her. She was to be my boss, however, in this new position.

I find it interesting to note that of all the letters written to my family and saved by my mother during years from different schools and different lands, for this period, there was not a single missive home. In retrospect, I'm not surprised.

Though I didn't realize it in September, my days in Chico were numbered. Even with the extra responsibilities of the RA job, my head and heart were in other places. I still traveled to Berkeley on a regular basis, and there I was learning that pot did indeed get me high, and getting high was what I was about. I set to finding how to score in this bucolic little college town and, to my surprise, found the answer at the local high school and the young girl who could procure it for me.

I can't remember her name but can still see her pretty little face and long stringy hair, her bell-bottoms, and sassy walk. Dangerous territory this, especially in my position of trustworthiness, to be flirting around with a seventeen-year-old. She would come visit me in my private dorm room, and we would hang out around town. It must have driven old Doris crazy! I even took her to Berkeley one weekend, and for some reason not clear to me, we took the Greyhound Bus. I think it was her mother's intervention as she felt the bus would be safer than riding the long distance in a car. I'm sure she wasn't imagining the sex we had in the back seat of the Greyhound on our late-evening ride—still one of the better offerings in any game of "where's the most interesting place you've ever *done* it?"

On that weekend in Berkeley, my young companion proceeded to have sex with a bass player friend of mine, Jack Dunn, and I was tremendously jealous. Reason won out, and I determined to score my drugs in the future from my less-risky colleagues in the Bay Area.

My weekly sojourns to Berkeley continued, as did my speedy taxi service. I don't recall much about my studies that semester, only that they definitely took a back seat to all the other interesting events in my life. I was making more new friends on the Avenue and even ran into Sue Remley, who had apparently gotten pregnant in her junior year and left school for a more liberal environment where she could carry her baby full-term and then give it up for adoption. I still recall the tremendous shame she seemed to feel in telling me her story over coffee.

The gorgeous Sacramento Valley climate did its usual thing: Indian summer afternoons, dramatic red skies at sunset from the burning off of the rice crops, the crisp evenings that forewarned of the coming cold. But my heart was with the vibrant culture of Berkeley and the changing times, which somehow hadn't even telegraphed their existence to Chico. By the end of the semester, and with the dread of how my folks would respond to this latest chagrin, I told them I was dropping out of school.

My folks had given up on trying to exercise any sort of control over me, other than financial. My dad and I barely spoke and our eyes almost never met. My mother was still obviously torn by being in the middle and chose to stand by her man, hanging on to the ludicrous story of how I had drugged him into misbehavior. It was the only reality she could admit lest she have to wrestle with how to stay with a man who could proposition his own daughter.

Though I didn't have an apartment of my own, I spent the majority of my time crashing with various friends in Berkeley, occasionally sleeping in my old room in Lafayette. When in my parents' home (it no longer felt like *my* home), I busied myself with painting with oils and writing poetry. But I was free to come and go at will, and Berkeley is where I would venture.

The atmosphere around the Cal campus was ever more lively, the drugs plentiful, and the emerging music scene a force we were sure would change the world. There were ongoing challenges to the power structure, the Establishment, be it protest against the war in Vietnam or the university politics. It would still be a few years before the need to quell the dissent became so extreme that violence was used against the kids on the street.

We were into the spring of 1966, and the times, they were definitely a' changin'.

Continuing Education

In order to escape any sanctions of parental control, the modus operandi was to ask for as little financial assistance as possible. I felt if I wasn't taking their money, then they had no right to judge my life choices. However, that averred independence meant I had to find an alternative source of revenue.

I had no recent work history, just the jobs I had held as a little kid working in my dad's shop. I decided to explore the unemployment office and put myself on their rolls. It didn't take long to realize that honesty about being a good typist could get me immediate placement in any number of dismal positions.

I was envious of the kids like Ronnie, who had crafted a regimen of attending Cal, flunking out, transferring to Oakland City College (soon to be the birthplace of the Black Panther Party), making up the deficit in their GPA, and transferring back to the university. It seemed ideal.

I held off, suffered through a couple of dreadful typing jobs, but planned eventually to lobby my folks to support me while I rented an apartment and returned to school at OCC. The course load seemed manageable and the cultural perks perfect.

During this time, my mom was well aware of my drug use. As I always had, I seemed compelled to share the most shocking elements of my life with her; I guess in some twisted way thinking my maturity would win her respect. I also enjoyed hearing my mother worry aloud about my health and safety—it actually resembled parental caring on some level.

When I screwed up enough courage to approach my parents about returning to school, the response was "You can go anywhere in the world, just get *out* of the Bay Area." This, ostensibly to get me away from the druggie atmosphere that Berkeley had become. But it also felt a lot like "Please go away and get out of our lives."

Around this time, an old friend from my first high school resurfaced—Pat Spingola, the friend with whom I had shared my first drunk. Pat had been attending school in Mexico City and was filled with tales of what a grand time she was having. "Come with me when I return," she says. "But what about the application process? Transcripts and all? What if they won't even accept me with my dismal grade point?"

"Not to worry," Pat had assured me. To hear her tell it, all the administration at this school, the University of the Americas, cared about was the cash to cover the tuition. All other details could be worked out while I was already enrolled and attending classes. And instruction was all in English as opposed to the curricula at the National University.

Pat lived in a *pensión* with the Flores family, a divorced mother and her four kids. The costs of housing were most reasonable, with room and board and laundry service all for 600 pesos a month, the equivalent of $48 (US) at the time. And the atmosphere was pretty permissive, with no curfew and no permission slip needed to go away on a weekend. La Ciudad (as Mexico City was called) was then a bustling metropolis of eleven million people, replete with a smog-laden atmosphere atop the plateau where the city sat. It fit the requirements; it was out of the Bay Area.

Pat and I spent the next week hanging out together while she regaled me with stories of her boyfriend down there, Chuck, or Carlos as the local kids called him. Chuck was part of a culture of kids from Southern California whose parents owned second homes in Mexico. In the case of Chuck's parents, their vacation base was in Guadalajara. Chuck went to school in La Ciudad and then would join his parents during holidays at their second home. He lived pretty independently and had a car and an apartment of his own in the city.

About a week before our departure, I took Pat to meet a friend of mine from Berkeley, Carol Ciullo. Carol was a nurse in the emergency room at Herrick Hospital near the campus and was one of my best acid buddies. She lived in an amazing little community called

Canyon, nestled in the Oakland Hills. Even today, many people still don't know of its existence. Up about one hundred steps from the nearest parking spot, Carol's house was largely a shack but nestled in the woods and seeming utterly remote. I had taken my second acid trip at her house, listening to Beethoven with tears streaming down my face as the music moved me to unbelievable heights.

While visiting Carol, Pat and I did a fair amount of drinking. Coming home to my folks on the winding Canyon road, she managed to get sick in my Mustang, vomiting all over the back seat. I was disgusted. After my futile efforts to remove all traces and odors, I left my folks with instructions to sell the car for me while I was gone and use the money to defray my living costs in Mexico.

Pat made the journey south by plane to Los Angeles where she hooked up with Carlos, then driving down into the Mexican mainland together in his car. I traveled solo with my two little suitcases from SFO to La Ciudad, direct, and landed there alone, the veritable stranger in a strange land.

A kind taxi driver helped me reach the address Pat had given me for Señora Flores in a busy urban residential block. She seemed a lovely person and introduced me to her kids: Patricia was eighteen and employed—the eldest. Raul was a small boy, and I was surprised to find he was sixteen as he was so diminutive. He took an immediate, flirty shine to me. Marta was thirteen and a rather predictably sullen early teen. The youngest was Margarita who was just nine and a sweet, sweet child.

The apartment wasn't large, but somehow we all fit in it. As best I can recall, two of the kids slept in the living room. The señora had her own room, and there was a separate bedroom where two students (Pat and I) slept. So perhaps it was a three-bedroom home. Certainly only one bathroom.

After introductions, pleasantries, and unpacking and settling into my room, I was eager to head out into the exotic urban evening to explore my new environs. I was also impatient to consume the rather large joint I had smuggled along on my travels in the plastic body of a ballpoint pen.

An enormous boulevard runs the length of La Ciudad, called El Paseo de la Reforma, or the Reforma for short. Not far from our abode was the portion of the Reforma where the enormous monument to Mexican independence was erected by dictator Porfirio Díaz—*El Ángel,* or the Angel of Independence. It's a stunning golden angel sitting atop a column that is thirty-six meters high. It was an impressive sight, standing there in all her glory, in a *glorietta* (or roundabout), amid five lanes of honking, streaming, anarchic traffic. The base, with its carved statues of various heroes of the independence and noble inscriptions, seemed a perfect spot to sit down on the steps and light up my joint.

I remember it as a brilliant evening, here in a part of this foreign land utterly new to me. No Baja this! La Ciudad sits high atop a plateau at 2,240 meters, or 7,349 feet above sea level. It shimmered with light and bustling activity, and I'm sure the altitude contributed to the heady feeling of being on such a grand adventure. Of course, the higher I got, the grander the adventure seemed; I didn't even feel the need to finish my smoke but put away half for later enjoyment.

From *El Ángel,* I began to roam the Reforma, watching the pedestrians, particularly interested in the way the men of this culture ogled foreign *gueras* (fair-skinned girls) while openly fondling themselves via their trouser pockets. The women were a flavor of submissive that was entirely unfamiliar. Economic distinctions were obvious, with the *indios* wearing more traditional dress and obviously the class who lived and worked at the behest of those in more modern garb. It was probably the first stark juxtaposition of classes I'd ever noticed, more obvious to me than the fact that a woman once cleaned our home who dressed and looked different from us.

In my mildly euphoric state, I continued down the Reforma until I came upon a large building that was the obvious destination of a large number of folks and saw the sign that announced the *jai alai* matches that evening. Cool! I had no idea what such a match might look like other than a vague impression from movies. I knew it was a sporting competition, and it sounded like fun. Paying a nominal admission fee, I entered the building.

Inside the arena was a small court on the ground level, then bleachers rising high up to the ceiling on only one side. I chose a seat about halfway up and took my place while the competitors were warming up. I had no real sense of the rules of the game but could tell from the preliminaries that the action would be fast-paced and fierce. But the most amazing part of the evening was just starting to get underway.

A couple of men worked a catwalk at the bottom of the bleachers, about ten feet above the playing surface. Each man had an apron about his waist with what looked to be a collection of tennis balls within the pockets. Then things really started to heat up. Moving my attention from the players to the men with the tennis balls, I realized that this was the way spectators were placing bets on the game. Someone would raise their hand, one of the catwalk guys would put some paper chit into a slit in the tennis ball and then throw it up to the man wishing to place a bet. In turn, the bettor removed the chit and placed currency in its stead, throwing the ball back to the betting agent.

That might sound straightforward for one transaction, but now imagine two men working the spectators at the same time, then multiply this vision with a speed factor like stockbrokers calling out bets on the floor of the New York Stock Exchange. It was complete pandemonium to my pot-addled brain. I was fascinated, at least when I wasn't ducking, imagining that every ball flying overhead was about to hit me.

I never did quite get the gist of the game but eventually made my way back to the *pensión* and the Flores family. My first evening in La Ciudad had felt like quite the adventure.

Pat eventually arrived and classes began. I was enrolled to take Shakespeare, trying once again to muddle through this literature requirement I had attempted twice before. It seemed every time I took the class, I had great difficulty with the instructor though I felt I loved the plays and sonnets. Perhaps this time would be my lucky charm. My other class was Philosophy 430, or Spanish Mystical Thought. It seemed a very cool title; I was excited about it without having any notion of what it would entail.

Each day, we would ride to school with Chuck in his VW Beetle, a distance of about six miles outside of town on the road to Puebla. Generally, we would smoke dope on the way, and I couldn't really tell you much more about the course of the day. The philosophy class was enthralling; both our texts were books by St. John of the Cross: *The Ascent of Mount Carmel* and *Dark Night of the Soul.*

The class had only four students beside myself. I hadn't realized this was going to be religious mysticism, but I remember being profoundly impressed with the readings. I still own those two paperbacks though I've parted ways with most of my library a number of times. Occasionally, I've cracked one open to be reminded that I had underlined a vast majority of the passages in them, with margin notes as erudite as "Wow!" I keep telling myself that I really must revisit these tomes one day to touch base with what apparently affected me deeply.

I fondly remember that, during the summer months, it would rain almost every afternoon, at 4:00 p.m. on the dot. My memory is of walking down the street, perhaps buying a torta from a sidewalk cart, and when it would begin to sprinkle. I'd duck into a neighborhood café with covered outdoor seating while the thunderstorm accumulated momentum. Soon it would be pouring with ferocity. Within a half hour, the storm had passed, the pollution washed away, and everything smelled pristine. In the time it took to drink two beers, the entire city had been cleansed.

Acapulco Gold, at this time the most potent marijuana known, was ours to be had from the source, as close as a six hour drive in Chuck's car. We would head south to the resort town on a Friday, arriving late in the evening.

Acapulco was an amazing landscape of contrasts: the luxurious hotels sitting on unspoiled beaches, arranged in several crescent bays on the one hand. In the surrounding hills over which one arrived, dropping down to the oceanside, were little shanty residences and enormous poverty. These conditions were the harshest I had seen, other than the migrant workers in Marie's cherry orchards. But it was among these shacks and hovels where we would score our dope.

I remember sitting in the car, waiting for Chuck while he negotiated our purchase. Perched along the dirt curb was a small, wide-eyed child watching me. She had terrible sores on her face and mucous running from her eyes. The thought passed through my mind that, likely, even the most minimal health care or immunizations could avert the suffering of this little girl. My vision of enrolling in the peace corps and doing service in poorer lands resurfaced momentarily, but then Chuck arrived with our drugs. We were off to think of sunnier things.

Night on the beaches of Acapulco were stunning. Balmy and tranquil, clear skies, and shooting stars, we would find a spot under one of the *quitasols* (the large umbrellas constructed of palm fronds) that were a permanent fixture along the sands. There we would light up our dope and lie on our backs, listening to the American rock and roll wafting from the local discos. I missed my music from home acutely; the discos playing the current hit "Mustang Sally" served to remind me not only of the car I had left but also that, yes, I would soon have to *put my big, flat feet on the ground.* In the benign climate, we just smoked until we drifted off to sleep, awakening in the morning without having ever even needed a blanket.

The bulk of our purchase came in the form of a *mita*, a quantity of pot rolled in newspaper, measuring about an inch in diameter and approximately six inches long. Due to the beachside humidity, the package was pliable to the point of almost being soggy. By the time we had made the trip back to the city at its 7,000+ feet, the herb was completely cured and ready to smoke. Sometimes for a lark we would just put a match to the end of the *mita* and toke. This premium crop, and at such an altitude, one hit had us pretty stoned.

In spite of all this frivolity, I was making a sincere effort to do well in class and would write home about my good intentions of spending less time with Chuck and Pat and more time hitting the books. I had been exchanging letters with Dianne, and she seemed interested in coming down for the second session of summer school. I was thrilled at the prospect.

Pat had enrolled in two art classes as her grades the term before had both been Ds. She apparently thought art subjects would be easy as her lack of attention to school and focus on partying conveyed very little concern about how her studies were progressing. Chuck was tiring of her, as was I. She dovetailed perfectly into my plans by flunking out after the first session of summer school.

Plans got firmed up, Dianne had applied (and gotten accepted) to attend the second session, and now she would be able to room with me at Señora Flores's. Pat headed Stateside, and I don't believe I ever saw her again.

As the time of Dianne's arrival approached, I realized I had harbored great hopes that our affair might rekindle while she was with me. I received news that my parents had sold the Mustang, and letters home were filled with references about wanting to use some of the money to take Di somewhere nice during her stay in Mexico. That plan eventually morphed into my parents venturing south for a visit and taking both me and Dianne to Acapulco for what seemed (by comparison to previous visits) a five-star weekend.

Chuck loaned me his Beetle in order to pick up my folks at the airport upon their arrival. My dad uncharacteristically swallowed his pride, stepped aside, and assented to let me do the driving as we headed to their hotel through the frenetic, madcap experience of traffic in La Ciudad. All maneuvers were accomplished through the cacophony of blaring horns and shouted admonitions to (freely translated) "Watch where you're going!" My passengers hung on tightly and, I'm sure, silently admired my cool comportment while weaving and bobbing and doing my own share of honking and swearing.

Once safely at their hotel, my dad arranged for a rental car for the trip to Acapulco we would make the following day. Never one to hold still, Dad was always a man on a mission; if Acapulco was the ultimate destination, then no time was squandered by seeing the sights of La Ciudad other than a planned ride out to visit my campus, which was accomplished before the end of their very first afternoon in town.

Living most of my life in Northern California, with all climates and landscapes seemingly within the range of a one-day drive, I was always astonished with how unique the vistas were on the journey to Acapulco. For the first time, I was unable to correlate everything

I saw with something familiar from home. The highway was narrow and winding with frequent roadside memorials where autos had plunged over the edge; scraggy little conifers grew out of crevices in sheer cliffs of rock. It was most singular.

The resort weekend was lovely; it was great to be with my parents but also have along Dianne, whom they really enjoyed as well. Her presence afforded me the opportunity to avoid awkwardness with my dad, and I think Mom appreciated that I had a friend of whom she approved more than Pat. We dined adventurously at small restaurants I had discovered on previous trips, and until her last years, my mother repeatedly would ask me, "What was the name again of those really hot, hot enchiladas we had?" "Enchiladas Meridana," I would reiterate: enchiladas with a sauce from Merida on the Yucatan Peninsula. Other than one evening sequestered in the bathroom in reaction to some local food or other, the long weekend seemed idyllic.

My folks were in town another week after our Acapulco adventure, and typical of my dad, very little time was spent holding still. It was reminiscent of our family's first trip to the Hawaiian Islands in 1961. Dad's notion of relaxing was to rent a car and drag the entire family on a circumnavigation of Oahu. In Mexico, our travels extended like the legs of a spider from a belly of the Distrito Federal, the capital where La Ciudad was situated.

First we had driven to the southeast to visit my school, the University of the Americas, which lay 16 kilometers from the city on the highway to Puebla, then back through the city to emanate south and west, into the state of Guerrero, stopping to shop in Taxco (*the* place to buy silver goods) to reach our holiday weekend in Acapulco. Again, we headed back through DF to head north, through the states of Hidalgo and Querétaro on Highway 51, destined for San Miguel de Allende in the state of Guanajuato, a four-hour drive through the Bajio Mountains of central Mexico, and covering a distance of 146 miles.

San Miguel is a beautiful little town in central Guanajuato, filled with American expatriates, retirees, and artists. The Instituto Allende is a highly regarded fine arts school where I had hoped to transfer in order to study creative writing. My parents wanted to see this latest fantasy in the flesh. They were impressed with the town's beauty and tranquility, a stark contrast to the bustling urbanity of La Ciudad.

Somewhere I had gotten a lead on a small cottage for rent, situated in the garden of a New York couple who had relocated to San Miguel. This spot was like a dream come true: a fully furnished studio in the corner of their walled courtyard, covered with bougainvillea; an adobe structure sporting a tiled roof and terra-cotta veranda. I could easily picture myself creating great things in this cottage, this town, this institute.

The only snag was the outside possibility that some friends of the landlords might be visiting in the coming month, in which case they wanted to have the cottage to offer their guests. We left it at that. If the friends were able to travel to San Miguel, the cottage would not be available; if they couldn't make it, I could have the rental for the coming school year. It was a thrilling prospect.

The disappointing outcome was only a few days in revealing itself—the New Yorkers would be visiting and I would be returning to the States at the end of summer session in Mexico City. The topic of a renewal with Dianne had been dispatched with a couple of conversations which left it abundantly clear that she had now moved on to her life in Sacramento and had no plans to be romantically linked with me. Friendship would have to suffice.

Avenue Redux

My return home in the fall of 1966 was a shock to my system. Again, I resorted to crashing with friends in Berkeley rather than fully inhabiting my old room in Lafayette. The first place I headed was to Patti and Susan's on Fulton Street south of the campus by a few blocks.

Typical of whatever, be it the lax times or my utterly undeveloped sense of any personal boundaries, when I walked up to their apartment and found no one home, I merely jimmied a window and let myself in, assuming I would be greeted enthusiastically. It wasn't an overwhelming welcome upon their return, but a little pot, the great equalizer, left them glad to see me.

I was granted permission to crash for a few days, but it was made clear I needed to find my own place after that.

Checking in on the Avenue, I found it a disturbingly changed place: speed had arrived from Los Angeles in my absence, and the innocence and *agape* I had left at the beginning of summer seemed to have gone underground. In its stead was a proliferation of biker gangs and hypodermics, a drug trade now controlled by the Oakland-based Hell's Angels, and a toughness on the street that was wholly unfamiliar. I sought out my old acid buddies to get their take on the current situation.

Accomplishing a double task, I found my old pal David having an espresso at the Forum café and got an update on current events, as well as the promise of a roof over my head at his place in the hills north of campus. David concurred about the rough new element in town, but the flower child in us (a term yet to be coined by the media) was still represented on the street. Acid was plentiful though its possession was imminently to be made a criminal offense.

Until the autumn of 1966, possession of LSD was still legal unless the law could establish an intent to sell. I recall a lovely fall day, the day before the new laws were to go in effect, when everyone I knew on the street was stoned on acid, and yet several people were handing out free tabs in celebration of its waning legal status.

"Care for a hit?" a friendly passerby would ask. "I'm already high." "Then have a little more." It was a vivid, Technicolor kind of day, and memory of it is warm and particularly fuzzy, for obvious reasons.

I prevailed upon David's kind offer of housing, where he had a large upstairs studio in a gorgeous Maybeck house that had been hacked up into rental units. Many apartments like this existed in Berkeley, in these butchered yet still stunning architectural master-pieces, for which Bernard Maybeck garnered the credit even though they had in truth been designed by his *protégé* Julia Morgan. Just one more raw deal for the women of an earlier time.

David's studio was up a number of stairs, meandering through lush gardens and along paving stones between flights. At any point in the ascent, you could turn around and see breathtaking views of the Bay beyond and all three bridges: the Bay Bridge, the Richmond-San Rafael Bridge, and the Golden Gate behind which the sun would set every evening. Once in the studio, it was just a large room with French doors opening to the bay view, a little hotplate-style kitchen unit in one corner, and a gigantic round bed.

David and I were to bunk together, but this included no assump-tions of sexual activity. He was the ultimate in platonic pals, largely, I believe, because his various disabilities from childhood polio left him hesitant to make himself vulnerable to rejection or rebuke from women. His large head and shaggy beard sat above a torso where only one half of one arm was fully functional. The other arm stayed stuffed in his pocket, and the operational limb only had mobility from the elbow down.

I remember being in an ice-cream parlor with him one day while getting cones. David was juggling change into his pocket and jockeying for the opportune time to take the cone from the hand of the teenage server when some impatient kid behind us started heckling, "What's the matter with the other hand? Doesn't it work?" with great sarcasm. David turned and calmly replied, "Thanks for asking. No, it doesn't."

It was to this studio in the hills that I, one day, took a couple of new friends who had arrived from Los Angeles to become part of our Avenue community. Once ensconced on the big round bed, they pulled out an array of stuff I'd never seen up close: some white powder and a hypodermic kit. The offer was on the table to sample the new phenomenon in town—speed. This was the only time in my life I ever shot up drugs, and though I found transfixing the ritual of preparing the needle, tying off one another's arm, and watching the small rivulet of blood enter the syringe, the high didn't impress me at all.

About Patti and Susan

Patti had spent her first year of college at Chico, coming from the small Southern California town of Ventura. We met when I was in Craig Hall playing my Bob Dylan records on a neighbor's phonograph. While all the other girls were plugging their ears, wondering what the dreadful sounds were emanating from down the hall, Patti instead ferreted out the sound and came looking for its source.

Patti was instantly smitten, as was I, by the powerful lyrics and rebellious tenor of this edgy folk radical. We became friends. Patti became a regular on my weekly forays into Berkeley, joining in the speedy taxi rides for a weekend steeped in counterculture. Before the end of her freshman year at Chico, Patti had applied to and been accepted to do her next year at Cal, Berkeley. So by '66, she was a bona fide denizen.

Once ensconced in this lively university environment, an old high school chums of hers, Suzie, came up for a visit and decided against leaving. Much by default, I believe, the two became lovers as a predictable outcropping of the necessity of sharing a bed and roof over their heads. To my best recollection, it was the first relationship for either of them with another girl.

Suzie got a job at Herrick Hospital as a ward clerk, I believe, on the strength of having been a candy striper in high school. It was at Herrick that she discovered, and came to share with us, her coworker Carol Ciullo.

Ciullo was an older woman—all of twenty-four! We were still in our late teens and hugely impressed with the fact she had a real job, had already had and divorced a husband, and lived in the woods in Canyon in the shack I have previously described. Carol was great fun and a fairly reliable source for drugs, some of them exotic and pharmaceutical. The memory comes to mind of the time she managed to steal opium from the hospital though it was in a tincture form, meaning we had to cook it down to smoke it. A powerful headache is the predominant memory.

So Patti and Susan lived on Fulton, right around the corner from her job at Herrick. Many afternoons before they reported to work, Suzie on the ward and Carol in the ER, we would be getting stoned in the Fulton Street living room.

I sought out the unemployment office in an effort to get a paycheck rolling in. This was before I appreciated the death knell it was to let the agency know I could type. Ugh! Instead of a lovely unemployment benefit check, they immediately sent me out to interview at a direct-mail advertising house on San Pablo Avenue.

Among my variegated employment career, this had to be one of the dumbest jobs I ever held. Direct mail meant junk mail. And my job was to wield a pair of scissors and snip apart postal routes from an endless stream of paper tape with addresses printed upon it, dividing it into segments to be applied to junk mail, corresponding with different carrier routes. It took less than a week before I was supping at the bar around the corner on my lunch hour, where they served a hot dog and a draft beer for a quarter. Many days I didn't make it back to work; I just popped in to say the rotten food next door must have poisoned me and I was going home sick.

But it was at this job a couple of weeks later that my boss walked by and inquired, "Have you ever had jaundice?" I didn't know what he meant, but he explained that I really looked rather eerily yellow and I should have a peek in the mirror. My eyeballs were bright as urine on vitamins! I called Ciullo at work, and she told me to come up to the ER so she could have a look at me.

I had no medical insurance—one of the few times in my life that was the case. There was no lab work she could do for free, but Carol's considered opinion, after asking if I had shared a hypodermic with anyone recently, was that I indeed had hepatitis. She did direct me to Berkeley Public Health Department where a blood test confirmed her diagnosis.

At this time there was no classification of hepatitis A, B, and C. Rather, they referred to infectious, serum, and viral. I was conferred the title of viral hepatitis, quit my job, dropped about twenty pounds in two weeks, and sought refuge with my good buddies Patti and Susan.

By this time, the girls had left Fulton Street and crossed the bay to live in the Haight-Ashbury at 720 Haight Street. Again, a studio apartment, but this time, they took pity on their sick friend and let me stay with them. With no health care beyond the initial diagnosis, I had no idea that sharing eating utensils and plates with others would communicate the disease. I promptly infected both my caring and compassionate friends.

We were nearing winter now, and things get rather blurry for me. I believe I bunked in a small twin bed about four feet away from Patti and Susan, and my best recollection is that Patti became more infected with the hepatitis than Suzy. As I grew envious of their connection and more and more fond of Patti, things between her and Susan began to show strain. Eventually, there was a critical moment that was an all-time low in my personal integrity. Knowing the result it would produce, I gazed in Patti's (yellow) eyes and said the words I knew would capture her heart: "I need you." Like magic, Suzi was soon moved out of the apartment and settling somewhere in Berkeley once again.

Though we lived in what was known as the Lower Haight, bordering on the ghetto neighborhood called the Fillmore District, we felt completely swept up in the social and cultural activity that was germinating in the Haight-Ashbury.

Tour buses were cruising up Haight Street, bringing tourists from the Midwest who were hearing about these *hippies*. City authorities experimented with making Haight a one-way street, first in one direction and then in the other. The street kids were literally laying their bodies down in the street, presumably holding protests by attempting to block the traffic. The police department merely hauled them off to jail.

On January 14, 1967, the Human Be-In was held in the polo fields of Golden Gate Park, the first massive free concert of its time, numbering an attendance of thirty thousand and officially marking the portal to the Summer of Love in San Francisco. The impressive lineup featured Alan Ginsberg, Timothy Leary, Richard Alpert (later known as Ram Dass), the Jefferson Airplane, the Grateful Dead, Quicksilver Messenger Service, and stage-side security provided by the Hell's Angels motorcycle gang. The new movement signaled a coalescence of the current generation of student unrest from local campuses at Stanford and Berkeley and the beat poet generation that had been the pulse of the North Beach neighborhood in San Francisco.

Comedian Dick Gregory performed as well and, by the following year, would be a presidential candidate to represent the Peace and Freedom Party, formed later that summer. It would still be a few years before the Twenty-Sixth Amendment to the Constitution would pass lowering the voting age to eighteen. But by Gregory's run, I would be twenty-one, and he was the first presidential candidate ever to get my vote in a California primary.

Federally Funded

Somewhere in the preceding months, Patti and I had taken civil service exams in the hope of getting a job with the US Post Office. It was not yet a private corporation, and the cost of sending a first-class letter was still a nickel. We tested well, got placed on a list, and eventually we were called in for jobs at a point where we felt fairly recovered from the hepatitis.

At the post office, the pay seemed exceedingly good and the dress code suitably informal. Just my kind of place! The job was a haven for longhairs and hippies, at least those not dodging the draft as the US military cranked up its efforts in the nonwar in Vietnam. The draft was probably one reason there were so many vacancies in domestic federal jobs at the time. Friends terrified of being called up were routinely fleeing to Canada and surrendering their US citizenship.

We began work at Rincon Annex in San Francisco, the main post office at the time. We came on the payroll with the position of postal clerk, and our duties were to sort mail in the closed-in, dusty, multistoried building, with amazing and dramatic Anton Refregier murals on the walls of the lobby below and cutthroat, paycheck-robbing poker games among the younger Chinese American clerks on the upper floors.

As a couple, Patti and I had the bliss I'd not previously known of living with my lover, sharing a bed, riding the bus together to the workplace, and schlepping to the Safeway store where we were astounded that three full bags of groceries cost the enormity of $30. Toward fall, we determined that we missed the warmer climate across the bay and sought a rental that would return us to Berkeley. We settled in yet another Maybeck masterpiece hacked into units and took up residence in a basement studio, probably at one time a maid's quarters. Even closer to the north gate of Cal than David's place, we were within a stroll of the Avenue by cutting across campus, and the bus across the bridge to our postal jobs was a mere walk down the (fairly steep) hill. By most accounts, we seemed blissful.

But storm clouds were brewing at the post office. Our calm little gig of mindlessly tossing letters into little slots was shaken by the news that we were expected to learn a more complicated scheme, where mail would further be broken down into individual carrier routes. This meant the daunting task of memorizing not only street names but also block numbers and addresses which divided the various destinations. Our minds could barely grasp how numbingly boring that sounded.

A more worldly friend hipped us to the inside information that if one really didn't want to perform this feat, the memorizing of the city schemes, that it was possible to separate from the job and still receive unemployment insurance. The first of many such times I availed myself of the subsistence benefit, it seemed a perfect solution to returning to the more satisfying routine of drugs, sex and rock 'n' roll. "Don't just not show up for the test," we were counseled. "If you do that, then you can't get unemployment. What you have to do is take the test and fail it, proving that the job was *too hard* for you. Then you can collect."

In mid-November, we did just that. Both of us. Patti and I took and failed our city scheme exams and got the news of our separation on my birthday. I remember gleefully riding home on the bus, crossing the bay with the entire vista of lights in the hills twinkling at us while I giggled and chanted, "I'm free, white, twenty-one—undecided and unemployed." Happy Birthday to me!

In our home on Scenic Avenue, our little basement, I again went into nesting mode. Our bed was in a tiny airless closet, where the double-bed mattress just fit and overhead were pipes which I assume were the plumbing for the upstairs unit. I proceeded to paint our bedroom a sky blue with the plumbing offset in a compliment of lavender. The other feature by our bed was a low table I had deliberately adorned with melted candle wax until it was quite vivid and colorful.

The living room had an actual fireplace, even if the tiny kitchen was barely functional. Rent was an extravagant $250 a month, the first time I had ever lived in such an expensive apartment. Were it not for the Maybeck moniker and the lush surrounding garden, as well as the cachet of being a Northside address, I don't believe it could ever have fetched such a hefty price.

If You Remember

I've always found charming the axiom, "If you remember the sixties, you weren't really there." Fittingly, I can't remember to whom it is attributed.

The energy of the time, the rising dissent surrounding the Vietnam War, the thrill of the seemingly endless concert offerings at the Fillmore, the Avalon Ballroom, Winterland, the air of (we hoped) true and lasting social change all took on a momentum of their own, and time became an accelerated vortex of people, places, and adventures.

Not long after that separation from the post office, I had a ghost from the past cross my radar: Norma Kwestel. Norma brought in her wake an entire cast of characters who would become future lovers, landlords, and acid buddies. Through Norma I met Gail Waechter, a highly regarded painter who had dropped out of art school just two weeks prior to graduation, dismissing as superfluous the conferring of a degree.

Gail touched that place in me that always was longing for the next adventure, the next possibility of a wild ride. Before long I began an affair with her, Patti threw me out of the house, and I moved in to share Gail's basement apartment in North Oakland which in itself was a huge art installation, replete with holes knocked in the walls providing a window into another piece of the artistic puzzle.

By Christmastime, Gail's ex, Peggy, appeared. She was a photographer, a lover from their time at California College of Arts and Crafts, and she lived in Manhattan in the West Village. On Christmas Eve of that year, 1967, we shared an outdoor feast with Peggy's family on the coast of Big Sur. The family had property poised on the cliffs; turkey was cooked in a Chinese pottery oven, and we supped at a picnic table in a balmy seventy-five degrees. Hard to believe that, a week later, we would be in the snows of a wintry New York.

Peggy extended an invitation for Gail and me to come stay with her and try life in the Big Apple. With the offer of a roof over our heads, I had the necessary ingredient of safety to make the journey. Piling in a 1957 pink Lincoln with two gay boy friends, André and Bob, we headed out a few days before New Year's.

We were a scruffy lot, none of us handy, and when we encountered blizzard conditions in Wyoming, no one knew how to install the tire chains we had packed along. In the dark, making our best effort, we managed to get the chains wrapped around the axle and had to spend the night in the car, wrapped in our sleeping bags, afraid to run the heater for fear of running out of gas. The next morning, a passerby helped us get underway and informed us of just how severe the storm had been. Apparently, yet again, we were lucky to survive.

Arriving at 105 MacDougal Street on December 30, Peggy welcomed us, and the boys went off on their own. A cold-water flat, only one small bed, a bathtub on a platform in the kitchen, and a commode at the end of a long hallway past Peggy's darkroom—I'd never seen anything like it.

It seemed only days before we got a call from Gail saying she had committed herself to an institution called Daytop. Today, we would say she entered rehab. Gail and I had dropped a lot of hallucinogens together and smoked copious pot, and apparently she hankered for a different worldview. Daytop went on in the end of that decade to produce revolutionary theater, exemplified in an off-Broadway play called *The Concept*, where residents acted out their own personal dramas on the stage.

I was left in residence with Peggy, got a job waiting tables in the downstairs Feenjon Café, and also was hired at an ad agency near Times Square where Peggy worked in production at a storyboard house. Wages were in cash as the company's employees had revolted against their many bounced paychecks.

Drinking became the popular modus of altering consciousness, supplanting drugs for the time. We were in infamous company; directly across from our apartment was the Kettle of Fish where folk notables such as Dave van Ronk and Bob Dylan hung out, drinking themselves into the next creative project. The Café San Remo at the corner of Bleecker and MacDougal had the cleanest mirrors I'd ever seen in a bar and was where, after work, we would drink into the late hours, discussing ideas for photo projects for Peggy or storyboards for short films that seemed to materialize from the deep recesses of my mind.

In February, a citywide garbage strike (the collection cans lived under the stairs in our apartment building) sent me home to California for a brief visit for some dental work. I returned when the strike was settled.

By April, Martin Luther King Jr. was assassinated, and before my mother could call me June 6 and tell me about Bobby Kenney's killing, she had also phoned to inform me that Greg Busch, Liz's younger brother, had murdered his own mother in a fit of rage. It was a pretty crazy time. Late in June, I returned home to Berkeley; six months in the Big Apple had been enough for me.

Back in Berkeley, there was a whirlwind of addresses, automobiles, sex partners, and more unemployment insurance. Reacquainting with Patti, we both, once again, got on the postal clerk list and managed to land jobs at the Berkeley Main Post Office. This time, we knew to request being RPO clerks, thus needing to learn schemes that were a memorization of all the cities in the state as opposed to individual addresses. It was a fun time.

Patti met Michael, a retired Air Force lesbian single mom, who also worked there. I moved from one place to another, often at the first of every month, and took up the usual diversions of hanging out, going to concerts (for $2.50), doing drugs, and drinking.

By late in 1968, I was settled in a little studio over a garage on Bancroft Way, paneled with knotty pine, and a short walk from the post office. During those times when I did own a car, they frequently were not running, often not registered, and even sometimes abandoned on the side of the road when they no longer served me.

It was in this apartment that my predominant memory of the times was the Democratic National Convention that August in Chicago, where police quelled rioters/demonstrators with tear gas, bludgeoning, and pitching young people through the windows of the nearby Hilton Hotel. They were protesting the war in Vietnam, the single most decisive issue of that election year.

My neighbors on Bancroft, in the house to which the garage was attached, were Roger and Julie. They were sweet Berkeley types and also the first heroin addicts I knew though that came as quite a shock to me as they seemed unlike any preconceptions I might have had about junkies. Through Roger and Julie, I met Ron, a member of a local band whose name escapes me. Ron and I had a brief thing; perhaps part of what I call "kissing frogs." Regardless of my untiring research into the opposite sex, I continued to find them remarkably under-stimulating and generally unfulfilling.

I remember Ron taking me to band rehearsals on a 250 retired commuter ferry boat docked and mothballed at the San Francisco pier. That was a fun adventure, living aboard for a couple of days and experiencing the whole world rocking and swaying for several hours once back on terra firma.

I got pregnant.

Well, the good news was I was finally confident that my body functioned normally. The bad news: no way did my self-indulgent lifestyle have room in it for a baby. I asked Julie for counsel; she advised not to say anything to Ron unless I planned to go through with the pregnancy. That settled that.

The day I got the results of the pregnancy exam from my gynecologist is still vivid in memory. It was just before work and I had gotten the bad news, only to have to hitchhike to the post office while still stunned by this revelation. A man picked me up; it was one of our baking September Indian summer days.

Making small talk, we began the short journey of less than a mile. He remarked several times about how hot it was, and then I noticed he was starting to remove items of his clothing, tie first, then shoes and socks. The next thing I knew, as I watched in horror, he was trying to remove his pants while driving the car and had begun to fondle himself. Great! As if the day hadn't already been horrific enough.

At the first available red light, I bailed out of the car and veritably ran the rest of the way to work. Maybe I'd even get lucky and naturally abort as a result of the jog. You perhaps can grasp the extent of my naiveté.

Along with the devastating news that I was pregnant came the quest for a legal abortion, no simple task at the time. An expectant mother had to obtain letters from three psychiatrists, pricey visits even then, recommending an abortion based on the woman's state of unfitness to be a mother. Those letters were then to be reviewed by a panel of physicians, in this case at Alta Bates Hospital where my gynecologist practiced. That panel would, in turn, decide whether the procedure would be granted. Between the cost of the independent shrinks and the overnight hospital stay, plus the procedure, I was going to be out of pocket for over $1,000.

The first shrink visit was a disaster. His probing questions as to the reasons I couldn't carry and deliver this child were invasive and confrontational, and my answers didn't seem to satisfy. At the end of our hour, he informed me that he could not give me a positive recommendation and perhaps I didn't want a letter from his office. Then I *really* started to panic.

One of the favorite questions was "So what will you do if you're not granted the abortion?" It didn't take long to deduce that the magic answer was "I don't know. I guess I'd just have to jump off the bridge." Okay, I get it. The next three psychiatric visits went more smoothly while I played up the lie that I was a potentially suicidal, homicidal young lesbian who couldn't be entrusted with the blessing of a dependent human life.

As the autumn days grew shorter, I awaited the decision of the hospital board. Eventually, they set a date for the procedure: November 2, 1968. I was to go into Alta Bates the night before to be prepped for surgery. I especially didn't want my parents to know anything about this passage in my life though I longed for the sort of mother-daughter comfort that I only knew through reading novels and seeing films.

The night before going into the hospital, I had gone by myself to the movies at the nearby art house on Shattuck Avenue to see

Roman Polanski's *Repulsion*. If you're not familiar with this work, it was a chilling tale of a young woman's descent into madness stemming from her sexual nightmares, fears, and fantasies. I was riveted by the brilliant film, wanting several times to leave the theater but compelled to remain in my seat. When the film was over, I left the theater and was swallowed into the Halloween night to walk home by myself. I was pretty freaked out.

The following day, I showed up and checked in at Alta Bates. I found the nurses sneering and judgmental, hardly angels of mercy. It was stormy as night fell, and frightened to death, I was feeling very alone. That night from my hospital bed, I decided to discard my pride and try to phone my mom but couldn't get through at all, later learning that their phone had been out of order until the following day due to high winds and heavy rains. When I was discharged the next evening, I simply walked home to my little studio with more emotions than I was equipped, on any level, to process.

The solution to the ensuing post-partum depression was the Christmas rush at the post office, with its increased volume of mail and endless opportunities for overtime pay. It worked for me—I would be able to settle my debts for the abortion.

It was in my little knotty pine nest and on my twenty-second birthday that I heard for the first time, from the Beatles' White Album, the anthem "Today Is Your Birthday." What a year it had been!

Ready for a Change

More address changes ensued, bringing a string of rentals. This compulsion to create a feeling of home over and over again. I've always just assumed it came from the same heart space as my annual childhood forts in the yard: a need to find a locus where I could build the home I wanted, attempting it over and over again, the mere act of creation being the seminal aspect.

Frequently I moved on the beginning of each month. At one point, filing a police report for some items stolen from my studio on College Avenue, the Berkeley Police recited a list of addresses where I had resided; I was pretty impressed with my own restlessness to say nothing of my apprehension as to why the police had so much knowledge of my whereabouts.

I amassed a fair amount of savings (relative to the time) from the Christmas season at the post office, and thoughts turned again to my desire to seek some strain of psychotherapy. Maybe it was the phone book, perhaps a free newspaper, but somewhere I came up with a phone number from an ad that appealed. I called to see about an appointment.

A young man answered and engaged me in dialogue, "Tell me a little about yourself and your situation." I recounted the past months, the abortion, touched on the issues with my dad and my teeter-totter between sexual orientations. "I think you'd better come in immediately," he urged. I was impressed, both with the speed of service and the tone of the exhortation. Someone was actually responding to my life with a touch of melodrama, and I have to admit it made me feel cared about.

His small office above the North Berkeley Post Office was comprised of a sitting room where he greeted me, and we chatted for a bit. I asked about his licensure and qualifications and actually was roped in by his explanation that he chose to avoid licensing bodies as their rules and restrictions narrowed his ability to ply radical and experimental approaches to therapy. The other part of the upstairs complex doubled as his living quarters. Don't ask me how on earth it happened, but he ended up taking me into the inner sanctum which contained (what seemed) a huge bed where he instructed me to lie down.

I'm still vexed by my own innocence and stupidity but relied on what I trusted was this man's *professionalism* and put myself, literally and figuratively, in his hands. My repulsion at the memory makes me unable to recall if there was any part of the experience that was gratifying. Perhaps there was extended foreplay, along with sweet, seductive whisperings that had me convinced his actions had any clinical merit. He took me without resistance.

As I left to walk the mile or so home, I do remember the predominant emotions were rage and disgust. I *paid* for this! To be taken advantage of once again, while incredibly vulnerable, under the guise, it was in my own best interest! I felt compelled to find someone to call and explore whether anything could be done about this guy. All I discovered was that the fact he had no professional accreditation merely meant that there was no governing body responsible for disciplining actions such as this. God! I hated men more and more.

I moved again. What the hell else could I do to get the taste of this most recent betrayal out of my mouth, my life? I moved to a small, ratty cottage down in the flats of North Berkeley—no cachet to *this* address. Fritz, a friend at the post office, had told me of the rental which was situated behind where he lived. It seems I still had a couple of men friends, but Fritz and I, for some reason, had clear boundaries.

I bought an older Volkswagen bus, and Fritz helped me build a sleeping platform in the back. I laugh to think of its construction of 2"×4" s and heavy-grade plywood; it made the vehicle incredibly heavy and slow-moving, given its relatively underpowered engine. The engineering feat was accompanied by bouts of copious wine consumption.

We headed north one night, Fritz and me, in my newly completed four-wheeled project, armed with a couple of gallons of red wine, and somehow headed up Highway 101 somewhere in proximity to the Eel River. It was still winter, and we hit some light snow. If you've owned an older bus, you know the wipers are utterly inadequate as is the heater. But we were warmed from within when we encountered a patch of black ice.

Fritz was behind the wheel at the fateful moment, and we spun out of control, skidding across the lane and off the edge of the highway, tumbling at the first sharp drop in the surface and rolling over and over. We finally came to rest at the base of a tree that put a stop to an inevitable plunge into the icy waters of the Eel. We were unhurt and conscious, but the open jug of wine had spewed all over the headliner of the roof. Our first concern was that we avoid a bust for drunk driving. Ah, youth and its skewed priorities!

The rest of the journey is a blur: perhaps a friendly motorist with a pickup and a winch. We seemed able to drive the beast and safely returned home to Berkeley. Why we were even on the road is anyone's guess.

That journey, like my many forays as a young hitchhiker, seemed to be about going places for no particular reason at all—just to go. The fact that I never ran face-to-face with peril while taking rides from semi-truckers, I think, is a testament to a safer time with perhaps fewer sociopaths lurking.

It was in this same period that a mutual friend gave me some bad news about my old friend Ronnie Franck, the man I considered in many ways to open the door for me to all the adventure that had ensued in the past three years. I was told, "Remember how you said, Lin, that you thought some of us would make it and some wouldn't?" referring to the occasional reports of friends who had committed suicide, purportedly because of their hallucinogenic explorations. Ronnie had taken sedatives and lay down on his parents' living room floor, leaving them to discover the horror of their drug-casualty child.

The Decade Closes

As we moved into 1969, things were getting fervently political, and Vietnam was being fiercely protested in the Bay Area. Then Governor Ronald Reagan had promised the voters that he would crack down on the perceived laxity of the UC administration, and as the atmosphere of political actions picked up heat, Reagan dug in ever further. By May of '69 things had gotten so tense that an effort by students and townsfolk to transform a junk-filled vacant property into People's Park developed into an armed occupation of Berkeley by the National Guard.

Reagan had called the Berkeley campus a haven for communist sympathizers, protesters, and sex deviants, true to his cold war paranoia. Angered by the community action two weeks prior, where hundreds showed up to clear rubble and plant trees in the new park (a park albeit on university land), the governor took action. On May 15 at 4:30 a.m., a chain-link perimeter was established around the property to keep people out. The response was angry and immediate; three thousand protestors showed up in Sproul Plaza.

As angry protestors spilled out of the plaza and continued their action down *Telegraph*, tensions were running incredibly high. I was oblivious to the activities, merely coming up to the Avenue to visit the record store, when I saw a throng of young people approaching, running ahead of an ominous cloud—tear gas. My curiosity waned as gunfire broke out right across the street from me. The sheriff's department officers were opening fire with shotguns and buckshot on the demonstrators. I was stunned, but not too stunned to run like hell. One young man, James Rector, died from those shootings; another, Alan Blanchard, was permanently blinded.

Terry Tall

Reporting for the swing shift at the Berkeley Post Office in mid-1969 was a little like entering occupied territory. The People's Park riots had erupted, and by the nineteenth of May, the National Guard was called in, bringing 3,700 troops and tanks to the streets of Berkeley. It was pretty surreal to have to walk through a cordon of armed soldiers surrounding the post office in order to get to work. The latter part of that week saw sweeps of the retail establishments on Shattuck Avenue, some blocks from the hubbub, where even senior citizens were indiscriminately dragged out of stores, forced facedown on the sidewalk, handcuffed, and shipped off to Santa Rita prison. The community was in an uproar and the armed presence was psychologically stretching folks to the point of snapping.

Under Reagan's rule, the boot heel of repression was still firmly on the neck of my generation. It was getting clearer by the minute that we weren't going to be good kids and behave. The post office bustled with activism and diversity, interracial relationships and long-haired, underachieving hippies with Phi Beta Kappa keys. A motley crew, but I felt at home there.

Once through the soldiers, we enjoyed a sort of sanctuary inside the post office, sharing a united sentiment of dissent toward the Vietnam War and national politics, as well as the broadest spectrum of cohorts in my experience: socialists, Red Diaper babies, revolutionaries, do-gooders, and outlaws.

Martha Stoddard cased mail just down the row from me and didn't seem to fit in any of those categories. For one thing, I had heard she played the cello. And she wore skirts and dresses. She had caught my attention and my daily amusement became endless furtive glances and stolen opportunities to engage in frivolous conversation with her. Oh, she was *so* bright! That almost turned me on more than her shapely legs peeking out from under the skirt made of some exotic Guatemalan fabric. As she leaned her head forward to read more closely the address on an envelope, her little half-glasses would slide down the bridge of her nose, and deftly, unconsciously, her index finger would dart up to meet them, returning them to their proper place.

Her profile had a patrician aspect and moved me to want to photograph her. I fantasized of picnics in the Berkeley hills where I might capture her likeness among our tall grasses and grand eucalyptus trees, catching some of the splendid light that the expanse of the bay seemed to impart on everything. Though her hair was short, there was a most demure quality to its styling: little short curls that framed her face and a pesky wisp that continually escaped captivity to the middle of her forehead.

"Martha, have you seen the new Bergman film?" *Cleverly, I shall engage her intellect*, I thought. "Not yet, but I'm hoping to." Grand! Perhaps she would consent to a film with *me*. But courage for the next step, the actual move into an invitation, eluded me for the moment.

Head bowed, back to casing mail.

When I first noticed Terry, she was sitting just to the other side of Martha at the cases, and she, too, was trying to engage my *inamorata* in conversation. This, I thought, could be problematic. Terry was fresh, bold, and just nineteen years old, I came to discover. Tall and lanky, when she crossed the mail room floor, there was a rolling bounce to her step and her gangly arms swung freely at her sides. Her quick, easy smile curled up the corners of her mouth, and she possessed impossibly deep dimples under her rosy Swedish cheeks—dimples that tripled in depth when she broke into a free-falling laugh. Blond hair, cropped close and careless, stuck out at all angles from her skull as if she'd just rolled out of bed after some playfully vigorous lovemaking in a pile of straw. She exuded cocky confidence and a teenager's assurance that she has seen everything and knows it all.

"Hey! How you doing?" It could have been either of us, but I was doing the asking. She peered across Martha's bow and gave me a nod of recognition. "Cool. How's with you?" Anything to interject myself into the conversation she'd been having with Martha.

Other than my guarded pangs of jealousy regarding Martha, I liked this kid.

Like me, she had a tomboyish aspect, an androgyny that found its home in blue jeans and flannel shirts, cowboy boots, and colorful language. A mere handful of us in the post office were lesbians, and we could have all passed as clones of one another but for a variation here and there of our length of hair. Mine was baby fine and chestnut brown, shiny, and halfway down my back. I would tie it in a ponytail to satisfy postal safety requirements with a thick government-issued rubber band. (And did I mention how terribly shiny it was? I was quite proud of my hair then.)

Terry was clearly one of us, and I vowed to find opportunities to know her better. One afternoon, a chance came to work a shift at the parcel post facility where I had seen she was being detailed for the day, and I jumped at the change of scene and a chance to know Terry better.

On the way to parcel post, I got to burn an easy half hour in travel time—a half hour of cheating the government out of its due—a definite plus and my version of anti-government protest. Through the swinging double doors, the big cavernous warehouse opened on a scene of large canvas tubs, akin to giant laundry hampers, spread about the floor in loosely lined-up rows, and enormous conveyor belts streaming packages in from their trucks at the loading docks. A handful of postal clerks were delightedly playing free-for-all, tossing the packages into their respective basket destinations, much as they would a basketball to the hoop, to the tune of loud rock and roll. Apparently, the parcel post supervisor was pretty cool.

Terry was already there and clocked in. I went to the time clock and punched my card, scoped out the floor, and found where I could work myself into a position next to her. "Hey, watch this!" She had noticed me sidle up next to her spot and was welcoming and engaging. I watched as she took up a large flat parcel in her long fingers. On it was marked "Photos: Do Not Bend." She shot me a sly grin as she turned the envelope to share its message, like a magician's flourish to assure the audience that there are no hidden rabbits or trap doors—a gesture that said, "Behold." Then she folded the manila envelope in half and secured it with a rubber band, writing on its exposed face "Oh yes, they *do*." Truly a badass! Though I was a little horrified at her boldness, the rebel in me won out. I *like* this kid!

She tossed the parcel to its destination tub, shot an electric smile my way, and winked as naturally is if she'd just drawn a breath. What a tremendous flirt she was.

"I see you checkin' Martha out pretty seriously," she invited. "Having any luck with that?" "Nah. Fun as it is to entertain the notion, someone told me she's dating Art Levine, that union rep guy. But if I had a shot at her, I bet I could turn her to women." So full of myself, but the reality was that every woman I'd been with so far was one that I had brought out. My version of public service, I reflected as I flashed a smile right back at her.

"Wanna get loaded at lunch break?" She slid a joint partway out of her shirt pocket as evidence of her earnestness. "Sure. Count me in." I appreciated the unselfconsciousness of the exchange in contrast to how awkward I felt trying to chat up a girl like Martha.

Lunchtime found us out back at the edge of the loading dock, reclined on a pile of empty canvas mail pouches. "When did you get hired? I haven't seen you around before this last week or two."

"I'm a temp," she offered. "Limited Duration Appointment or some such. That's okay. I'm just looking for a couple of months' work and then hope to go back home to Washington state."

By the time we finished the joint and wolfed down the bag lunches we'd each brought, we were laughing hysterically about who knows what. She was easy and fun. And had a pretty quick mind which I appreciated. I could feel we both hated to let the moment go when it was time to go back indoors to work.

"Hey, I could score us some beers after work if you're up for it," I plied her, secretly knowing she was too young to purchase booze on her own. I was the Seriously Older Woman here—all of twenty-three. "Sounds good to me. When we get inside, I'll write down my address for you."

The rest of the shift glided quickly through the evening. We wouldn't get off work until 11:00 p.m., but by then, I was armed with Terry's address, a house in Oakland she shared with a room-mate and the roommate's boyfriend. Beginning a social call at close to midnight held untold potential for an excuse to spend the night with her.

The rundown craftsman house on the Oakland-Berkeley bor-der was easy enough to find, and Terry answered the door before I knocked. I was quickly introduced to her roomie Sue and Sue's African American boyfriend, Teddy. A fellow photographer, Teddy was enjoyable to chat with as I admired some of the large-format black-and-white prints he had strewn about the floor. Sue, a sweet blond girl with long hair, was a friend of Terry's from Bellingham, Washington, who had come here to go to college and found love among Berkeley's diversity.

Furniture, never a priority, was typically absent except for a double-bed mattress on the floor of the living room that did dou-ble duty as a couch. Covered with one of those typical thin-cotton Indian-print bedspreads, it was where we all parked to get stoned— the customary communal ritual of greeting new friends. A small, low table was where the stash box resided, along with rolling papers, ash-tray, and a quaint hand-thrown ceramic dish of roaches to be saved for scarcer times.

But this couch was also the conjugal bed of Teddy and Sue, and after a bit, they invited us to leave them to their lovemaking. Terry and I headed off into a small pantry space near the kitchen that was her bedroom, simply by the declaration of placing a mattress on the floor. Another beer. Another joint. Aimless chitchat as we gradually reclined our bodies to a greater and greater degree.

Terry languorously slid back, reaching an arm behind her head to fluff up a pillow for greater support. Damn, she was cute like that, fingers laced behind her head, elbows flung out to the sides. Her twinkling brown eyes telegraphed that she was fully aware of the fact, and as I propped myself up on one elbow, her grin was so broad beneath me that it felt I could fall right into one of those dimples. It was the most natural thing in the world to lean down and tenderly kiss her mouth.

Oh, she was sweet! Her taste, her tongue, her softness all made me a little giddy, but that didn't stop me. What a great kisser! This was a good deal more fun than the mere fantasy of Martha, whom I quickly put out of my mind to focus on the girl at hand.

Ah yes, *hand.* Mine began its exploration with Terry's face, slowly stroking her cheek while I kissed all around her mouth and into the softer reaches of her throat. I slid my hand down to where it covered her Adam's apple with the slightest suggestion that her very next breath was dependent upon my generosity. She eagerly met my lips, but everything about us maintained the most exquisite restraint: the kisses small, quick, tender, and fleeting. My fingers left her throat and sought out the buttons of her shirt. She smiled through a kiss with her complicit approval of my intentions to undress her. She pulled away just for a moment, "Say, I sure would like it if you could spend the night." "Done."

Her open shirt revealed small, milky white nubile breasts, but the nipples were all grown up and hard as rocks. I nuzzled her, alternating between flicking her nipples with my tongue and taking the entirety of a breast into my mouth for a deep suckle. She was obviously loving this every bit as much as me. I used my free hand to slide her belt out of its western buckle.

Once past the metal buttons of her Levi's, I could see before me this incredible terrain of milky white belly, slender to the point of protruding hip bones, and an invitation to move my kisses southward. Her taste was unfathomably fresh and clean, her skin so luminescent and tender that I wanted to cry. I wiggled her jeans lower so as to slide a free hand down between her legs, down to the thick, warm wetness that eagerly waited for me.

We went on for hours, teasing, prodding, licking, and sucking, then stopping to grin widely at each other. There was no rush here; we were in agreement on that point. Though I had briefly languished in her moistness, I slid my hand away to prolong the tease. She responded by flipping me over on my back and starting an exploration of her own. She was every bit as artful in action as in surrender.

Terry climbed up on top of me and got between my legs, which came as a bit of a surprise, albeit a pleasant one. Her bony pelvis thrust into my vulva, and the pressure felt like heaven as I arched up toward her. My every fiber longed for orgasm but didn't long as loudly or insistently as my desire to reach greater and greater plateaus of excitement. I was in her hands for the moment and happy to be there. At last we deemed it time to get rid of the rest of our clothes and crawl into the sheets.

I was crazy with sex, wet beyond recent memory, but I wanted her to come first. I wanted to exert that psychic power over her: to reduce her to a quivering mass of sensuality. I pinned her arms up over her head while I climbed on top of her, kissing her one last time and cautioning her to be a good girl and come when I commanded. I bid adieu and slid my mouth down the length of her torso, finding the homing beacon of the plump little pearl of flesh between her labia. I set to work, slowly, methodically, suckling, tugging, traversing her clit with my tongue. With a free hand, I teased the perimeters of her vaginal opening, darting gently in and out, then withdrawing until her gyrations clearly begged me to return. We were close *now*, all right!

Terry's orgasm was beautiful. Unable to replay the images, I chose instead just to luxuriate in it. She wracked, she shuddered, waves of involuntary muscular contraction rippled through her abdomen. And then she was still. I slid from my outpost between her legs, up to gently fold her into my arms and she quietly wept a bit, but as I pulled back to notice, her smile reappeared, broader than ever, and those incredible dimples! Yeah, I *liked* this kid!

"Mind if we get a snack before we move on to business with you?" I, too, was famished and appreciated her suggestion as we padded into the kitchen to raid the icebox. More beer (Christ! We could put it away) and some cheese. There was an icy cold green apple in there, too. As we trundled back to bed, she gently ran her hand down my bare back and caressed my bottom, grazing the wetness literally dripping from my cunt. She was thrilling, but hunger commanded allegiance.

Terry laid me down, made a gesture that I should be still, and, pulling out a Swiss Army knife, proceeded to cut up the apple and lay the slices on my belly. Repeating the movements with the cheese, my body became a smorgasbord for our delight. She would take a slice in her teeth, using no hands, and manage to grin up at me from the corner of her eye all the while. "Hey, feed me some, too. I'm the one who's been doing all the work." "Sorry," she countered. "Did you really think what I was doing back there was without effort? But I'm happy to feed you just the same." She brought a slice of apple, between her teeth, up to my mouth, and I took half of it with a loud, crunchy snap. "Great apple!" "You should taste them up in Washington. These things are lame." Just the same, it hit the spot.

It was getting really late by now, and I wasn't sure if I still had the drive to continue making love. But all she had to do was sweep her hand down my thigh and caress between my legs. God! I was so incredibly wet! Yeah, I had the drive.

She was artful and she was sweet. I really liked her tenderness as, even now, it's not easy for me to come. It's one reason I always prefer to make love to my partner first—at least that way I'm good and primed. But she took me slowly, climbing, climbing, my hips arching up. She led me so naturally I felt like I was on a guided tour up a stairway to heaven. She kept her lips on my mouth, but it really was where I wanted them. Her kisses were long and deep, yet still with that restraint that told me she would never run out of interest or staying power.

Her hand moved from clit to cunt to clit and always just at the right time. I was getting huge, and she began to experiment with fitting more and more fingers inside me. I was taking them easily and still calling out for more. She took her mouth away from mine and started whispering in my ear, "Do you want it? Do you want it, baby? Tell me how much. Tell me when you want me to make you come. You can have anything you want." A wave swept over me, a consciousness that we were so in sync, and then a deep, deep craving—a feeling I could never get enough of her—just before I exploded in orgasm. Waves and waves of contractions and I heard myself moaning as if my disembodied spirit were in the room next door. She just kept working me, and I just kept coming. Glorious!

As my body wound down and I recovered my breath, my heart felt so incredibly exposed, as if it had been torn open. Tears were flowing down my cheeks and draining into my sheepish smile. I barely knew this girl, and she had touched the depths of my soul. Life at the post office was going to get a lot more interesting.

We were an item now. Things were just that simple in those days. Lesbians today, products of feminism, don't really understand what it was like back then. These were prefeminist times, and our dissolution of gender distinctions was more egalitarian than anything. Boys looked like girls, girls looked like boys, and though we were aware that in the 1950s lesbians had had some rigid gender roles, ultra-butch and ultra-femme, we eschewed that culture. We were born of the hippie revolution and we were set about to change the world for good and for the better.

Yes, Terry and I were together now. She liked me, I liked her, the lovemaking was great, the future was wide-open, and it was the simplest thing in the world to say "I love you" and never spend another night apart. I still rented the front bedroom in the flat of some friends who lived near the post office, and sometimes we made love there on our lunch break. Other times we spent the night at Terry's. Work was fun, glancing and winking, sharing our secrets and the smells of each other on our hands. Martha was forgotten for now, and before long, she married Art Levine, the union rep guy.

Other changes were in the wind. Terry's Limited Duration Appointment was coming to an end, and it was time for her to figure out her next move. Her friend Mary Connor had written Terry with news of an opportunity to caretake a thousand-acre cattle ranch in central Washington. A veterinarian friend of theirs, a woman with whom they had grown up, needed someone to stay on the property she owned with her husband and a third partner.

The three owners were breaking up their household; the husband was being drafted and sent to Vietnam while his wife was taking a veterinary job in Spokane. The third partner, a cowpoke, would be working on a nearby ranch and would come to tend the herd when needed. Essentially, they were looking for someone to occupy the house and protect it from vandals. Adventure called.

Terry was interested and wanted to know if she could count me in. Did Hoppy wear a studded jacket? How could I pass up an opportunity to live out my own cowpoke fantasies? And why would I let this sweet young woman out of my life when I'd only just found her?

This wasn't a deeply considered or tortured decision for me. Much as Terry and I had fallen thoughtlessly and naturally into being lovers, we tracked the scent of adventure just as easily. I had been planning to work my unemployment scam again for a while—just needed to fail the RPO scheme test (as I had at the San Francisco post office), establish that the job was beyond my abilities, and I would be eligible for the dole. The date of my last chance to pass the exam was so near Terry's official separation date that it seemed just one more sign that the Washington Adventure was meant to be.

As fall approached, Terry and I packed up, piled into the green GMC panel truck I had bought to make the trip, and joined her friend Mary on the Washington coast. I liked Mary immediately, especially her classic Irish looks, with soft black shoulder-length hair and the greenest of eyes set deep into the china-white skin of her pretty face. High cheekbones set off the adorably pointy chin that seemed to lead the charge of her every sentence. She was articulate and kind, warm to this stranger, and obviously a very dear friend of Terry's. With very little aforethought, I was certain she would make a perfectly lovely roommate.

Gazing out the window of Mary's parents' house, the saplings of Bellingham were turning bright yellows and scarlets; the woodsy landscape of the Northwest starkly delineating the change of season as it never did at home. A few days later, the three of us headed for central Washington near Ellensburg and met up with Mike the Cowpoke in a local coffee shop.

Whoa! I thought as I took Mike's measure. (And delighted at my easy fall into the vernacular.) Mike was the real deal—western shirt and tight Levi's, a bulge in his shirt pocket containing a pouch of rolling tobacco, and the permanent round imprint in the seat of his jeans where a can of chew resided. The legs of his pants were shredded at the bottom where they constantly greeted the earth, and his boots were well-worn and cracked, caked with dried mud. The Stetson hat cocked back on his head summed him up, with its permanent ring of sweat stain and a beat-up old feather sticking out of a leather headband. Everything about him smelled like straw, sweat, and manure. This was a workin' man.

Terry had cautioned me that Ellensburg was a fairly conservative town, but it wouldn't have even occurred to us to tone down our behavior. Though we later learned of town gossip about our strange unmarried status and the oddity of girls living on the plains without benefit of male protectors, we felt comfortable with who we were but nonetheless conceded not to rub anyone's nose in our relationship. In 1969, this was familiar territory for us; folks, straight folks, didn't really think about lesbians. We were just single girls come to babysit the ranch.

Over coffee, Mike filled us in with details of the property and assured us he would always be nearby if any contingencies came up in the maintenance of the ranch. Then picking up the check and giving us the order to follow him, we caravanned to our new home about fifteen miles northeast of the college town.

It was ratty, run-down, extremely isolated, and just perfect! This was an entirely new sort of romance for me, just like I imagined the Wild West. The ranch house consisted of a mudroom where one entered and shed dirty boots in a space shared by an extra refrigerator, a deep freeze, lanterns, large plastic garbage cans, and some miscellaneous tack. Mike was engaging Mary with a stream of details in his clipped, no-nonsense speech while Terry and I shot questioning but excited glances at each other. I half listened to our ranch orientation while reaching up to finger a bridle hanging on the wall inside the screen door. Trying to remain cool, I could barely contain my delight and flashed Terry another huge grin. "Mike, what are all these refrigerators for?" I queried. The mudroom looked like it was a part-time used appliance store. "Just one is a refrigerator. Oh, I dunno. It works. It's just older than the one in the kitchen and comes in kinda handy for extra stuff. Gail (the veterinarian) used to keep medications for the cattle and horses in it. The other big box is a deep freeze. The green can is dog food for Ringer who lives under the house. Happy to send some venison steaks your way once I get time to hunt."

We moved into the kitchen where we encountered a big wood-stove (the only stove, I noticed) where we would cook our meals and where yet another refrigerator stood. A simple, unfinished wooden table was the only other furnishing. A small living room contained a free-standing fireplace where the lumps of coal we burned would be our only source of heat throughout the house. Multiple layers of old linoleum were coming up off the floor in places and together with the many different patterns of peeling wallpaper cataloged the years of neglect. This was a working ranch as opposed to a ranch-style home.

After brief discussion, Mary was granted the one habitable bedroom downstairs. It made sense in its own way. Mary was single, without the warm arms of another for the cold nights ahead. The downstairs put her right near the fireplace. And she was a bit of a girly girl, deemed having a greater need to be close to the one bathroom. Terry and I had romantic visions of using a slop jar upstairs when necessary.

The other downstairs bedroom was purportedly for storage but was more accurately employed as a breeding ground for mice. The ranch owners had stacked spare mattresses and rolled-up rugs to the point where clearing the room out would just present new problems of where to put their stuff. Terry and I opted for the privacy of the attic where we later rolled out a threadbare Oriental rug we'd discovered downstairs and used it to delineate a place for our bed on the floor. The other half of the garret, separated by the chimney coursing through the room, was a perfect site for my darkroom and also a place where I could write.

Ever since Chico and my introduction to the workings of a darkroom while editor of the yearbook, I had loved this nuts-and-bolts aspect of photography. Just a whiff of developer transported me right back to stolen moments with Dianne, the red light outside the door warning all others to stay away while we, together, witnessed the marvel of images coming into being in the tray, as if by magic. Then with Peggy in New York City, I humbly became her student as she explored avant-garde forms of expression for the medium.

Peggy was skilled and passionate about her art, and she loved to think aloud while she experimented with exposure times, contrasts, and paper types. I listened intently, asking questions here and there when there was no fear of breaking her concentration. I learned a lot from her during my six months there, and when I returned to Berkeley from New York, I set about acquiring equipment of my own. It had been sitting in storage, awaiting a permanent home, and now I had the time and place to make photography my own. In addition to my faithful 35 mm camera, I had brought with me my enlarger, trays, chemicals, and all the other trappings of the aficionado.

Yes, this space would be perfect.

Coming out of my musings, I turned my attention once again to Mike and his final instructions. But the part of me left in my photographic reverie began framing shots I wanted to take: the few bare trees set in relief against the sagging clapboard corner of the house; Terry's 1951 Chevy pickup, acquired before we departed the coast; the barn with its list to starboard. Perhaps even Mike might consent to being the subject of a photo series about life on the ranch. Our little trio waved goodbye in the direction of Mike's tailgate as his pickup rolled down the gravel drive and out the great swinging gate that, once closed, encapsulated us in our "life on the plains" fantasy.

We fell into an easy rhythm on the ranch, and everyone helped with various chores as we set to work preparing for the approaching winter. Our cocooning of the house consisted of plastic sheeting on the outside of the windows, ostensibly to keep out the wind. Hardly. Before long, we augmented this by nailing blankets over the inside of each window; blankets we watched progressively blacken over the wintry months from the coal dust escaping every time we stoked the fire in our potbellied fireplace. Proper venting seemed an art that eluded us, and my poetry of the time is filled with references to at last understanding what spring cleaning is all about as I dreamed of months in the future where we could, once again, see out our windows.

Things were good with Terry. Her playful nature and waiflike qualities allowed me the indulgent fantasy of being the older, wiser woman. With her quiet smile and twinkling eyes, she delighted in our stoned nightly entertainments of playing with the kitten we had taken in.

Rosie was spunky but slightly pathetic, having lost one eye to some infection she carried when first appearing on our doorstep. Mary joined in the revelry as we even attempted to get Rosie stoned. Life seemed simple; we rolled our own cigarettes, hauled our own coal from the depot in town, focused on nothing more essential than keep the fire stoked.

Mary and Terry would be taking some classes at Central Washington State University in Ellensburg, and I would be collecting unemployment insurance from my stint at the post office. While the girls toiled in town, I sat down in my newly created studio, dusting off the trusty little powder blue Smith-Corona portable typewriter. I commenced work on a lesbian western, beginning with the characters I fantasized us to be: Terry became Terry Tall while I, in turn, was dubbed Legs Latrine.

We were prostitutes from St. Louis, wily and resourceful, who had squirreled away enough money to effect an escape from our life of servitude. Buying passage on a departing wagon train headed West, we taught ourselves along the way to ride and shoot and fend off the unwanted advances of men. We were tough and clever—everything I imagined us in our real-life adventure in Ellensburg. Later in the narrative, Terry and Legs would meet up with Torch MacLaine (obviously Mary needed a role in our saga) who was sold by her impoverished parents as a mail-order bride, only to jump off her stagecoach in the night, be discovered near death by a local Indian tribe, and acquire her own skills set for survival in the Wild West. We made our encampment in Jarbidge, Nevada—a real town but a name I loved because *who gives a town a name that rhymes with garbage?*

I was having a great time working on this story and would regale the girls each evening with the latest installment to the accompaniment of their cheers, requests, and suggestions. I worked long into the night with the wind blustering outside and Ringer giving the occasional warning howl that coyotes were near. It felt only fitting that I purchase a .30-30 rifle. Hopalong Cassidy rears her head once again.

Some nights I worked quite late in the studio, Terry sleeping in the next room. I was happy and filled with a love of the girl with whom I shared this country adventure. Romantic expression seemed to elude us, except for the frequent erotic chatter during lovemaking. I turned to poetry to vent my caring, to give it a voice. Other times, prose filled my heart and spilled onto the page:

> *"I don't know who you are, but I know you're beautiful, and I know we know each other from a time before, and I know you to be mellow." Some people have always wanted the moon or big cars or pure spirit. I have always wanted the mellow woman. Don't you remember? Let me turn your head. We lived on a river, and we almost never spoke, and we made love in the moonlight—your small breasts so firm from the cold night—and we drew pictures in the sand, and we would put our mouths together and breathe each other's air until all the energies of one breath were expended. And sometimes you would read to me. Oh, I loved it when you would read to me. And we collected berries. And we kept the fire going. And we loved each other so much. "Don't you remember?"*

It seemed the energy to create never abated: poems, photography, song lyrics, the work on my novel. I hadn't known this kind of fire since, as a college freshman, I had adored Dianne and crafted a volume of poetry from my nightly exercise of verse springing forth from aching young love.

My little Smith-Corona seemed able to say all those things which I could not. But we drifted along merrily and life seemed good.

Carol and Tommy were friends who lived in town and harkened back someplace in the history of either Terry or Mary, I never was quite sure. But they were simpatico, they were dopers, and they were a delightfully cheery couple. They were also our source for scoring drugs in this new community.

"Hey, guys!" We rushed out to the yard when we heard their Ford approaching. Taking care to dry off my hands, especially well from the dishes I'd been washing, I joined the girls to greet our buddies. It was a difficult lesson to realize how quickly the dry Ellensburg winds and cold environs could seriously chap one's hands. I had recently been taught the virtues of Bag Balm (meant for the chapped and bleeding teats of dairy cows) to address my earlier carelessness.

Carol was that prototypical Earth Mother that seemed to inhabit and define the straight women of the time. Long, flowing skirts and handwoven lumpy sweaters, bright, colorful leggings and shoes I can only describe as elfin. Tommy—coal black hair, fringe-like about the ears and softly framing his face—had one of those marvelously droopy mustaches that looked like it would never tickle if it got a chance to get between your legs. Clear-eyed and cheerful, they exuded the love ethic of the era. We were *always* happy to see them.

"So great to see you guys." We hugged and kissed all around. Each Sunday, when Tommy and Carol would venture out to the ranch, was a welcome draft of civilization—a reminder of a hippie culture thriving beyond our barbed wire. Our ritual of communion was to prepare a meal together, take hallucinogenic drugs, and listen to music, some of it new and delivered by our guests.

When the weather permitted, comic relief was provided by pestering the poor, hapless livestock, the horses in particular, only one of which, Mike had told us, was harness broken. The game was the trial and error of discovering just *which* horse that might be. Emboldened by the bone-warming elixir of straight Scotch whisky, we would each take our turn at pursuit, with a variety of styles ranging from Wild West maniac to clever and cunning Redskin brother. We didn't really care if we ever harnessed the horse, but one afternoon, Tommy actually did, only to be promptly thrown once he vaulted himself onto the mare's back.

As a matter of course, the minute Tommy and Carol arrived, we set about to explore the day's options in terms of drugs. Always there was pot, and increasingly our favorite diversion was psilocybin mushrooms, a perfectly organic complement to what felt a most organic lifestyle. Naturally, it was important to drop the mushrooms before any other order of business so as to maximize the time we had to trip as a group.

Tommy and Carol were with us that Thanksgiving; Mary had gone to her parents' on the coast. Carol said, "Guys, you need to stoke the fire a little more to the back. I need *indirect* heat for the oven but need it direct under the back burners."

"Crap! Whoever dreamed there was more to this than just building a big-ass fire?" That would be me, the Queen of the Huge Blaze, the pyro in the group, and always the first to claim the assignment of Fire Goddess. "Put some thought into it, girl. This is an *art*, this cooking-with-wood business." Carol certainly seemed to know her way about the stove. The rest of us put our energies into prepping the vegetables, peeling potatoes, constructing the dressing, and getting the bird stuffed and ready for the oven. Terry, surprising me, had informed us that she was expert at making the gravy when that time came.

The four of us working in concert produced a pretty fine feast, and after a day of getting stoned, managing to roast a turkey in a wood oven, bringing all the elements together, and then stuffing ourselves, a lively hand or two of poker seemed a perfectly fitting and absurd occupation for the remains of our mushroom high. As the cold of the night crept through the blankets on the windows, we were all pretty drowsy. Soon, our two city dwellers headed back to Ellensburg. "Bye, guys! Love you," we chorused as we waved them down the drive.

I noticed both Terry and me, whenever outdoors, had fallen into the habit of keeping one hand warm at all times in a jacket pocket so as to keep the chapping ritual singular and manageable. And we learned together to lubricate our hands just as much as our boots and belts. For us, there was Bag Balm, for the other a regimen of Sno-Seal, diligently applied to all seams with an old toothbrush before setting the items near the fire to soak up the welcome lubricant. The elements were a vivid piece of our existence in a way we'd never known as city girls. Reminding me, the wind whipped a loose corner of plastic on the outside of a living room window.

It was late, bitter cold, and the fire had burned low. Terry and I treaded upstairs, sated, and destined for a heavy slumber.

Something god-awful awoke me a few hours later. In my stupor, I couldn't tell what brought me to consciousness; some searing sensation in my nose and throat but switching on the bedside lamp, I saw a green fog cloud rolling up the stairs and into our bedroom. Sight came first, then I smelled it. Skunk. Apparently, Ringer had trapped a skunk in his lair under the house and it had discharged its payload. Terry woke with the lamp, and when together we realized just how bad it was going to get, we threw on our jeans and flew downstairs, where the odor was only more intense.

"Christ! Let's get out of here!" Terry choked out through the bandanna she held over her mouth and nose. "To where? It's 20° outside," I said, glancing at the thermometer in the mudroom. "Let's head out to the barn. Maybe we can pile up some straw to sleep in and get warm." I had my doubts. This seemed a notion much more romantic than practicable, and I caught myself in a moment of exasperation with Terry's uncharacteristic impracticality.

Though on paper my love grew strong, in actuality I viewed her more and more as the ardent teenager, the kid I felt I was caretaking, projecting that I was nursing her into her adult lesbian persona. The irony of my arrogance didn't elude me, and I once again wondered just how well *I* was able to show up for a mature and committed relationship. Underneath her twinkling, charming self, Terry could also be quite brooding, and at times, I felt we could barely connect.

Musings aside, we bundled up, throwing on our coats and mittens and grabbing sleeping bags. We actually went to the barn to attempt sleep, climbed a permanently placed wooden ladder, and ascended into the drafty loft. Picking a corner and huddling together we struggled to craft a nest. "Ouch! The straw! Whoever said it was *soft*? And give me some of that blanket, dammit!" We knew the bags wouldn't provide enough warmth and brought blankets as well to roll up in. We were cold, we were cranky, and even if I could have abided the straw poking me everywhere, it was piercingly raw out, and it only took about half an hour before we quit pretending and admitted we had to get out and away from the ranch.

While Terry secured the house, I set out a large bowl of kibble for Ringer under the front porch, barely able to approach through the still-potent cloud of skunk vapor. Hastily throwing a few items in a duffel, my Pentax, and most current notebook included, Terry assembled her own bag of essentials, and we piled into the Chevy, headed toward Ellensburg and Tommy's house.

In the morning, we took a flight to Berkeley to visit friends, hoping that a week away might give our house (and maybe our relationship) a chance to air out. I still laugh to think of the miasma that escaped from our bags six hundred miles later, making us fairly unpopular houseguests.

Returning to California for that short visit made me more keenly aware of our isolation in Ellensburg. I missed the street action, the immediacy of a bustling student population, the energy directed toward protest of the war. By comparison, Washington felt confining in its conservatism. I enjoyed the life on the ranch, but something about it felt as limiting and cramped as the sooty, claustrophobic blankets on our windows. I was ambivalent as we planned our return trip north; maybe this little Hoppy was done playing cowboy for now.

My feelings for Terry were beginning to feel conflicted, and I'm sure she could sense it as well. My Terry, my adorable girl, had essentially become more a character to me—a cowpoke in my western, a love object for pining verse—than a real woman with a need for some depth with her lover.

In the day-to-day, in our reality, I was becoming increasingly restless. My photography work grew more internal—experimental exposures, abstract images—rather than focused on capturing the open expanse of our landscapes and the enduring vitality of the livestock. I dreamed of living again in Berkeley, nuzzling against the political unrest of demonstrators in the streets and students holding campus buildings hostage. *That's* what I yearned to see through my lens, what I longed to capture on film—the sheer, vibrant energy of the times.

When we returned to the ranch and Ellensburg, the morphing of our relationship was evident, at least to me. I was shutting down sexually, emotionally and withdrawing more into my darkroom and late nights in the studio. Letters started to arrive from Karen, an old friend from grammar school, who lived in the Humboldt area of northern California. Her missives gave evidence that shifting cultural times were reaching even the farthest outposts of our home state as she related her desire to explore the loving of women.

> *Dear Lin,*
>
> *You seem to be the only one I know who I can talk to about this. My friend Jana, who is hanging out with some folks in Oakland called the More House, has been drifting through Arcata in her travels. She is everything my life isn't: traveled, adventurous, free as a bird. She is living in a commune with this bunch of folks, the More House folks, and tells me of all their amazing workshops about everything from how to masturbate to how to have a deeper sharing with one's mate. Oh, how I envy her freedom as I turn again to folding laundry and chasing down my two year old.*

I placed her letter on the desk and sighed as I rubbed my tired eyes. Her tone was achingly poignant.

In her freshman year at Humboldt State College, Karen became pregnant, married the dad, dropped out of school at nineteen, and was now raising two young children while hubby Richard taught elementary school in McKinleyville, the next town over from their home in Arcata. The daughter of fervent intellectuals, I think Karen was every inch as disappointed in herself as her parents had probably been. The consolation prize was two beautiful and bright children: son Dana was six at this time and Meghan was two.

The letter continued,

> *Richard is a good man. I would never say he isn't. But late at night, I wonder, what else is out there in this big world? Jana talks about her workshops, the almost prayerlike devotion to sexuality, and she talks about making love to other women. Her eyes light up as she pries me about whether I have a healthy relationship with masturbation. "Treat yourself to the greatest lover you know," she urges. Jana even asks outright if I would care to try it, to have sex with her. And as I lay there in my marital bed, having serviced my husband like the dutiful wife my upbringing would have me be, I seriously consider it. You know about these things. What do you think I should do?*

> *Love, Karen*

Thoughts tumbled about in my head; I couldn't shake Karen's letter. I decided to play the voice of reason opposite Jana's devil's advocate. "Don't do it, Karen," I feverishly typed. "My gravest concern is that you will find it's where you're meant to be, and then what happens to the lives of those who depend on you? Making love with women is no joke. It is a powerful and life-altering path, and I think you should tread very, very lightly."

The theme carried on through a continuing stream of letters. Jana was lobbying fiercely to bed Karen, that much was clear. And though I pretended altruism; in fact, I was determined that if Karen were to take a woman as her lover, it should be me. My restless heart, tiring of the relationship with Terry, entertained fantasies of bedding my old friend from the eighth grade. While Terry was in town attending classes, I was doing my own diligent masturbatory research, and Karen's was the face I saw floating above me.

As the spring thaw subtly insinuated itself onto our ranch, bringing quietly dripping eaves and soggy gravel roads, the temperatures began to creep on the occasional marvelous day all the way to crest 40°. Mud-caked boots, fear of bogging down in the driveway muck, so sick and tired of coal heat poorly drafted, I thought increasingly about California. Whether visions of Karen or scenes of student unrest, I felt a powerful longing to be back in my home state.

Also, my unemployment was running out and Terry and Mary's school term was nearing an end. Mary wanted to return to the coast, home to her family, and had heard of a job opportunity in a letter from her mom. Unbeknownst to us, she had filled out an application and actually been to an interview while she was in Bellingham over Thanksgiving.

She never said a word, and I guess follow-up was slow coming. In February, she had received a request for a second interview, and then she shared her hopeful reservations with us. "It seems like a really cool job and looks like they might actually be interested in hiring me." Though the prospect of a career track in banking wasn't anything that would have appealed to either Terry or me, Mary seemed eager to enter the grown-up world of chasing a profession. Her studies had been geared to learning management and business, and it seemed it had all been to good end.

Mary's scheduled departure sort of shook things loose in our world, and though our rent was only $45 a month, Terry and I seemed hesitant to consider staying there without our third. I think we felt the ranch too cloistered for just the two of us. "What do you want to do, Lin? Are you thinking of looking for work here when your unemployment runs out?" Terry was ever the pragmatist. "For me," she continued, "I don't think there's that much here. Even the coast would be a better shot at a job. This economy is *depressed*, man." She was right, of course.

The unspoken fear wasn't the economy so much as the topic neither of us wanted to broach; our relationship was losing its luster and would soon gasp its last breath. We deemed it time to pack up the ranch and move our act someplace else. As far as our future as a couple, well, more would be revealed.

I used the next week to dismantle my darkroom, taking time first to develop those rolls of film which were still captive in their little canisters. I had loaded them myself, from bulk, my Tri-X and Plus-X, now containing images yet to be brought to life. I needed to minimize the risk of them getting exposed to light during our packing and moving and was nostalgic as I poured the developer into the stainless steel cylinders, the acrid aroma of potentiality stinging my nostrils. A good smell, though, a bouquet that attached another sense beside sight to my manifest creativity. I could never envision a time when that odor wouldn't make me feel self-satisfied and productive.

As we collected our belongings, dividing, organizing, boxing, and labeling everything, we unconsciously grouped our two worlds separately. I noticed it and Terry did, too, but we still didn't speak of an imminent breakup.

We didn't really own much, but what we had elected to drag north with us were possessions we obviously cherished: my *Winnie the Pooh* in Japanese and other treasured texts, my Smith-Corona, darkroom equipment, the novel in progress. For Terry, it was even less: a couple pairs of Tony Lama cowboy boots, her leather working tools and materials, a funky little stereo phonograph, and some records. We each had our own truck, and we each packed them separately, confirming the division of our household.

We reached out to Mike the Cowpoke at the local phone number where he was living and working. Thanking him for the time on the ranch (and the unexpressed opportunity to entertain a fantasy of a life that was his reality), he assured us that soon he would be moving back, as would his partners, and the timing of our departure couldn't be better. Gail's husband had gotten an honorable discharge from the Army and was headed back Stateside to pick up his former life. Gail was happy to return to the local veterinary, large-animal practice where she had worked before the draft and the war had turned their world upside down.

Mary had already departed the day before. Terry and I stood in the yard, basking in the welcome sunlight, so absent the last few days. "See you when we get to Snoqualmie Pass. We can stop for coffee." She sounded as if everything was just as it always was. "Deal," I called out to the back of her head as she ducked into her truck. With her Chevy in front of me, engine cranking, I opened my driver's door and prepared to climb into the Jimmy, looking over my shoulder to frame one last shot in my mind's eye of the home and the adventure we had shared. I scanned the clapboard, the majestic elms, even the faithful-but-elusive Ringer, always ready with a greeting but never a farewell. Today, no one was left standing there to wave at our receding tailgates.

Terry had decided to forgo staying on the coast and was also eager for the revolutionary action of a more urbane setting. But our first night's stop was in Bellingham, where Terry would pick up a few odds and ends from her mother's house and we could spend the night and start fresh in the morning for our journey to California. As we huddled in the bed, listening to a gentle rain outside the window of her childhood bedroom, Terry delivered her requiem for our partnership. "The sky is crying for us," she spoke quietly in my ear. It was the most poetic thing she'd ever said to me.

It took this moment of poetry to finalize our situation. True to the times, as naturally as we fell *in* to love, we fell *out*. Just as naturally, we assumed we would be good friends and harbor no ill. How did we *do* this? How did we move through strong attachments and out, never feeling the loss, the devastation of unrealized dreams and unfulfilled promises? Of course, we always had the next joint, the next beer, the next mushroom or acid trip. We seamlessly, mindlessly skimmed over the oceans of our emotions, somehow never thinking we were getting wet.

We chose our next stop as Arcata. I had been talking about Karen and Terry was curious to meet her. As we caravanned through Oregon and headed for the border of California, we would stop occasionally for a meal or a beer, check in with each other, fuel up our trucks, and share a quiet moment. Terry was sweet and tender. Wordlessly, we acknowledged the sadness we shared at the loss of our lover relationship through the soft touch on a cheek, a wistful smile, a friendly pinch on the butt. We were gonna be okay. We knew that.

Though we were both eager for the energy of the Bay Area, Arcata in general, and Karen and Richard in particular, presented an opportunity for one more adventure. We never did seem to tire of adventure. I had queried Karen about opportunities in the area—

work, college, dope, a music scene—and she confessed she was pretty out of touch. But, she encouraged, hungry for woman companionship, we were more than welcome to stay there and sleep on their floor while looking for housing and work in the Eureka area, if that's what we chose to do.

Their little two-bedroom apartment, Karen had written, was on the outskirts of Arcata, which was home to Humboldt State College. In a few years, this county would become world-famous for its ideal pot-growing soil and climate, but for the moment, it was just a country school with a burgeoning population of hippie students. It was evident from our first stop at a coffee shop that there were plenty of kindred souls in this town, and our spirits were buoyed as we followed the step-by-step, hand-scrawled directions to Karen's house that the waitress had given us.

I had called ahead before we left the coffee shop, and when we drove up, Karen was waiting. She'd been watching for us at the mailboxes, feeling we might get confused about the way the apartment units were numbered.

It had been a lot of years since I'd seen Karen—not since high school. I'd forgotten how diminutive she is. Her personality had a force to it, and one could never quite believe so much power was packed into her slight frame. Only 5'3", her eyes were the brilliant green of her father's, and like my memory of his, forever darting about, inquisitively and intelligently, taking in all the information available. Karen's blond, thin (some might say stringy) hair clung close to her skull and hung down to her shoulders in the long, straight style of the day. She was always embarrassed by her nose (I had remembrances of endless keening in front of a junior high school mirror), again a gift from her father, which she protested was a large, misplaced hook of a thing marring her visage. It looked fine to me. I'd always thought her complaint a bit silly.

But here she was before me, arms open in greeting, as if I were a long-absent lover home from the war. A bit self-consciously, I submitted to her embrace until such time as it grew awkward. Time to introduce Terry and then to take on meeting the husband.

Richard greeted us at the door. A bearded, hulking giant of a man, we learned shortly that his favorite pastime was knitting afghans which he entered in county fairs. He appeared a nice enough fellow; he played the recorder, helped Karen with the cooking and laundry, seemed to thoroughly delight in his children, and was actually quite handsome behind that unruly full beard.

We were invited to bunk on the floor that night, a Friday night, and in the morning, Richard was delighted to show off by making pancakes from his private stash of sourdough starter. The kids were adorable, and Karen doted on them. I was impressed with how verbal she was with her young daughter and how mature Meghan's budding language skills seemed in turn. I cracked up when Meghan referred to her own private parts as *my vulva*. Both children, learning young the niceties of being upstairs neighbors in flimsy, modern apartment construction, had been taught to walk with quiet feet. No small trick for a toddler and a six-year-old boy.

That night, as Terry and I quietly conferred from our sleeping space on the living room floor, we decided we'd stick around for a bit and that Monday we would drive the few miles to Eureka and seek employment. Karen was delighted for the new faces and fresh personalities to join her brood when she heard of our decision. "Richard, they said they could actually do some babysitting and we could go *do* something." He was pleasant about it, but the unspoken truth was they didn't have an extra penny with which to *do anything*. As a fourth-grade teacher, his salary was minimal beyond belief.

Several surprises ensued. Monday morning, following Karen's suggestion that the shrimp-packing plant in town was always hiring, we went there to fill out applications. To our astonishment, they asked if we could start work immediately. Terry smirked, "I guess they called *our* bluff."

"Yeah, I wasn't really thinking I was *that* eager to get a job." We shared a cackle as we signed the W-4s, out of earshot of the supervisor.

Picking or cleaning shrimp was an unbelievably stinky enterprise for which we weren't prepared. We learned that we would be paid commensurate with the *quantity* (measured in pounds) of shrimp we picked, removing their tails and deveining them, and for the beginner, this was exceedingly slow work. We watched with quasi-horrified fascination, witnessing the deftness and speed of the experienced—the women who had done this job for their entire adult lives—and the sheer quantity they could amass of cleaned shrimp.

We felt doomed. This was a grim lot, the pay and the environs stank, and we couldn't quite envision a future for ourselves in this time-honored local industry. Still, after a backbreaking nine hours, we resolved to at least try returning the following day.

Trudging back to Arcata, feeling we sullied everything we touched (I was glad we had chosen to drive in Terry's truck), we had to shed our clothes on the front porch of Karen's apartment before we even dared enter. Quickly we each showered and still felt odious, if not odiferous. The kids held their noses, and the parents took us in good humor. "I'm not so sure how long we'll last at this game," I apologized. "Hey," Richard countered. "There's a reason they're always hiring." We all had a good laugh and a great home-cooked meal.

The other failed experiment was trying to indulge Karen's lesbian fantasies. Richard and Karen had been grappling with her developing sexual interest in women since before our arrival. He wasn't exactly a huge fan of Jana's but sincerely considered his wife's needs and struggled to expand his vocabulary for how to address them. All of us felt our distinct duties in this era to rethink the paradigms of our upbringing. Richard was as thoughtfully pursuing personal freedom, in his own restrained way, as the rest of us.

Now that we were on the scene, the discussion on the subject expanded into a family sort of meeting to include me and Terry. After the kids were put to bed, it was time to gather on the living room floor, share a joint Terry produced, and address the issue as a group. We were a little uncomfortable, knowing why Richard had called this powwow, but he was our host and this was his house. His will be done.

Richard opened the conversation. "Lin, I know Karen has been writing you, telling you all about Jana, and asking for your advice. In fact, Jana came through town a couple of weeks ago, and she and

Karen had some time alone." I tried to hide my astonishment. The bitch had beaten me to the prize! But Terry felt the ripple go through me and gave me a subtle nudge as she passed me the joint.

I had shared with Terry that I felt *myself* the proper initiator of an old dear friend. And in turn, Terry shared that she also had an interest in helping Karen discover the joys of women. We had chuckled about three ways in our more off-color moments, right under Richard's roof, right on his living room floor.

Continuing, Richard kept the topic rolling, "It's important to me what Karen wants. And I want her to be happy. But I need to be happy, too." He tentatively declared that he didn't mind if Terry or I slept with his wife, but we would be required to make love with him as well. Ugh! Guys can be so one dimensional, but we determined to humor him. We nodded assent and let him drone on about bed and lovemaking schedules he'd dreamed up. I guess we all have our ways of keeping the hurt at bay—the hurt that your wife would want another, the pain and worry that life as you know it might be disintegrating.

The air was pretty heavy by the time we finished the joint and the sit-down. Terry and I had mostly mumbled, not offering much but giving Richard his say, while we could sense that Karen, notwithstanding our collective insecurities about the future, was pretty excited about the potential this new arrangement held for her. She was about to get more than she ever bargained for in this new realm of women loving women.

By the following day, after a second shift at the shrimp plant, I declared I was through with the job, but Terry determined to stick it out for the rest of the week. I was ecstatic as that meant that, on Wednesday, with Richard at work, Karen and I would find time at last to crawl into bed together. Dana was in first grade, and Meghan still took naps, bless her heart!

Oh, why is it that *sweet* seems to be my favorite superlative for a lover? But sweet she was. Karen was so ready, so ripe, so willing. She seemed as a person who'd never been satisfied though I knew that not to be true. Panting, sweating, heaving, coming, and then coming up for air. "Oh my good God! Where did you ever learn to make love

like that? Jana and all her workshops can't hold a candle to you!"
Maybe it was the art of flattery, maybe the years of faking orgasms
with her husband, but I chose to take her at her word. "You are truly
a beauty," I mumbled into her breast. "I could do this for a long, long
time. When did you say Meghan wakes up?"

"Soon, but please, please, *please* fuck me one more time! I don't
think I could ever get enough of this." Duty called; I was milady's
servant.

Terry hadn't been fooled by my precipitous departure from the
shrimp plant and, in fact, told me she had stayed on in large part to
give me an opportunity with Karen. Now *that's* a good friend. She
was a good egg. She also knew that she was going to get her turn with
Karen soon enough.

The next night, once the kids were settled down, Richard produced his finely crafted calendar of connubial bliss and declared that
either Terry or I, he didn't care whom, would sleep in the bedroom
with him while the other would sleep on the living room floor and
share the night with Karen. Well, with a glance, Terry and I knew
what the fair course was. After dessert of homemade apple pie (Karen
certainly had a lot of energy today), I bid the girls good night and
trundled off into the bedroom with Richard.

The bed seemed small and Richard was a big man. He probably
rang in at 6'2" and 240 pounds. This was no king-size mattress, and
I felt like I was suffocating already before he even switched off the
light. He was much what I would expect and remembered about
being with men: didn't talk much and seemed to think he would
intuitively know just what would *get the job done* as he called it. I
stifled a groan.

I lay there with him on top of me, grunting where appropriate, letting him pump away and feigning increasing excitement as
he predictably ground his way to climax. I faked orgasm well, with
years of practice, both with men and women. I once jokingly told a
woman, "Hell, I even fake it making love to *myself*," and that wasn't
very far from the truth. Richard seemed convinced by my performance, kissed me a bit (that god-awful beard!), rolled off me, and
was soon snoring. I wished it were only a cliché and not the reality of

my friend's marriage bed. Muted sounds from the living room told me that Terry also was treating dear Karen to a heaping serving of bliss. As I lay there with Richard's heavy, unconscious breathing, I could hear past him to their passion: the muffled moans, Terry's soft undercurrent of love talk, the crescendo of small escaping cries that just couldn't be contained. I was happy for my friends and happy that they provided a proper soundtrack by which I could touch myself and finally get wet, finally come, while Richard snored on by my side. Well, we had survived the first night of this new arrangement, and Karen was sure getting her opportunity to have some great sex!

As we moved into the third week of this, Terry and I were now both unemployed, and did we ever enjoy Karen. Richard was a small price to pay for the days of filling Karen with love and eroticism, gently teaching, coaching, talking, answering her every question about making love to women. We shared three ways, sometimes me busy kissing Karen's mouth while Terry took Karen's clit into hers. Karen's slender fingers proved perfect for fisting me, and she was so astounded, and my orgasms so stupendous all of us would simultaneously collapse in tears of joy and giggles of delight when we finally crashed, exhausted.

Sometimes one of us would make love with Karen while the other did duty babysitting Meghan when she rose from her nap and took her for long, long walks in the stroller. Both women, mother and child, delighted us. Still, we had to pay the piper when Richard beckoned.

I'm fairly sure he hadn't grasped that the women were getting a lot more sex than he was, but his bed was shared every night, and that was way more sex than he'd been enjoying in his marriage to date and with three different women. Wasn't this *every* man's fantasy after all?

Of course, it began to wear thin. The tension in the little apartment was high, and the sexual energy just heaped on more. We entertained the notion of getting our own place. Though it might mean less time with Karen, it would definitely mean even less with Richard. So we spent some time with Karen and Meghan as we dallied in coffee shops, perusing the classifieds and driving around, looking at places for rent. We still had a little money from closing out our respective bank accounts, and rent was very, very cheap in this economically depressed community.

Terry and I settled on a small Victorian house in Ferndale, a bit to the south. An adorable town of seeming miniatures, we found a little gingerbread house, yellow with white windows and all manner of decorative bargeboard, intricately tooled fascia, and ornamental shingles. It was perfect for us, and though it would minimize love-making opportunities with Karen, it would also provide a welcome refuge from sex with Richard. The rent was high for the area—all of $125 a month.

Ferndale was interesting and quintessentially picturesque. An old established community of Swedish dairy farmers, it dated back in the area beyond many of the earliest settlers, perhaps on a par with the Russians who had discovered much of the California coast. Its lush green meadows and lowlands were dotted with ambling bovine herds while clear blue skies dropped down to kiss the rocky and vis-ible coastline.

But in its history, its longevity, it also contained a very closed atmosphere, one quite unwelcoming of newcomers. Where long-time residents would be greeted by first name in the local grocery, with hearty invitations to just "put it on your tab," we were met with suspicion and curtness. Complaining to Karen, she explained that it was just a function of the Ferndale culture.

"They don't care much for new folks. Yeah, I've heard that" was all she had to offer.

We were single women, both butch in our way (though Terry had the advantage of her obvious Swedish ancestry and looks), and momentarily unemployed, all of which made our prospective land-lady nervous and the townspeople distant. Before the first month was served out in our cute little home, we found the cliquishness of the entrenched community singularly suffocating and unwelcoming. Back to Karen and Richard's and the rotating bedfellow's schedule.

They were willing to take us back into their home, but as antic-ipated, Richard still clung to his planned lovemaking schedule as tenaciously as Karen held on to her desire for the two of us. Both husband and wife seemed desperate to get what they wanted—as urgently as if their lives, individually and as a couple, depended on it. That wretched quality bred anxiety and tension and created a palpable air of unease in the tiny apartment. It seemed even the children were affected.

Before even a couple of days had passed, Terry requested a family meeting after the dishes were done and Dana and Meghan were put to bed. She offered, "Karen, let me take care of drying the dishes while you help Dana finish up in his bath. You work too hard, anyway."

"Thank you, dear one (she loved this manner of Victorian eloquence passed on to her by her parents. I found it charming). It's most kind of you. You are such a big help around here." Richard seemed rather sulky as he sat in his overstuffed chair, squinting broodingly at his latest afghan project. I never could quite get used to the sight of this behemoth, furiously at work, knitting needles flying.

It took another half hour or so before the kids were tucked in and we had each, in turn, tiptoed in to wish them sweet dreams. Finally, the time had arrived for our sit-down. Terry was the first to speak. "Richard, it's about the lovemaking stuff. I'm just not really comfortable anymore with the way this works." She cleared her throat, and though to most folks she forever appeared composed, I detected the slight flush in her fair cheeks that always attended any moods of discomfort. "I've been doing a lot of thinking, Richard. And the bottom line is, I don't think I want to sleep with you anymore."

There, at last, someone had put it out in the open. I adored and admired her in this moment for her candor, for the courage to say what I couldn't. *Say*, I thought to myself, *why couldn't I?* Emboldened by Terry's honesty, and before Richard had much opportunity to react or I had the time to reconsider, I piped up, "I'm really sorry, Richard, but I've been having the same feelings. I feel the same way. I know you want this, but it just doesn't feel right to me." (*He's* what didn't feel right, I mused. I could fuck his charming wife from here to Sunday and then back through the days of the week!) I kept *this* thought to myself.

A thick, dark quiet descended as we all turned to Karen, now fidgeting and coughing a fake little cough into her lacy handkerchief.

We awaited her turn to speak, to comment, but I'm sure, without exception, we were all floored when she joined the chorus, "Richard, I don't really want to sleep with you anymore *either*." Stunned silence describes it adequately.

There wasn't much left to say. The remainder, the future, would have to be hammered out between husband and wife, father and mother. This was no longer the affair of mine or Terry's in which to meddle. We, at least, knew enough to bow out at this point.

The meeting broke up and we said our good nights, Karen and Richard heading into the bedroom for (most likely) a sleepless night. Terry and I inhabited the floor and whispered late regarding both our astonishment and our imminent departure. The days and weeks to follow were not ours to witness.

It was quiet the next morning. As was his habit, Richard rose and readied Dana for school, dressing him, fixing a nutritious breakfast, packing a little Batman lunch pail, making sure all the cowlicks on his tiny red head stayed plastered down. Also as usual, Meghan, at this hour, crawled into the bed with her mom for some tender time of cuddles before the onset of a new day.

Terry and I pretended to sleep through the departure of father and son; we weren't going to figure out any answers until we had our opportunity to join Karen and Meghan in the big bed. With veiled conversation, we explored any developments since last night's bedtime.

"What did he say? How did he take it? You really surprised us by being so brave, but, Karen, *whatever* do you think you're going to *do*?" This, while trying to keep any note of urgency out of my voice for the benefit of blissful little Meghan, delighting in all the woman flesh assembled for her delight. Karen began softly to weep as Terry and I alternated caressing her tears away. "It isn't looking too promising. I think I really want out of my marriage. I just feel so *dead* here even in spite of how much I love my children. I've never seen *anything*, gone *anywhere*. I know it's almost sacrilege, but maybe as an individual, I'm worth more than this." Meghan was busy fiddling with Terry's hair, smiling contentedly, perhaps consciously choosing not to perceive her mother's pain and confusion.

"Terry and I are going to take off today. I hate to leave you in the lurch, but I'm pretty sure Richard doesn't appreciate our presence while you two try to figure things out."

"Yeah, I think we need to give you guys some space," Terry contributed. "There really isn't any work for us here that we *want* anyway, and our money is kinda runnin' out. Better off in the Big City, I think." Karen's face revealed her pain at the thought of losing so soon a pleasure so newly discovered. We all knew the truth of it: there was work to be settled here, and we weren't a part of it.

By noon, we had packed our few belongings into our trucks. We decided to spend some quality time visiting with Karen and playing with Meghan and then quietly disappear while the golden child took her nap. Finally, it was that hour.

We cried, we hugged, we smooched a little. Karen gushed at how much this past time had meant to her, how much it had changed her life. *Yeah*, I thought. *I'm not so sure how great an idea that was.* But it was done. I asked Terry to take a photo with my Pentax—a last shot of me and Karen leaning against the Gimmie. I, in turn, would do the same for Terry as she embraced Karen in the open door of her trusted Chevy.

"Ladies, start your engines." We were heading south to Berkeley, back to the action we better comprehended than the intricacies of the marriage of friends and strangers. Though surely no one could settle all the blame at our feet, Terry and I had definitely had our roles to play in this drama. Karen had longed for change; Richard, in wanting more, had perhaps lost all.

Terry and I continued on our course of perpetual movement, always running two steps ahead of our consequences, forever opting for adventure where others might have stopped to take stock and perhaps reflect. In our wake was a family, likely shattered but certainly shaken forever by virtue of our having passed through it. The prophecy was borne out; as I had told Karen from our earliest letters, the loving of women was no trifling matter. It had, in fact, proven life altering for her.

Return from Arcata

Once back in the Bay Area, Terry and I were clear about going separate ways. She had been invited to crash with Patti and her partner, Michal, but being an ex of Patti's, I was viewed with greater suspicion. I returned to the roost of my parents' home. Dad put me to work at his business, a shop in a metal building out at the airfield, where I would be the entirety of the front office, learning to do the payroll taxes, keeping accounts receivable and payable, and answering the phone. Karen was a great deal in my thoughts.

After a few weeks, I worked up the courage to phone the Arcata apartment to see what I could learn of their current situation. "She's not here." Richard's voice was frosty. "When will she be back?" I couldn't imagine Karen having a long enough leash to be running errands without Richard by her side. "No, she's not *here*. I'm not going to tell you *where* she is, but she and the kids went away for a bit. Karen's trying to figure out what she's going to do next." Ooh, this sounded pretty serious. And what sort of dope did Richard think me?

Just how many options does a single mother with no income have? I was certain my next call would be to Karen's parents' home in Walnut Creek, where, sure enough, Karen herself answered the phone.

Taking advantage of the long cord, she took the phone into a bedroom and shut the door, the better to be able to freely converse. Her parents, loving a prolonged visit with their grandchildren, were nonetheless concerned and watchful in their anxieties for Karen's future.

"Oh my god! It's *sooo* good to hear your voice." She sounded breathless, but I think she was merely whispering. I thrilled at the sound of her. "We're here for a while. I'm not sure how long. I don't have a car or anything, but at least I have some space to sort out my feelings about everything that's happened."

I ached for her—for the heavy days, conversations and decisions that still awaited her, but also for the longing and memory of her slender, sweaty body up against mine. "What a pig!" I chastised myself silently. "Don't you care anything about her marriage falling apart?" The worst of the metaphorical little devil on my shoulder was quick with a succinct reply, "Nope."

We spoke daily on the phone without much flak from her parents. I wasn't clear whether Richard had not implicated me in their marital troubles or whether the *parentals* (as Karen called them) thought she was having reconciliatory conversations with her husband. But within the next two weeks, it was time for action.

Another sibling, Karen's younger brother, was now embroiled in a marital meltdown. He needed to move home to sort out *his* thoughts, and Richard was clamoring for the return of the children. Dana needed to get back in school, he insisted. My suspicion was that it was more about forcing Karen to experience aloneness without her kids, and the cynic in me felt he was also setting the stage to claim Karen was *abandoning* her children—pretty strong language but frequently the view courts took if a woman wanted to explore any manner of personal freedom. And that she did.

Karen consistently bemoaned the fact that she'd seen so little of the world, and we began to talk about taking a road trip together while she sorted out her feelings surrounding the domestic situation. I had used my first paychecks from Microwave Engineering (Dad's firm) to purchase a 1967 Suzuki motorcycle. It was red and shiny, only two years old, and the engine, though not terribly powerful at 200cc, was still legal to ride on the freeways. A friend assisted me in learning the fundamentals of riding and road safety; I acquired a good helmet and passed my DMV licensing exam. Hey, I was ready to *rock*!

She urged me to take her on a motorcycle odyssey. Her parents fretted, Richard harrumphed, and the children pleaded for picture postcards, but we packed up our gear and made plans to head for the Rocky Mountains.

And what a sight our chariot was! This poor little motorcycle was incredibly weighed down with the enormity of all the supplies and equipment we could imaging requiring. On the front handle-bars, we affixed one sleeping bag, wrapped in a tarp and fastened with a bungee cord. Then on the rear luggage rack (don't mistakenly think this apparatus was large, by any measure), we lashed the frame of a backpack in order to extend its capacity. This, in turn, was laden with another tarp and, on that, the bag portion of the backpack, which held all our cooking utensils.

These were not the days of slick, lightweight, compact back-packing equipment. We carried a mess kit that was enormous by today's standards, unfolding to reveal two cooking pots, two plates, a lid which doubled as a fry pan, and a couple of drinking cups. On top of the backpack bag was lashed another sleeping bag and a duffel with some clothes.

Poor Karen! As well as all this, she was required to carry a sec-ond backpack, bag on frame, on her back while we rode; it contained the remainder of our necessities. Just the thought of the wind resis-tance her body must have endured gives me a backache to this day!

Hitting the Road

We were a sight as we headed for the highway, both sets of parents in their turn wagging their heads in disbelief, but we were aglow with the spirit of adventure. On the first day out, pointed south down the coast highway, we soon realized that our burden (and the small size of the bike) would necessitate a rest stop every 50 miles, just to let some circulation back in our butts. The most we could eke out looked to be about 200 miles of distance by the end of a day of travel.

South down Highway 1, turning inland near Santa Lucia, up the winding mountain roads through Fort Hunter-Ligget (with scary signs warning of overhead military maneuvers), across the interior valleys to the south fork of the Kern River, we crept along.

At Lake Isabella (a bit northeast of Bakersfield), we fished with green willow branches fashioned into fishing poles, affixing the bit of nylon line and miscellaneous hooks we'd brought along. I actually caught a rather lovely eight-inch trout which Karen was able to prepare luxuriously. We cooked it over a campfire while neighboring campers voiced their envy at our catch.

We rested there for a couple of days since the route along 178 to 395 to Interstate 40 in order to reach Needles was going to be 280 miles! We met the challenge with frequent rest stops and sheer perseverance, excited to exit California and be at last on a multistate odyssey.

Farther south, crossing through the desert and entering the town of Needles, renowned for frequently being the hottest spot in California on any given day, we came up against temperatures of 117°.

The poor little bike was barely functioning against these challenges, and while it rested, we took shelter sitting in a river with all our clothes on. An enormous thunderstorm loomed on the horizon, and we watched intently to assess whether it would cross our path. After some hours of this, we still couldn't discern its intentions and figured we'd better get underway.

Maybe the storm had been suspended in its journey, maybe we just sucked at meteorology, or perhaps it was just lying in wait for us, we two girls who had no idea whether a lightning strike while on a motorbike would kill us or we'd be insulated by our rubber tires. But no sooner did we get underway than we had the distinct impression that the storm, complete with its distant flashes of lighting, was fast on our heels. We rode on with steely determination.

This was Karen's first real *adventure* in life since marriage and children had eliminated the vagabond option for her. She wanted to see and visit a long laundry list of places, and my task was to open up the world for her. We cut across the bottom corner of Nevada in order to take in Hoover Dam, which, indeed, was impressive. We flirted with going to the Grand Canyon, just because she had never seen it. Near as I can recall, we got a peek from the edge which satisfied Karen, but no major adventures like a trip down to the canyon floor.

Remember, everything we owned was on the little Suzuki, and we had to keep a protective eye on it.

We ventured north to Page, Arizona, and it was interesting that the entire town was built in 1959 to support the community of workers constructing the Glen Canyon Dam on Lake Powell. This was my first awareness of the *Company Town.*

We crossed the Arizona-Utah border through the little town of Kanab. As we entered Utah, we were awed by the marvelous landscape. A bit off our path were the spectacles of Bryce Canyon and Mt. Zion National Parks to the east, but we were traversing the lush plains up through Mt. Carmel and Long Valley on Highway 89.

It was a lovely toasty day of the sort that makes a young woman on a motorcycle want to ride in cutoff jeans. I was. Suddenly, I was hit with a jolt I couldn't identify. The inside of my left thigh was burning with pain so intense I thought perhaps I'd been shot and had difficulty maintaining control of the bike. When I was able to safely pull off the highway, I discovered a bee had hit me in the bare leg at a speed of 50 mph, his feeble little corpse still clinging to my flesh. I was shocked that a bee sting could hurt quite this much!

It was late in the afternoon, and my enthusiasm for continuing was waning. We were on the outskirts of the tiny town of Panguitch, with less than 1,300 inhabitants. We spied a quaint country church, and across the street were two old women in rocking chairs on their front porch. We stopped to address them and ask if, perhaps, they had any sort of topical remedy that would help with the pain and swelling at the site of my beesting.

Parking the Suzuki and removing our helmets, the women seemed quite friendly which was a welcome relief. Not many pairs of women on motorcycles were traveling the highways in 1970, and we couldn't assume our reception would be warm.

"Oh, we're so relieved you are girls! So many awful boys come roaring through here on motorcycles!" one of them said. Big sigh on our part.

They invited us to sit a spell, and one of them came out of the house with some baking soda and a cup of water to apply to the beesting, along with some lemonade on a tray to slake our road-weary throats. We told them our eventual destination was Boulder, Colorado, though I'm not sure we had formulated that idea even to ourselves at that point. It probably had to do with Karen's desire to visit a reputedly hip college town, where some of the earliest mobi-lization of student activism was blossoming around environmental concerns.

We inquired about local campgrounds or recreational facilities where we could park ourselves for the night. "Why, right across the street on the church lawn." Glancing at the lawn, lush and green, we couldn't quite trust what we heard. "You can park your motorcycle inside the fence, too, but you must be out before morning services at 9:00 a.m. Don't worry, the church bells will summon the town about a half hour before that, and if you wait for us here on the porch, we can feed you before you continue your travels."

The next morning, after a restful night under the watch of the church steeple and a canopy of countless stars, we moved the Suzuki across the road and perched on the porch, awaiting their return from services. Over breakfast, they offered to help us chart a scenic journey as we moved ever eastward and north.

They were proud of the Utah countryside and delighted to share their love of it. They said it would be like taking a journey themselves.

We needed a route populated enough for refueling but really wanted to avoid a path limited to major highways, especially with our max speed of 50 and the need to rest our butts at regular intervals. We shared a warm goodbye and hit the road.

We traveled up Highway 89 amid some lovely plateaus and greenery until reaching Salina, Utah, a good-sized city and then headed east on Interstate 70.

The poor little Suzuki struggled a bit crossing over the Wasatch Plateau at an elevation of 8,825 feet. We figured the carburetor troubles were related to the elevation rise but hoped that, after our descent into lower terrain, the sputtering would resolve itself. It mostly did. We stuck with Interstate 70 until it was time to rest and recharge in the dinky town of Green River (with a population under 1,000). Being a little over 100 miles from Salina, we only had to rest our backsides once along the route.

Sometimes our progress seemed slow; other times the beauty of the landscape was sufficiently impressive to turn our minds from our physical discomfort. We stuck with 70 and crossed over into Colorado heading for Grand Junction, where we might find a motorcycle shop to bring the tiny bike back to its full power. As suspected, the boys in the shop told us that our points were barely gapping. Hmm, I had no idea what they meant, not being much of a mechanic myself.

They explained that carbon buildup on the points and spark plugs resulted from having fuel too rich for the higher elevations. An adjusted fuel mixture and new spark plugs were accompanied with a short tutorial on how to adjust the mixture further if needed. We were on the road again with much more pep than when we pulled into the shop.

From, there it was only 85 miles to Glenwood Springs, where we had decided to turn south so Karen could experience the unique charm of Aspen. I had only visited in winter when skiing with my family, so I, too, was curious to take in the glory of its aspen groves in full leaf.

When we departed Aspen and continued southward, we had more climbing to do, up to 12,000 feet, and my fiddling with the fuel mixture seemed to be a lesson not fully grasped. On one long climb, Karen had to get off the bike and walk alongside, still donning the backpack she wore while riding. The decrease in overall load let me limp up the hill on the indomitable little machine.

We turned toward the north, still at mountainous elevation, and were lucky to encounter some kind lads with bikes in the spec of a town called Leadville; they helped me get the mixture adjusted more appropriately. Leadville was adorably picturesque. Originally named Silver City, it was the first proposed capital of the state of Colorado and known for being the last place that Doc Holliday was a lawman.

We learned our ultimate destination of Boulder was a mere 112 miles away and chose to spend the night in Leadville so as to be fresh for the final leg of the trip. I was definitely ready to get out of the saddle and settle into whatever adventures awaited us in the college town.

When we arrived in Boulder, it was actually a pleasant shock to find ourselves in a bustling city of 67,000. We hadn't been in that much humanity for a month. The university area was vibrant and alive, with young folk everywhere sporting ponytails on the guys and tie-dye on almost everyone. We felt at home in the counterculture. Pulling over near some student types and inquiring where we might be able to set up camp, we were directed to Four-Mile Canyon on the southwestern side of Boulder. We headed there.

It was a picturesque and forested winding road with Four-Mile Creek running alongside. With very little vehicle traffic, we picked a spot right off the road and along the stream to establish our temporary home. Since Karen and I were both compulsive *nesters*, we had a tidy functional camp within about an hour.

We formed a suitable firepit for cooking, leveled an area for comfortable sleeping, and unpacked our gear onto a couple of makeshift shelves of flat rocks. Resting for a moment and admiring our organizational accomplishment, we decided it was time to head into town for provisions get the lay of the land.

We were looking through the lens of perhaps wanting to return to Boulder one day to set up a more permanent home.

Once we got into town, we saw signs and posters everywhere advertising a big Earth Day celebration. There were special green flags flying and every once in a while we'd see some student type wearing a gas mask. This was the first event of its sort: a massive teach-in with speakers and groups discussing *pollution*. It was founded by Gaylord Nelson, a Wisconsin senator who had been deeply affected by seeing firsthand the devastation caused by the Santa Barbara oil spill in 1969.

Nearby federal labs provided tours and speakers covering topics from polluted streams, polluted foods, noise pollution, and radiation. All talks and workshops were free and attendees were encouraged to use public transportation. Chatting with university students was very informative. Elementary school children rode their bikes to school and helped to pick up trash. There were guided *ecology walks* led by teams of a scientist paired with an architect or designer that would educate the public about effective or ineffective use of space. All pretty fascinating.

Neither Karen nor I had really participated in any activism of the sixties; she was busy with marriage and child-rearing and I was busy going to rock concerts. If I wasn't at the Fillmore Auditorium or Longshoremen's Hall or the Avalon Ballroom, then I was parked on a barstool or hanging out on Telegraph Avenue in Berkeley. Maybe it took immersion in a totally new environment to have an awakening of incipient consciousness about larger issues.

We went shopping for some food items and then headed home to our camp. When we got back, we found a handwritten note on our table area, weighed down with a rock. It read, "This is private property. But your clean use of the space assures me you will take care of my land. As long as you are considerate, you are welcome to stay here." Wow! Actual permission. Our initial panic at the first sentence subsided.

The seminal issue about our arriving in Boulder was that for the first time we were actually *alone* together. Not sleeping at our respective childhood homes, no kids or Richard demanding attention, and though our little home was primitive, we could feel truly *coupled*. The most intimacy we had on our journey was the warm feeling of Karen's arms tightly wrapped around my waist and the sign language we had developed to point out significant sights or personal needs to each other. Talking around the winds and our helmets just wasn't workable.

So rather than engage in the environmental activism once we were in Boulder, we were more focused on enjoying and embarking upon the joyful experiment of living together, building a home. We would together forage for suitable firewood along the banks of the stream, and the task of building the fire would usually fall to me. What can I say? I was just quite good at building a fire. She would cook on that open fire while I would make repeat trips to the creek's edge to fill our largest containers with water.

I had discovered troves of blackberries, elderberries, and other items we used to boil into colorful liquids, then attempt to tie-dye a couple of our T-shirts. (The colors couldn't survive any sort of subsequent washing, alas.)

Since it took so long to heat a large pot of water over the fire, we would do our bathing and hair washing in the very chilly water from the stream, taking care to lather up both hair and body away from the creek's edge. Taking turns, the other would do the freezing-cold rinse while we both shrieked with delight. Invigorating doesn't seem an adequate description.

She taught me how to mix up our Bisquick, take the dough, and roll it into a long snakelike shape, then wind it around and around a green twig, holding and rotating it over the campfire until golden brown on all sides. Once suitably browned and if thoroughly cooked, it would slide easily off the twig, awaiting butter and honey to be dripped into the center. Such a simple thing, but the result was a delicious miracle!

Karen started dinner while I took out my longhand manuscript of the lesbian western I had been working on since Ellensburg. We were pretty happy.

During our stay in the canyon, we met some interesting locals. One who has remained in memory was a hippie type who told us he had been struck by lightning *twice* and had been to conventions of people who had also been struck by lightning. By his account, everyone in attendance was a little strange.

Our only negative experience while camped in the canyon was that, returning one day, we found someone had stolen one of our backpacks, unfortunately, the one with my manuscript inside. I was crushed! I had worked many wintry nights in Ellensburg, up in our garret/darkroom, weaving a fantastical tale about we three living on the ranch—Terry Tall, Torch MacLane (our roommate Mary) and Legs Latrine (myself). The greatest part of the experience of creating this story was the discovery of how easily words flowed from me and that, without any particular self-consciousness on my part, it was also hilarious.

Additional injury was that the backpack taken belonged to a friend back home who was reticent to loan out her nice pack to begin with. I felt terrible. To this day, I haven't had the courage to try and recreate the yarn for fear it would never be as good or as effortless as the original.

On top of the discovery of the missing pack, Karen was longing for her babies, her only contact being a couple of collect calls from a phone booth. For the moment, they were staying with Karen's parents in Walnut Creek. That day, before we returned to camp, she was told that Richard had filed for divorce and sole custody of the children on the grounds that they had been abandoned by their mother! She was a mess.

It began looking like the sensible thing to do would be head back to California in order for Karen to fight to keep her children. Concurrently, I was starting to worry about our funds getting low. All indicators pointed to our adventure having to take a back seat to cruel, harsh facts. We started making plans to pack up and be on the most direct route to the Bay Area in the next day or two.

The task was clear and urgent; we needed to get back home. Karen went into a steely resolve and focused on organizing our gear. I took on the navigational chores, studying our meager maps with an eye to efficiency. It looked like Interstate 70, heading a bit south, was our best exit route, then making our way north toward Salt Lake City so we could pick up Interstate 80 for a straight shot home. We were both in *action mode*.

Planning to leave the canyon at first light and having fueled up the day before, the route I chose would be our longest day yet— about eight to ten hours of riding, connecting with State 89 up along the eastern boundary of Provo, north to Salt Lake City where we could pick up Interstate 80. One hell of an exhausting ride.

Thoroughly shot, we made it and camped the night on the southern end of the Great Salt Lake in a state park. My body felt three times older than its twenty-four years. Karen was pretty quiet but stayed close, seeking comfort. I didn't know how I could help with her heavy heart except to just be there and available if she wanted to talk.

In my own impotent way, that was the best I could muster. It was more than a decade before the amalgam of recovery groups, meditation, therapy and soul-searching would help me even begin to understand the phenomenon of compassion. We were both pretty awkward, perhaps the entirety of our generation was, at sharing our deepest concerns and fears with one another. I just knew my mission, once home, was to advocate for Karen to be reunited with her children.

We had some cold food to eat, not wanting to unpack much, and slept pretty well and fairly long. In the morning, we gathered ourselves and went to a nearby café to get some breakfast and things to munch on along the way.

Once west of Salt Lake City, with the massive body of the lake itself to our north, we had the Great Salt Lake Desert to cross. This is one incredibly barren stretch of land. It seems to go on forever when, actually, in our direction of travel, it's only 75 miles. But it's 75 miles of *nothing*! Think race cars and land-speed records and terrain where even sagebrush won't grow in the acidic earth. This is the kind of hard, beaten surface where anthropologists say they can still find tracks from the Conestoga wagons that traversed here during the western migration of the eighteenth century.

Around noon, the entire atmosphere seemed like it shifted. The sky grew dark and ominous, where the last time I looked overhead it was bright blue with a few puffy clouds. The wind started to pick up to the point where it was affecting my ability to control the bike. It was coming off the lake, hitting us broadside, and began gusting. Gusting hard. We were getting blasted by what I thought were grains of sand. Pulling off to the side of the highway, we tried to take cover on the leeward side of the Suzuki.

Jesus! This wasn't sand; it was *salt*. We were in a salt storm. We had to take one of the tarps off the bike and pull it over ourselves as being pelted by grains of salt was very painful wherever it reached bare skin. We just stayed huddled like that for over an hour, maybe longer. At least our tiny engine got some time to cool off, and I hoped that salt hadn't invaded any critical bike parts.

When the wind died down and it felt safe to resume riding, we continued west on 80, eventually spying in the distance the giant neon cowboy figure in Wendover as we crossed the state line into Nevada.

We were one backpack lighter, but our mood was heavy. I could feel tension in Karen's arms wrapped around me—not warm and loose like before but a bit desperate and buzzing with energy. The worry and anxiety in her muscles conveyed itself to my body as well, tensing me up and piling on to the sensations still vibrating in me from the salt scare.

We hadn't really talked about Richard and the kids, and I didn't quite know what I could contribute. Rather, we were preoccupied with thoughts of what we would encounter back in California. We had no home to share, so we both had to seek shelter from our respective parents. Karen's parents only knew of our relationship whatever sordid tales Richard shared as an aggrieved and abandoned husband.

Since Richard taught school up in Humboldt County, Karen would at least get the chance to spend time with the kids at her folks' until Richard's school year was over. But she told me there were lots of pleadings, many sorrowful and tearful phone calls, and constant entreaties to come back to their little nest.

For my parents' part, they were glad we both returned from our odyssey in one piece, and my dad agreed to employ me at his company once again so I could earn enough to rent an apartment, hopefully for myself and Karen.

Building a Proper Nest

Karen was increasingly clear that returning to Richard and Humboldt County was not the direction she wanted her life to take. But she did want to fight for her children. The focus became creating a suitable residence for obtaining custody. I looked for an apartment while Karen sought employment. Both seemed to be achieved fairly quickly.

Taking the bus into Oakland, she found a job as a file clerk at the Capwell's department store on Telegraph Avenue. I was able to find a small studio apartment just a little farther up that same thoroughfare. Next step was the search for an attorney since Richard would hear no compromises. He wanted his wife back!

I don't recall how we settled upon Alan as our lawyer, but he came at the recommendation of someone we knew. In our first meeting, we learned a raft of discouraging facts: (1) there was tremendous antigay bias in custody cases; (2) our new little nest would never pass muster with any home investigator as being too small to house the four of us; and (3) I would have to recede into the background in any interactions to protect Karen from appearing to be a lesbian despite Richard's protestations. Every move was filtered through the lens of an anticipated court struggle for custody.

This last caveat was pretty humiliating for me, as I had *never* been in the closet since I was outed to my parents at age sixteen! I was also rather shocked to discover how much a legal retainer could be.

At this point, Karen's sister stepped in with a brilliant idea: why not look for a rental house and she could share the financial burden? As a flight attendant, she would rarely be home and her room could pass as a bedroom for the kids, who were still young enough to share a room without impropriety. Voilà! One hurdle met and conquered. I was charged with the real estate search.

This time, I did find a proper nest for our little family. It was a lovely craftsman-style house at the end of a cul-de-sac off Piedmont Avenue in Oakland. It was quiet, had a small backyard, a place for my darkroom, and the owner was amenable to my doing a great deal of interior painting, brightening up the place and keeping me busy enough not to butt in to the details of the custody case.

Once the painting and hardwood floor scrubbing were complete, I set upon the task of making the second bedroom look kid ready. I had to find a way to make a pair of beds and began keeping my eyes open for building materials. Aha! My reconnaissance focused on a construction site up the street, about a mile from our house. A large apartment house, there was a plethora of pickings on the site. I focused on a couple of 4'×8' plywood sheets and determined to come back after dark.

Late, late that night, I pulled my truck up to the curb near the plywood. As I struggled with the unwieldy weight and shape, I noticed some red lights approaching with no sirens. Clearly the cops! I dashed for the bushes to hide myself and hoped they weren't coming for *me*. Sure enough, they pulled up near my truck, hemming it in, and I was clearly their target.

I had no idea what to do until I heard one of the officers say, "Hey, the keys are in the ignition. Let's just tow the truck to the impound yard." That brought me sheepishly out of the shrubbery in confession mode. A man (the owner of the project, it turns out) had seen me from his apartment window across the street and called in the cavalry. I stood quietly, knees quivering, while cops and owner alike discussed whether charges against me should be filed, the owner declaring he thought I should be taught a lesson, the police declaring that it would be a felony arrest. I was pretty darned scared and began pleading as to how I was only trying to make beds for my kids and nine other types of whatever pitiful I could come up with. I had not yet managed to wrestle either piece of ply into the truck.

With stern warnings, they all concurred that I looked scared straight and sent me on my way. I was disappointed with the failed mission but felt extremely lucky not to be in handcuffs.

The Legal Fight

Alan assured us there were many steps before we needed to concern ourselves with children's furniture. There was a mountain of filings with the court, financial statements (ugh), and other hurdles which we might not even clear.

I provided what support I could, but my frustration with the slow progress in all this and the lawyer's propensity for not returning phone calls with our desperate questions had me agitated. In addition, I was hit hard by the consecutive losses of two rock icons, Jimi Hendrix and Janis Joplin, within two months.

Still working at Microwave Engineering for my father, I had an opportunity to address the mounting bills from Alan. Since I was the only person who worked in the office up front, I was able to apply for credit with various merchants, then field the phone calls from them to validate my claimed (and wildly inflated) earnings. I felt pretty slick and quickly accrued many charge accounts and gas cards. This allowed me to use my actual salary to help pay our bills. And I never defaulted on my accounts, thereby building a good credit history.

Unfortunately, I also discovered that the Macy's store near my work had installed a liquor department where I was able to indulge my burgeoning alcohol habit with my excellent Macy's credit and their excellent supply of booze in half gallons. Ah, foreshadowings.

Seeking a Challenge

I began to get impatient. It seemed like we hardly ever got an update from Alan about either the divorce or the custody case, and when we did, it was seldom news that made us happy or encouraged. Concurrently, as my annoyance grew, I happened to run into an old friend from the Telegraph Avenue hippie days, and his news was that he had been going to law school. I started pumping Chris with questions and learned some interesting things. For one, in California a person didn't need a bachelor's degree to get into law school. And if I could make up the few credits shy I was of half my degree, I wouldn't be required to take a bear of an exam called the First-Year Bar, or the Baby Bar.

Ooh! My favorite thing! Extreme action mode! Karen could sit and wait on news from Alan, but right away, I was enrolled in the local community college, taking a fun yoga class and introductory Spanish (which was a cinch for me). I also had to sign up to take the LSAT (Law School Admission Test) and admission to a school would be contingent on a good score.

Smugly I thought, *What is Alan doing for us with all these billable hours?* I figured I could also get in on a gravy train like this! I began studying for the LSAT and enjoyed it. Very different than anything I'd done before. It was not so much right and wrong answers and memorization but a challenge to *reason*. It suited me.

I saw an ad in the *San Francisco Chronicle* for an LDA (limited duration assignment) job to be a toll collector on the Bay Bridge. I applied and was hired, one of the first women to do this job since World War II. I knew it would end in six months, but the pay was good, even if only once a month. That part was hard as I was definitely a paycheck-to-paycheck girl.

The day I reported to the Bridge, I roared up on my little Suzuki and immediately was assumed to be a lesbian. Okay by me. I quickly bonded with Mr. James, an older guy who would go out to the parking lot on his break and drink whisky from a bottle he kept under the seat of his battered old VW bug. If our half-hour breaks coincided, I joined him. If not, he just left his car unlocked for me. The nights can get pretty brisk in a little tin booth on the Bay Bridge approach. We joked and called the whisky antifreeze.

James and I worked the swing shift, from 3:00 p.m. to 11:00 p.m. We got to be buddies, and he would come over to my neighborhood bar, all the way from San Francisco, and we'd drink beer and shoot pool. The name of the joint was Egbert Souse's, a dive bar no longer open. James would pay for everything (he sold real estate on the side), and I was delighted to have such a kind new friend.

On my days off and on weekends, I would put in quite a few hours studying for the LSAT. There was a large focus on comprehension in the practice tests, some math and work problems, and the essays (my stronger skill). I also had my community college classes which involved a bit of homework. Workdays, I would study a couple of hours in the morning until it was time to meet James at Egbert's. I also managed some LSAT review during slow times in my toll booth.

Anxiety over my performance on the exam as well as long hours left me in a state of exhaustion that was medicated with alcohol. I was still young enough to think it gave me staying power and perhaps even made me smarter. Youth can hold an amazing brand of delusion! On weekend nights, I also convinced Karen to come out with me to San Francisco and the newly gelling lesbian bar scene.

At last we had a place to congregate! Some played softball on various teams sponsored by the bars. There was Maud's in the Haight-Ashbury, Peg's Place out on Geary Avenue, and Kelly's down in the Mission District. Each establishment had its own culture, some more working class, some with more underage girls, and Maud's, my favorite and most enduring as sort of new progressive brand of lesbian which eschewed old-fashioned gender role-playing and divisions into butch-femme dichotomy. We were a *new* breed, a hip breed of queer.

I had never really had a social milieu where I was part of a whole, visible and accepted. I was a funny drunk. Not the morose sort or a tough girl itching for a fight. My wit was quick and my humor sarcastic. I got laughs, but I'm sure I also alienated many women. And man, could I ever hold my liquor (more delusion?).

Karen grew tired of this scene quickly and opted to stay home, bake sourdough bread, read, and do handwork. I chose to drink and flirt, with the comfort of knowing the little woman was waiting for me at home.

These days, I joke and say I pretty much spent the '70s on a barstool. I never engaged with the Free Speech Movement, the Women's Movement, or the radical political movements of the time such as the SDS or the Black Panthers. I just wanted to drink and get into law school. Karen waited patiently for developments in her divorce case.

Big Changes

The six months on the Bridge drew to a close just in time for a final push toward the LSAT. I took it, felt good about it, and had a bit of time to rest and recover. And drink. And wait for the results.

Fortuitously, one of the interest cards that I had put in with the city of Oakland sent word they were hiring for parking and meter checker (in other words, meter maid). I had previously taken a test and my number had come up; I got hired.

Not long after that, I was accepted to San Francisco Law School, a nighttime four-year curriculum for an LLB degree. I was excited and looking forward to great things in my future. I also discovered that out of 120 students in the first-year class, only four of us were women, three of whom in my estimation were there shopping for husbands. The year was 1972.

The legal studies were a grind. There was never any such thing as being finished or learning enough. The goal in a legal exam is to digest a set of facts, then be able to argue all sides of all issues contained in those facts and cite legal cases supporting the argument one is making. Acquiring this ability was about reading tons of historical cases in very large casebook tomes, then following the trail of all the cases cited to support the decision in the assigned case. Exhaustive and exhausting.

The meter maid job was like comic relief compared to law school. But I liked school and was proud of myself for getting in and happy to brag to anyone who would listen that I was a law student.

The crew was small, about a dozen women, almost all African American. The gals I bonded with were the only other white women, Catherine and Kathy, collectively called the Cathies. Our commonality was a love of current *rock 'n' roll* and a penchant for smoking pot. We also shared an aversion to work, which, as a meter maid, frequently involved taking verbal abuse from the citizenry.

When I was no longer on a short leash (meaning a beat that went 'round and 'round city hall all day), the girls and I developed a system. The neighborhood that was eventually to be the 980 freeway was a great place to hide out while they moved old Victorian homes out of the future interchange. The three of us would meet there, fire up a joint, and occasionally create fictional parking tickets. How could that be done, you ask?

To create the illusion of actually working, we devised a system. Since the first data entered on a ticket was a license number, we created a template, writing down the number and letter arrangements of a typical out-of-state plate. For instance, if we saw a car from Wyoming, we might note that a typical order was 123 XMF and make a note of it. Then if it was time to write a citation, we would give it to a fictional vehicle from Wyoming with the plate 456 XYZ. The beauty of this system was that the computers automatically deleted any citations issued to cars from another state.

Similarly, the parking computers would reject plates belonging to undercover police cars. To our jaded eye, these vehicles were extremely easy to spot. Thus, a citation was safe. We thought we were pretty slick. *And* to our knowledge, the scheme never was uncovered.

As time went on, I was allowed to roam out East where the only parking enforcement was of two hours, red, loading, or bus zones (as opposed to meters), and the expected yield was just a dozen citations or so per day. I would have my big law book in the scooter and find a nice quiet street up near the hills, and with the tome poised upon the steering wheel, I would study assiduously.

Close Encounter

My courses were the usual fare for a first-year law student: Crimes, Contracts, and Torts. I found Contracts the driest, but loved Crimes and Torts. Professor Jerry, my Crimes teacher, was in private practice with his wife but had previously worked in the San Francisco District Attorney's Office. He was a great storyteller and recommended to all of us that if we had any intention of being litigators, we should get involved in community theater or take public-speaking classes.

I mention him because halfway through my first year, I needed to call on him to get me out of a serious jam. He was the only criminal lawyer I knew.

Karen and I had gone out on a Thursday night to the city to visit our friends Barbara and Noreen. It was Barbara's birthday, and we had a small gift for her. They lived in the Haight in an old Victorian divided into two flats, upper and lower. Each floor had one long narrow hallway with a living room and two bedrooms branching off it. The living room served as a third bedroom and the kitchen was at the rear of the flat. Barbara and Noreen shared one bedroom, their roomie Sylvie another, and some guy used the living room as his quarters.

We were greeted at the door by Barbara and followed the birthday girl to the kitchen where the three women were drinking tea. We joined them around a small table for small talk.

There was a loud knock on the front door.

Barbara wasn't expecting any additional guests, so was surprised to see a couple of burly men in suits. They sure didn't look like anyone the housemates knew. They identified themselves as police officers and inquired about the third roommate, Dave, a young hippie guy who was out for the evening. The cops were told Dave was not home, but they just kept walking in the house, peering around corners, looking for him. Barbara repeatedly insisted the officers were not welcome in the apartment, asking them to remain at the front door, but they walked right past her and down the hall. By now, the rest of us were watching from the kitchen doorway, and we could feel the collective fear and anxiety mounting. There seemed to be no stopping these dudes!

By this time, all seven of us were gathered in the tiny kitchen: the three housemates, Karen and me, and the two cops. They ordered us to sit down while they scanned the space, including casting salacious stares at the rest of us. There was a certain ugly way straight men in those days looked at lesbians—some combination of predation and disgust. We were terrified and silent while they prowled around the kitchen.

Though I had my couple of encounters with police, I was never involved in any kind of search. It was creepy. They opened cupboards, pulled out drawers, strewing the contents on the floor, and looked under the sink, opening containers. And this not being my house, I had no idea if they were going to uncover some huge cache of an illegal substance. But I did know enough from one half year of crimes class that they had not shown a search warrant nor did they have permission to enter the flat.

"Hey, check this out!" One of them announced with joy. He had pulled down from a spice shelf a jar, twelve ounces or so, and in it was a handful of marijuana *seeds*. The eventual arrest record said it was twenty-eight grams of seeds. These guys were having an *aha* moment, realizing they had enough evidence to continue arresting us.

Though the *Miranda v. Arizona* decision was handed down by the Supreme Court in 1966, I have no recollection of being read my rights. Perhaps I wouldn't even recollect my own name. I was so frightened. They called in to dispatch for a paddy wagon, and we sat around waiting.

The ride in that wagon was even more petrifying than the totality of the experience thus far. A large windowless van the size of a UPS truck, no seat belts, and a seemingly evil delight in giving us

Mr. Toad's Wild Ride, the five of us were thrown about the back of the van while trying to hang on for dear life. I also had no idea where we were headed.

When the vehicle finally came to a stop, we were let out at loading dock where the officers led us through doors and into a receiving area. I felt like one of those spy movies where our protagonist is led to enemy headquarters with a hood over his head, thus keeping the anxiety and tension as long as possible. Apparently, enemy HQ was this time the San Francisco City Jail.

I don't recall what manner of processing we went through, but we eventually landed in a group area about twenty by twenty feet with many other women. Guessing by the various states of disorientation, resignation, and frustration among our neighbors, I deduced we were in the drunk tank. Reality and dread began to sink in; marshaling our meager resources became paramount.

Barbara agreed to put in a call to Professor Jerry for me, leaving the message that I was in city jail and needed help urgently. While she was still on the line, Jerry broke in and delivered the discouraging news that nothing could be done before morning when he would appear before a judge and try to secure our release. I needed to conserve my own phone call to reach Cathy. She was working the 7:00 a.m. shift, and I would need her to tell our supervisor I had called in sick. That call was pretty hilarious as, by now, it was well after midnight and Cathy was apparently deep in slumber.

"Cathy! Cathy! Wake up, Cathy! This is Gentry and I'm in jail!" I was still getting indistinct mumblings on the other end of the line and was terrified she wouldn't comprehend the urgency. Eventually, she sounded as if coming out of her fog. "Please tell Rocky that I called in sick in the morning! I don't want to be AWOL," I pleaded. When I was convinced she heard me, I surrendered the phone to the next needy defendant.

That night in the drunk tank was unlike any other I had experienced. Jammed in with about a dozen other women, we being the only lily-white detainees, it was probably the most concentrated diversity I'd ever been thrown into. Our bailiff was Caucasian, and all night long, I mean *all* night, one of our cellmates was hollering, trying to get her attention, "White woman! White woman!" If the night hadn't been so terrifying, it might have been hilarious.

On the phone, Jerry had said he would be in to confer with us after going to the police station in the morning to get the arrest report and whatever information he could. He also said that if we couldn't appear before a judge that day, then we would be stuck in the drunk tank until Monday morning. Yikes! I just couldn't let my imagination go there! No matter how hip I considered myself, in my bones, I was just a scared little suburban white girl. Needless to say, none of us slept a wink.

Around 11:00 a.m., the bailiff told me I had a visitor. Since only I had an actual relationship with Jerry, I met alone with him in a small interview room. Jerry said since our description of the search definitely sounded illegal, with the repeated requests for the officers to remain outside, then he would be filing a motion to suppress the evidence (the seeds). And if the evidence was excluded, then there was no case.

Jerry shared an interesting tidbit. Since he was familiar with the guys in the DA's office, he had gotten a look at our file, and inside on a piece of scratch paper was a handwritten note: "All five are dykes." So more than the presence of pot seeds, this was actually why we were arrested. I also shared concerns with Jerry as to whether this incident would make me ineligible to be admitted to the California bar. Though attitudes toward dope were relaxing a little, it still was an unknown whether possession would be considered a crime of *moral turpitude*. Jerry said it hadn't been tested, but our more pressing concern was whether we could get arraigned before the end of business so that we weren't stuck in jail all weekend. I asked about bail and Jerry said he was going to request we all be released on OR (our own recognizance) which would require no cash.

The five of us breathed a major sigh of relief when, around 3:00 p.m., the bailiff fetched us and led us to Jerry's location outside one of the courtrooms. We had gotten an arraignment before end of day! I was in a bit of a daze between fretting for my own future and getting a chance to experience firsthand the world of criminal procedure.

From the Hall of Justice to City Hall

As first-year finals grew nearer, I felt the time crunch and asked for a four-month leave of absence in order to study full-time. My request was promptly denied. Again, not thinking about consequences, I resigned. I filled out more interest cards for various city jobs and kept on studying.

I did quite well on the first year exams and mention city hall because, in Oakland, that's where job openings were posted and where one filled out interest cards to be kept on file.

Exactly four months to the day of resigning the meter-maid job, I received a notice in the mail that an entry test was being given for gardener I, for which I had filed an interest card. The test included a segment on physical strength, I think in the hopes that it would eliminate most female applicants. Undaunted, I pushed the loaded wheelbarrow up a short ramp. I won't say effortlessly but satisfactorily. It's the only aspect of the test I recall.

I was only the second woman to be accepted in the position, and not only did I get to spend the days outdoors but also could go to work in jeans! In the meter-maid job, we all had to wear uniforms, but now it was just jeans and a tacky polyester City of Oakland shirt and comfy boots.

Gardeners either reported to a particular park or showed up in the mornings to ride with a roving crew. Both assignments consisted mainly of picking up litter and trash left behind by picnicking citizens or thrown from their car windows. Occasionally we would weed, mow, edge, or prune. We were closely supervised by someone higher up the gardener food chain, and the pleasantness of the day was entirely dependent upon just who that person was.

My first assignment was with a salty and profane older Portuguese man of minimal intelligence but merely a satisfactory performance for a year elevated one to gardener II. Lou (my II) and I rode alone and mostly cleaned center strips in the streets or swept broken glass from public tennis courts. It was not the work, but the chatter, that made the day intolerably long.

Lou was a classic chauvinist pig and, in the early '70s, allowed to freely spew his putrid attitudes and resentment about me taking a job that rightly belonged to a man. He knew he could really get my goat with remarks like, "You should be home baking cookies." As a cocky young lesbian, I could barely contain my rage and frustration.

When I finally drilled it into his thick skull that I was gay, that opened up wondrous new avenues of abuse he sent my way. Phrases like *hostile work environment* were still far in the future; I felt I was a captive audience in the truck to his misogynist rants and especially his disgusting objectifying of women we saw on the street.

Coming out in that era usually elicited a couple of categories of response from men: either grossly personal questions such as "What do two women *do* together?" (frequently asked even by therapists) or the men who assumed I was just as misogynist as they. They just considered lesbians dickless versions of men—the kind of men I viewed as disgusting, overbearing and predatory. And without exception, all would offer the cure of their magical expertise! God, it became so tiresome. I eventually complained about Lou's language and behavior but was summarily diverted with the news that my assignment was being changed to a large park in the east end of town. Here I was supervised by a gardener III who actually resided in the park. His language was an improvement over Lou's, but I was still regarded as an anomaly in this male occupation.

Ironically for a gardener, my supervisor's first name was Romaine. But whenever I was in conversation with Romaine, rather than looking at my face, he would just stare at my breasts. Eventually, I took to chucking him under the chin and saying, "Hey, Romaine, I'm *up here*." He was quite a bit shorter than me.

Not Exactly a Picnic

The daily grind continued in the same way, but it was a bit of saving grace that Cathy (remember the Cathys?), my old meter-maid buddy, had also gone over to the park department. Interestingly enough, it was Bill, husband of the other Kathy, who had encouraged both of us to take the gardener exam while Bill himself had his number come up on the city firefighter list.

At this time, Bill also had an opportunity to promote within the park department. What settled it for him was that Kathy told him she decided she was a lesbian and wanted a divorce. In Bill's words, he lamented, "Hey, why not turn my *whole* world upside down?" So he took the job with the fire department.

Even though Kathy vanished into the corporate world, Bill and I remained good friends, sharing a love of baseball and watching other sports. I was his confidant as he nursed his hurt feelings over the end of a marriage that had been challenging at best. And he would also share with me the rigors of a new career at fire.

While working out East in Knowland Park, the quiet days of raking up fallen leaves and picking up the trash of citizen visitors, I had quite a bit of time to continue my prodigious drinking habit. The work day ended at 3:30 p.m. when I would go home, clean up, and head for the dyke bars in San Francisco.

The pattern was always the same. The evening began at Maud's (now a place of legend) with the after-work set. Then as it got later, many of us would drive down Seventeenth Street to Kelly's in the Mission District where we could dance. Since Kelly's had no license for dancing on the premises and also hosted a number of underage drinkers, a sentry would stand at the outside of the door. She would possess a switch that controlled the jukebox.

When our guard would recognize police approaching, she would hit the switch, the music would cease, and the younger pups would scurry to hide in the ladies' room. When the coppers left, the music and dancing would resume. I think the police mostly enjoyed disrupting our merriment as the routine really didn't fool anyone.

A Change of Scenery

I learned from others in my law school class that were I to transfer to Lincoln University, another night law curriculum, I would be able to attain student loans. This was not available at San Francisco Law School due to their lack of ABA accreditation. They were accredited by the state, but not the national association—an issue of library size and the number of full-time faculty.

Always on the hunt for free money, the allure made my decision for me. I transferred to Lincoln and applied for financial assistance. My thinking at the time was that once I was pulling in big bucks as an attorney, these $2,500-a-year loans would be a cinch to pay off.

Now at Lincoln, my second-year courses were Property, Equity, and Criminal Procedure. Procedure was fun, Property arcane and challenging, and Equity was a total snooze. Even today, I don't think I could tell you what equity meant or what the casebook reading was about.

The most notable and distinct memories I have of Equity class were a couple of cultural events that captured the attention of much of the country as well as my bored mates in class. These may barely be remembered by anyone under sixty today.

On September 20, 1973, we all were distracted from lecture that evening by a televised tennis match named the Battle of the Sexes where Billie Jean King had been goaded into competing against an old duffer of fifty-six named Bobby Riggs. He had been loudly and broadly bragging that, even at his age, he could wallop the thirty year-old star of women's tennis. The match was being broadcast in our school lounge while class was conducted next door. I and a few others slunk out of our seats and crept over to the lounge to watch the telecast where Billie Jean dispatched Riggs in three straight sets:

6–4, 6–3, 6–3. Hah! Vindication! Among my male classmates, many had thought the woman would be subjugated.

Mind you, at the time, I never considered myself a feminist so much as a detester of and a competitor against men, whether taking a job an old fart like Lou felt should be the domain of men or sexually conquering women whom men found desirable. The fact that I spent all my leisure time on a barstool had been my preference over all the culturally confrontational movements that you would think my rebellious nature would have me join. I watched passively during the Free Speech Movement of '64, was puzzled by the Freedom Rider friends who had traveled to the Deep South to help register voters later in the '60s, and, most heinous, thought my contemporaries in the Women's Movement were, "a bunch of whiners who just needed to get laid."

Now that was a very male-patterned, chip-off-the-old-dad bit that later filled me with shame. In the bars, I heard for the first time that I objectified women and didn't really understand what it meant. These things required years of argument, deep reflection, and therapy to unravel. But you would never find me at a march or a sit-in or flinging Molotov cocktails. My rebellion was always more of the "don't tell me I can't apply for a job or pass an LSAT exam or do *anything* a man could do."

The second district memory of Equity class was in the following spring. It was February 4, 1974, when Patty Hearst, the granddaughter of newspaper magnate William Randolph Hearst, was kidnapped from her Berkeley apartment by three armed strangers.

It was learned that her abductors were a group of armed radicals calling themselves the Symbionese Liberation Army, or the SLA. Quoting the FBI, they were "led by a hardened criminal named Donald DeFreeze and they wanted nothing less than to incite a guerrilla war against the US government and destroy what they called the capitalist state. Their ranks included women and men, blacks and whites, and anarchists and extremists from various walks in life."

Being Hearst's granddaughter and Hearst being the publishing company of the local *San Francisco Chronicle*, she made a perfect high-profile target for grabbing national attention to the group's cause and demands. On April 15, 1974, members of the SLA robbed Hibernia Bank on Noriega Street in San Francisco, and security footage showed Patty Hearst armed and in concert with the robbers. Questions swirled: Was the kidnapping a hoax to extort money from the wealthy Hearst family? Was Patty romantically involved with DeFreeze? Or was she suffering from Stockholm syndrome (a term that was new to most of us)? For whatever reason, it appeared that Ms. Hearst had become aligned with the group and their agenda.

One month later, on May 17, the group was involved in a shoot-out with the FBI in a house in Los Angeles—six members of the SLA were killed. I mention this because coming into equity class that evening, some comedian had written on the blackboard at the front of the large classroom: FBI 6, SLA 0. It was a moment of comic relief in a tense standoff being closely followed by the news media throughout the afternoon. It wasn't terribly funny, but our dry class needed all the levity it could get.

Is This Really What I Want?

During the summer break, I continued working for the park department, hitting the lesbian bars in the city and aggravating my relationship on the home front. Karen had lost the custody battle which was additional tension. It wouldn't have occurred to me that she was grieving and depressed and could use my company let alone support. Hey, she was no fun! Time to head for Maud's.

While we lived in the rental house on Rio Vista, I occupied the weekend days repainting the entire interior of the house. When finished, the owners thought it looked so great they gave us notice to move and put the house on the market. Oh, irony! Through a friend, we found a large flat downtown on Waverly Street. It was a nice spot, just a block away from Lake Merritt.

The forays to the dyke bars in the city continued with regularity. I often went with a couple of old friends from my days at the Berkeley Post Office, Marilee and Cheryl, who were a couple. Again, Karen elected to stay home. The girls and I would get sloppy drunk, dance while hanging all over one another, and somehow make the journey back to the East Bay at closing time, managing not to be stopped for drunk driving.

During this time, Marilee and Cheryl broke up; Karen and I invited Cheryl to move into our spare bedroom on Waverly. As was rather embarrassingly typical in those days, one night, returning from the bars, Cheryl and I fall in bed together where Karen finds us the next morning and tells us she will be moving out. Inept at honesty and forthrightness, this seemed my habitual way of traversing from one relationship to another, with no ability to confront problems with my existing partner and swept up in the lust for new opportunity.

Change on All Fronts

Creating a household with Cheryl, we now included her pets—one big, old fat cat named Jokim (a bastardization of Joaquin) who had lived a long life at the animal hospital where Cheryl worked. Serving a lengthy career as a blood donor and now seventeen, it was time for him to retire. There was Cheryl's trusty pup named Beowulf who accompanied us on many backpacking trips. The remainder in the cast of characters was Bam-Bam. Adopted from the hospital when his two gay owners, constantly boarding the critter so they could travel, directed the staff to just put him down. Bam-Bam, was an exotic marsupial from Madagascar called a Galego. With the help of my dear old friend Bill Wittmer, we built Bam-Bam a huge enclosure in the corner of our spacious (and relatively without furniture) kitchen. Bill brought a magnificent branch of Leptospermum from Lakeside Park where he was a gardener II. It was Bam-Bam's delight to spring all about his cage from branch to wire fencing and back to branch. The one downside of this entertaining beastie was that he was nocturnal and right on the other side of our bedroom wall. The noise grew to be a symphony of sorts as he also gave us constant entertainment.

A Whirlwind Summer

I was delighted when my second-year grades were received in the mail. Finishing in the top 10 percent of my class of '85, it was equally good news that a student loan of $2,500 had been approved for my third year. Whoopee! We ate well but drank even better. Always behind on my now numerous credit cards, I breathed a sigh of relief to have a windfall coming in.

Filled with confidence, I registered for year three. Constitutional Law held the promise of being interesting. Ethics was a brand-new course along with the addition of an ethics portion on the bar exam for the first time. The class and the test had been deemed necessary additions after the scandalous Nixon/Watergate era. Wills and Trusts promised to have the same snooze factor as Equity. Dry, dry, dry!

On the job front, I had been transferred from Knowland Park to the garden center in Lakeside Park where I would be on a roving crew, which consisted of driving around our area in a double-cab truck and maintaining the center strips in divided city streets. In other words, weeding and picking up litter. It didn't feel much like gardening. We also covered a few parks, but again the work was picking up trash and sometimes edging lawn areas. The job was saved by the four of us inside the truck; we all got along well and spent a lot of time laughing, reading, stopping for coffee, and generally goofing off. I was starting to realize that this was the essence of city work: labor as little as possible and avoid being caught by a supervisor. Not much different than the meter-maid gig.

Meanwhile, Cheryl had a new friend at work. Claire was a shy young lesbian and my gal was happy to take the youngster under her wing, both in the hospital job and also in the lesbian culture. She visited our home frequently, and we all enjoyed watching football together. One problem, I thought Claire was pretty cute too.

Claire's face tended toward the cherubic, again with irresistible dimples, and eyes that conveyed the quickness of a very bright mind. But overall, in posture and in dress, she revealed the insecurities of youth in unfamiliar territory—baggy clothes and slightly stooped posture, seemingly wanting to blend into the background. It was fairly clear that both Cheryl and I were infatuated, and Claire loved the attention. With my third year of school approaching, my attention turned to more pragmatic things than the next football season, and in my withdrawal from our little courtship dance for Claire's attention, she opted to become Cheryl's lover.

In reflection, it's bizarre how quickly we could shift emotional gears and move on to the next whatever. I have no recollection of emotions beyond frustration at my defeat in competing for *the girl*.

The Decisive Year

Though I would be defined as a high-functioning drunk, my performance in school miraculously happened through a haze of consistent drunkenness.

Cheryl and Claire moved to a tiny house in Benicia, and I roomed temporarily with some friends in North Oakland. As with my time in Knowland, the routine continued to be leave work at 3:30 p.m., change clothes, and head for San Francisco for an evening at the bars. When those establishments closed at 2:00 a.m., I would go with a small cluster of bar pals to an all-night restaurant in the Mission District for breakfast.

Staggering home around 4:00 a.m., I would be up at 6:45 a.m. and at Lakeside Park by 7:00 a.m. Herculean! The workday would be survived by a copious intake of coffee, cigarettes, and sugar in any form attainable. (More miraculous than surviving this regimen is the fact that, in the thirty years of drinking and driving, I had never once been cited for drunk driving, been given a sobriety test, nor been in an accident attributable to alcohol.)

For one reason or another, I decided to move back to San Francisco, nearer to school, and begin my third year. Again, I was in the Haight-Ashbury, this time right off the Panhandle of Golden Gate Park on Page Street. Now after end of class, I had not so lengthy or perilous a drive home.

Year three looked to hold promise with more interesting classes: Constitutional Law, Ethics, and Wills and Trusts. As with the previous two years, that last entry proved to be the ultradry one. The subjects were seeming a bit more relevant to our time and the classmates were maturing as well. We were beginning to consider what the future might hold for young attorneys.

Time moved toward midterms rather predictably: work, study, class, drink, crash. One evening during class break in Wills, a couple of compadres and I decided to head up to the bar on the corner of Geary. Leaving my books and briefcase in situ, we planned to return before class let out. Well, ahem, time passed and we lost track of it. I realized when we were done drinking for the evening that my books were still in the classroom.

The building was dark when I returned. All I had was a number for class-related emergencies and soon found myself on the phone with the dean. Shit! Well, she trundled back to school in her after-hours attire and let me in with a very scary frown on her face. I'd like to think I had learned something but probably just never to leave books in class when I snuck out.

I was hearing things in school that were giving me pause. For one thing, there was a strict dress code both in a law office and appearing in court. Men must wear ties and suits (no sport coats), no loafers, and never pout their hands in pockets while addressing the court. You can guess how primitive the codes were for women! Business suits with skirts and heels! Things would open up in the next decade, but for now, it was just draconian as my high school dress code.

I had entertained a fantasy when I first applied to law school. My plan was to get past the bar exam and move to an apple orchard and farm house in a picturesque location like Forestville in the Russian River area. I would tend my orchard until a large outdoor telephone bell rang, foretelling of legal business. Perfect, right? It took less than a week into my first year to realize that such a reality was perhaps available to a retired judge, but no such autonomy for a newly graduated lawyer.

So that path was not going to happen. Now my classmates were talking about conferences and meetings, we should begin attending outside of school. One sentence in particular gave me great pause: *I know this firm is a bunch of assholes, but they hire a lot of first-year associates*. It was becoming clear that the practice of law was going to be one more oppressive popularity contest, where the cutest and best dressed would be the women to succeed. School was losing its allure.

After the first semester and midterms, I grew anxious and bored. This wasn't going to be my path after all. As the year spawned 1976, I decided to drop out. I had proven my point: I passed the LSAT, I was third in my first-year class, and my succeeding academic record had been exemplary.

Through Karen, I met a friend named Lynne who was a postal letter carrier. As was the lesbian custom, it didn't take long before she moved in with me.

We still lived in the Haight, but now with no school and still commuting to East Oakland, I decided to lobby for a transfer to a roving crew at Lake Merritt. The transfer was approved, and then quite fortuitously, I got a rental opportunity in Alameda. For Lynne, it was a boon as well; she also was stationed in Oakland with a shift that began at 7:00 a.m.

My friends, George and Layla (the same friends who helped me get the flat on Waverly St.), had bought a large Victorian in the Gold Coast area of the small island town. Beautifully restored homes and tidy gardens, Alameda seemed like a refuge from Oakland and San Francisco, with the Estuary jokingly referred to as *the moat*.

In Lynne, I met my match on the drinking front. On my way home on paydays, I would stop first at the liquor store, having cashed my check during lunchtime. Before groceries or anything else came the booze. To support this expensive vice, I began growing pot in a couple of raised beds on our small patio. I grew excellent product, and the sale of those buds became our grocery fund.

Before supper, we would sit outside and enjoy a couple of gin and tonics. Then with dinner each evening, we would have one or two bottles of imported wine. (In 1977, we were way too stuck up to drink California wines which were yet to come into their own. Like many alcoholics, we felt that the more costly our poison, the less likely we would be branded drunks.) Since Lynne arose at 4:30 a.m. to get ready for work, we would retire upstairs to bed right after dinner dishes were done. Once in bed, comfy in front of our tiny TV, we would have multiple glasses of Kahlua and cream.

Lynne was a very withholding lover, and with this drinking routine, she would gradually become more affectionate. By the time I thought some lovemaking might actually occur, she would pass out and noisily snore, leaving me with the company of the TV. It was a lonely arrangement.

In the Woods

An opening came up to work in Joaquin Miller Park in the Oakland Hills. I jumped at it, thinking I'd be rescued from endless litter pickup, working in the median of busy boulevards and sweeping up glass on public tennis courts.

It wasn't a dream but still a huge improvement over downtown. Again, I was with a roving crew, but they were pretty great and our gardener III believed in the time-honored tradition of wasting city time. In the hills we were less visible when goofing off.

Among the crew, there was hilarity, beer drinking, and stopping to buy smokes. Sometimes one or two of us would be dropped off to do maintenance work at one of the lodges or other recreation department facilities. (This is where my deep familiarity with Oakland hiking trails began. If you don't know them, you definitely should!)

I was drawn to one crew member in particular—Jim or Jimbo as we called him. He was a very accomplished surrealist painter who had graduated from California College of Arts and Crafts. Bright, witty, cute, with long blond hair, cowboy boots, and a sexy swagger.

I surprised myself by becoming attracted to him. We would kvetch about our unaffectionate partners who never put out. He was married quite young and had a raft of complaints as did I. Both our partners were Libras, so we decided this lack of physical affection must be a characteristic of the sun sign.

Before long, Jimbo and I were requesting to be dropped off at the same assignments and soon began a sexual affair. I grew quite confused as I never claimed to be giving up women or even considered myself bisexual. By now, Jim's wife was pregnant with their first child, and he was *really* not getting any sex. We fed each other's strong drives throughout the park, discovering multitudes of pic-

turesque spots for lying down in redwood duff or blowjobs leaning against a tree. Aside from Jim being magnificently endowed, I
was on a self-appointed mission to rescue him from this marriage I
had decided was holding him back as an artist. I should have been
ashamed at my arrogance, but I wasn't.

It's too embarrassing to scroll through the humiliations of *the
other woman*. Lynne had moved out but rarely would Jim come over
or take me out for fear of Oaklanders who knew him and his wife
and would see him straying. I shed many tears while pleading and
complaining about how little we got to see each other aside from
work. This was a loneliness far worse than Lynne's drunken snoring
next to me.

To distract myself with a project, I decided to declare bankruptcy and avoid paying back my student loans from law school.
These were the good old days when student loans were *not* secured. I
found a young lawyer to help with the filing.

It was informative. I learned my ratty VW bus was not at risk
of being repossessed (I *said* I was naive) and that I could keep my
television. I didn't really own much else. Firstly, she noticed that I
was not behind in any of my credit cards or other debts. Since that
was highly unusual for someone seeking relief through bankruptcy,
she suggested I might incur a few months of unpaid bills. Of course,
she warned I could never say this was her legal counsel. I was aware
this would mess up my credit for the next seven years but figured I
needed external assistance to break my credit card spending habit.
Ludicrously, my total indebtedness was $7,500!

As we rolled into 1978, our workplace affair was becoming
obvious to anyone paying attention. The foreman called me in one
afternoon and suggested it might be less distracting for me to work
down at Lakeside Park. Of course, it was the woman who needed to
be transferred.

Lakeside Autonomy

For the first time at Lakeside I was not on a roving crew but rather assigned to a section of landscape on the shore of Lake Merritt. I shared a small boiler room in the basement of the old boathouse with one other gardener—a great guy named Dennis. Once a day, our foreman would drop by to pick up our time sheets and inform us of any particular tasks for the coming day.

Though we began the day together in the boiler room, we then went off in opposite directions to our various sections. If it rained, we'd just hunker down together, frequently smoking dope. One rainy morning, I grew weary of the leaks in my VW bus, which required keeping a bath towel in the shelf below the dash, wringing it out at each stop light.

Only a few blocks away was Oakland's Auto Row, so when there was a break in the downpour, I drove the short distance and shopped for a new car. An hour later, with my bus accepted as a minimal trade-in, I drove back to the park in a brand new '79 Mazda GLC.

It was such a transformation not even to consider the weather when I drove somewhere. What a delightful experience! Also this exciting new acquisition was helping distract me from pining over Jim. What better? I decided to go on a vacation by myself, stay stoned, and perhaps go skiing.

Adrift in Snow Country

It had been a good year for snowfall, so I decided to try cross-country skiing at Royal Gorge, a resort on the way to Tahoe. I booked a room at a nearby inn, rented some gear, and hit the road.

Royal Gorge is the largest X-C resort in North America with miles of tracks and panoramic views of the eastern Sierra. The Alpen Haus, where I was staying, was very near the trailheads and provided a snowy road upon which to practice maneuvering in the unfamiliar equipment. I figured it should be just like walking on my downhill skis. Not even close! But it was lovely to be out in the quiet while stoned and nursing my wounded heart.

The next morning, I had breakfast in the dining room, grabbed my gear, and drove to the parking lot at the trailhead. A solitary teen sat in a little kiosk and sold tickets to the resort. No one else appeared to be around, so I invited the kid to share a joint with me. We got righteously high and then I hit the trail. By myself.

The snow was soothing to my soul. I love the quiet, pierced by an occasional Steller's Jay and the soft thud of snow cascading out of the trees. The sky was a brilliant, cloudless blue. I never feel closer to God than when I am in the snow. The simple and pure elegance of nature.

Though I had been a sporadic jogger, I found I wasn't very well-conditioned for the rigors of cross-country. And I was still a heavy cigarette smoker. I plodded along slowly, enjoying the environment much more than the exercise; I was not going to last until the end of the day.

I made a very poor decision by diverging from the track I'd been traveling. Good old spirit of (foolish) adventure. I enjoyed walking in snow that wasn't already worked over by folks before me. I kept getting high, pausing to smoke and take in the glorious scenery, and began to think about calling it a day.

I must confess that the confluence of nature and stupidity had left me a bit disoriented. I began to guess which direction the trail-head might be by looking at the path of the sun as it was getting lower. I couldn't be confident about any of it. After a few false starts, reason stepped in and told me, "Just backtrack and follow the path that got you here."

It was becoming late afternoon, and I was getting worried I might be lost. I hadn't seen a single other soul since the kid in the kiosk. I fervently hoped that since we had gotten high together, he might recall that he hadn't seen me pass back his way. As I trudged I pondered what might happen if I didn't find my way back to the car before darkness fell. I just kept walking.

When I eventually realized where I left the main track and then rejoined it, I could see I was only about one hundred yards away from the car when I became lost.

I slept hard that night at the Alpen Haus, exhausted from worry and crying over Jim. I rose early, ate breakfast, packed up, and headed back to Oakland. And gloriously, my car didn't leak and had a great heater!

The Next Big Challenge

When I got back to work, Dennis was quite animated and excited. He told me there were rumors the fire department was going to be hiring and we should go for it. I was skeptical that a woman applicant stood a chance of passing the physical rigors of the qualifying exam, but Dennis was insistent. He claimed that the city was getting federal monies if the hiring list could evidence more diversity than in the past.

Before I got too excited, I decided to check in with my old buddy Bill who had joined the department seven years prior. He confirmed that the rumors were true and was encouraging that I should train for the exam. No date was set for when it would be administered.

This was it, my next big challenge. As with the LSAT and the rigors of law school, a good portion of my motivation was attributable to bucking the odds. I wanted to see if I could do what no other women had done before me. When I was hired as a toll collector, I was only the third woman on the job, with the exception of women who filled in during World War II. And when I was hired as a city gardener, I was just the second woman. I wondered if I could manage to be the first female Oakland firefighter.

I kicked into high gear, joined a nearby gym, and began running around Lake Merritt every day. I was thirty-two and in excellent health other than my smoking and drinking, so I decided to cut back on those activities. Feeling vigorous was a new sensation, and I enjoyed coming out of the fog of a drunk in a dead-end job.

One day, running around the lake with Bill, I felt proud and encouraged when he said, "Of all the women I know, I think you're the only one who could do the job."

Dennis had determined to train for the exam as well, but we took separate paths: he would ride his bike to the job every day from out in East Oakland and I started seriously weight training. But in the gym, I was self-conscious if I knew there were other aspirants there at the same time, especially men. Bill had warned me that men in the department were vicious gossips.

This is the seventies, and just as a woman was not expected to have ridden a motorcycle to Colorado and back, even more I was an oddity in the weight room. I had taken one weight training class at community college and felt confident on my own. But the guys just couldn't leave me alone, forever interfering and trying to instruct me. Later, I learned much of their information about form was faulty.

A Rigorous Routine

Since I was disappearing from my section around the lake to sneak over to the gym in Alameda, my foreman, Ray, complained that every time he looked for me, I was nowhere to be found. Sassy as ever, I told him, "Just because you can't find me, Ray, doesn't mean I'm not here."

Ray seemed to feel that were I transferred to a more precise area, he could better supervise me. He moved me to the Rose Garden, the very same garden where Carolyn Martin's murdered mother was represented on the Mothers' Walk.

This was the first assignment in my seven years in the park department where I actually learned some gardening. I loved the roses and was working with two other guys who were quite decent. The floribunda section was mine alone.

If not familiar with the Morcom Amphitheater of Roses, it's a lovely product of the WPA, one of several in town. (The Woodminster Theater and Cascade are another.) Filled with ficus-clad winding paths, staircases long and short, and a centrally located reflecting pool often visited by migrating birds, it is peaceful, serene, and a great place to get high.

But I dialed back the dope in the name of physical conditioning and mental discipline.

Ray's scheduled visits were fairly predictable. We began work at 7:00 and our foreman would come around to collect our previous days' worksheets around ten. Then lunch hour was at eleven. The only structure in the garden was a building containing the public restrooms and our office upstairs with a small table to lunch at and a shower. The latter because on days we used the three-hundred-gallon spray tank for the roses we needed some place to decontaminate.

So I devised a cardio routine to do on city time. I lapped the large reflecting pool five times, ran the long flight of stairs five times up and back, and traversed every inch of pathway. It was demanding, but I could finish in a total of forty-five minutes. That left just enough time to shower and hop back in my work clothes to meet Ray for his daily visit. He was delighted to finally know where I was.

But once he departed, I trotted to my car, zoomed through the Webster Street Tube, and hit the gym immediately on the other side of the Estuary. That left an hour and a half to lift weights and get back to the Rose Garden before our lunch period was over. I was making great gains in strength, endurance, and confidence. And my coworkers indulged my absences.

My Mentor

Bill continued to nurture me along. I visited his firehouse out by Eastmont Mall and was introduced to group meals and some of the various tools of the trade. I learned the difference between the engine and truck and was tutored about the brotherhood mentality where all crew members chipped in to help the others, even with their home projects. To demonstrate, Bill recruited me to come to his house to help pour a concrete pad for his hot tub.

Bill emphasized how new recruits were judged by their *hustle*, jumping up to be the first to help or showing up for duty as much as an hour early as a courtesy to the firefighter being relieved.

I was still living in Alameda, and Bill advised me to get an Oakland address for my application as city residents were given an additional five points on the hiring list. Some friends helped out with that. Veterans also got a leg up with five points, which would help out Dennis, having served in Vietnam.

Finally, a date was announced for submitting applications for City of Oakland Firefighter!

The Federal Connection

The federal government had committed to grants designed to improve to diversity in hiring. In return, they exerted influence on the design of the physical agility portion of the exam. Also, the removal of previous restrictions as to age, gender, and height. The city must design an exam with job-specific tasks. For example, rather than requiring applicants to perform pull-ups as in the past, they must devise events such as hanging a large exhaust fan high in a doorway to test sufficient upper-body strength.

The city also sponsored an educational program at the Drill Tower (training division) for applicants to learn basics of tools, hydraulics, firefighting techniques, and CPR, hopefully creating a more level playing field among gender, racial and age groups.

I learned the term *adverse impact*, wherein if an entire class of people could not pass one or more events the test was *prima facie* discriminatory. Eventually, dates were announced for the testing to begin, starting with a written exam. Five thousand applicants signed up for the written!

The process moved like molasses but move it did. Word was leaked that only two thousand of those who took the written would be moving on to the next phase—the dreaded agility test. This is where the women would be especially challenged, in particular climbing over a six-foot wall. As one compatriot cheered on, "Just pretend the man is after you." Oh well, another cultural disadvantage, I sighed to myself.

The agility took place over a few days at the drill yard. The tasks to be executed were dragging a 160-pound dummy through a tunnel low enough to require crouching, advancing a charged (full of water) three-inch hose line along an arc as it resisted you staying in bounds, running up the five flights of the tower, then raising a fifty-foot roll of three-inch hose up to the roof and lowering it again. Also, the challenging six-foot wall, hanging the aforementioned smoke ejector in a doorway, and removing (then replacing) very heavy folded canvas tarps called salvage covers from a lower bin in the truck.

All tasks were completed sequentially on the same day. Very, very exhausting but there still was compelling need to hit the gym and forever strive to become stronger.

The number was again cleaved in half, with one thousand hopefuls being cleared to take the oral exam. When my day with the examiners came, I must confess to being greatly assisted by a friend who had been interviewed the previous day.

Eventually, a list of eight hundred candidates was released. Dennis was #11, and I came out #13. Those extra points for residency and veterans proved significant as we, top applicants, all had scores separated by only hundredths of a percent. My final ranking was 99.54 percent!

Then we waited.

A Little History

The federal grants were contingent upon the department having sixty vacancies to fill. A slight hitch was that all throughout the ranks there were personnel *acting* in higher ranks due to grievances and lawsuits claiming racial bias in promotions. Therefore, until the cascade of promotions took place, the existing vacancies were zero.

Slowly, the legal challenges crept through the system. I would call HQ every day, inquiring about the hiring timeline, never realizing that my actions were wholly inappropriate.

By the end of February, we received notice that the first class off the list, my class, would show up for duty the beginning of March. We were to come prepared with black jeans, navy blue sweatshirts and tees, and some serious firefighting boots.

By the grace of God, number one on our list had deferred and left me filling the last slot in our class of twelve. We were properly representative with two women (one White and one Black), four White men (two with fathers in the department), one Latino male, and five Black men. Our youngest classmate was nineteen and the oldest thirty-eight. We ranged from five feet four to six feet four. These demographics were sure to please the feds.

The Next Six Weeks

It took years before I could pass the Drill Tower on Highway 880 without shuddering. These are not happy memories!

Our days in training would always begin with jogging through the produce district and Jack London Square, both nearby. Then into our jeans and T-shirts for some classroom time. Of course, the men could change in the locker room while we two women had to take turns using the restroom as a changing station. Then it was drill, drill, drill. Thank goodness it was springtime and not the height of summer as we dragged and coiled hose and threw ladders on the asphalt training ground. On-duty truck and engine companies would come down to train us on various extension ladders and extraction tools.

The 100' aerial ladder was erected in the yard every day. We were required to climb to the top, hook our legs in the rungs, spread arms out wide, and lean back as far as possible. Even given my life-long love of heights, this was fairly scary one hundred feet off the ground.

This had become a daily exercise due to a previous class when a recruit climbed halfway up and froze, unable to continue upward and afraid to descend. Training had to be certain this wouldn't happen on a fire scene.

Bill's admonitions to *hustle, hustle, hustle* stuck with me; I never needed to have it barked at me as did some other recruits. We washed department vehicles, checked and filled fire extinguishers and air bottles, assembled and disassembled a variety of equipment. All was accomplished wearing heavy turnout coats and gloves. If we would be wearing them at a fire scene, then we needed to train in them. I faked my way through tying various knots while wearing the bulky gloves.

We crawled on hands and knees in the basement of the tower, the room charged with smoke and hoses charged with water, relying on our breathing apparatus and hopefully a sense of direction. There was ample opportunity to observe where individuals might become frightened, claustrophobic or otherwise unsuited for the job.

Our duties as public servants were drilled into us. Never cheat, never steal from a fire scene, represent the department at all times, on or off duty. Always be on time for roll call. Don't hit off sick. Prove how hungry you are for this job because there's eight hundred more behind you, just waiting for someone to drop out or fail. And *hustle, hustle, hustle!*

We trained with wooden ladders even if they had been replaced in the companies by aluminum ones. Hardwoods, hickory and ash, and heavy. Straight ladders, extension ladders, attic ladders, and even a 50' extension ladder that took six members to raise.

The hose was cotton and Dacron jacketed and usually of the three-inch type. Once wet, it became very heavy. Due to the fact it could mildew, we were also trained in proper technique for hanging it up to dry as it would be in the companies.

This certainly isn't the sum of the curriculum, but it does comprise my least favorite parts. The hose was fitted with solid-brass couplings that seemed constantly to crack me in the shins when picking up a donut (a rolled fifty-foot length of hose). I had bruises and hematomas the full length of my legs.

I had to hold it together, but every evening when released, I prayed to make it to the first turn in the road before I burst into tears of exhaustion and physical pain. I was angry about all my classmates who either had wives or parents they lived with who would have dinner waiting and clean laundry for the next day. I sweated through two complete sets of clothing per day and would walk it up to the wash and fold a block away from home. That was a luxury I afforded myself.

The six weeks felt as if they would never come to a close.

The First Hired

Christine held the highest position on the hiring list after number one deferred. She has legitimate claims to being the first woman hired. I, however, was the first to successfully graduate into the companies, thereby being the first *on the line*.

Weekly, each recruit was called into the captain's office for a performance evaluation. As I said, there was another woman in the class, and the brass frequently spoke as if we were one individual: "the women" this and "you women" that. It seemed they were so gun-shy after the racial bias lawsuits that as Christine's performance (the Black recruit) was beginning to show signs of inadequate strength to graduate, it called us both into question.

"We're not sure the women will be ready to graduate on time" was what I heard the captain say as fear gripped me. I hadn't fought this hard only to falter on the threshold. And from what Bill had told me about the department gossip apparatus, I was determined not to begin my career under a cloud of insufficiency. It was bad enough that even fellow classmates would say, "I don't know what you're worried about. They would never fire you," implying that I was an affirmative action hire and somehow protected.

After the meeting with the captain, with just one week left to go until graduation, a fortuitous event occurred on the yard. During an exercise called the LPG drill (for liquid propane gas), my mettle was seriously tested.

This drill was to instruct us in advancing two hose lines, down in a crouch, toward a Christmas tree structure. Each branch of the tree (made of pipe) was spewing out an ignited stream of gas. Since the drill would be performed by more than one group the flames were not extinguished but instead we advanced, used a fog stream to push away the flames, and the person on the nozzle would simulate turning off the valve at the base of the tree. I was on the nozzle position and, therefore, closest to the flames.

The roar from the gas was deafening! Behind me, one to each hose line, were two mates, each of whom I had evidenced showing substandard courage. We made it safely to the shutoff valve, but as we began to retreat, the lads got anxious and began backing out too quickly. Still in a crouch, they pulled me backward and off my feet while the heat from the flames singed the entire front of my hair and left me with very rosy cheeks. I was furious!

I requested to see both the captain and our lieutenant at lunch break. My voice was shaking with emotion as I said, "Please don't group me together with these guys! My entire career would be tainted if I were held back!" They quietly took in my words, then reassured me that the coming week, the last week, would be focused on drills requiring moxie, of which they felt I had plenty.

Rappelling and climbing from floor to floor on the outside of the tower with pompier ladders were definitely exercises that took a lot of nerve; I felt more confident. Christine was notified she would not graduate on time and quietly left the group. However, I still had not been ordered to the tailor for a proper uniform for graduation, whereas all the men had. I can't quantify my anxiety.

On Friday, I was called into the office and told to take the afternoon off and go get my uniform! Graduation was the following Monday!

I would wait until I was safely home to collapse into sobs of relief.

Graduation Day

On Monday families arrived and were directed into our classroom where spirits were high and the air was crackling with jubilation. Everyone was so proud—the recruit class shone in their new uniforms and parents and loved ones beamed approval. One by one, the chief of department called us forward, pinned badges on our breast, and administered the oath of duty. My badge number was number 111, and I really liked that.

For the first time in my life, I felt my parents were actually proud of me and my accomplishment.

After the oath ceremony, we all filed out into the drill yard for cake and coffee, milling about and congratulating one another. I was interviewed by Wendy Tokuda, a local news personality with the CBS affiliate. I had been cautioned by the officers to play down any media attention as it would set me apart and perhaps cause hard feelings among the men.

Later that evening, my parents watched the Tokuda interview on television, and my dad even took snapshots of the screen.

The date was April 19,1980, and it had been exactly one year since the written exam. The wheels of bureaucracy grind slowly.

A Critical Incident

After graduation, we each were assigned to companies. Our schedule for the next six weeks was to report to the Drill Tower for roll call, but at the end of a day of instruction, travel to our individual companies where a twenty-four-hour period was completed. We would be immersed in firehouse culture, get a taste of the schedule, respond to fires, and continue to drill with members of the house. Those drills were then signed off with comments on our progress.

It was on the drill yard one day, just a few months into the job, when a truck company came down to train us on power tools. The truck was typically very burly dudes who considered themselves the manly men of the force. I was approached by one such firefighter.

He seemed huge to me, definitely a weightlifter, and he made a beeline straight for me. Just two inches from my face he stared me down. "Do you *do* girls?"

I was totally taken aback at the inappropriateness of his aggression. I held my ground. I had never lied about being a lesbian and wasn't about to start now. Since sixteen years old, my story was available to anyone who asked, but I had hoped in this new culture to reveal my sexual identity on an individual and interactional basis.

I was stunned by this truckie's boldness but felt compelled to stay true to myself. Maintaining our proximity while thinking quickly, I looked right in his eye and said, "I do what I like!" 'Nuff said.

The most successful people I know
have figured out how to live
with criticism, to lean on the people
who believe in them, and to push
onward with their goals.

—Michelle Obama

Epilogue

Though it might seem that I entered this new world in an elegantly insouciant manner, that braggadocio was short-lived. The incident where I was outed on the drill yard was just the first red flag on the minefield.

This acculturation was met with an endless stream of hostility, insults, isolation, and a firmly held belief that this was no place for a woman. My sole defense was to grow even thicker protective armor while striving to prove I was one of the boys. In many ways, it felt like tiny pieces of my soul were being chipped away as I strived to join in with the misogynist and racist firehouse chatter.

If the lads were crude and coarse, I could meet them head-to-head. If they invited women into the firehouse to dine and then spend the night, I would find a date as well. I accepted the hurtful and backhanded compliments about my cooking ("Well, this will build a turd") with guffaws to evidence what a great sport and team player I could be.

Having been cautioned during training that a new recruit, or FNG (fucking new guy), was subservient and noncontroversial, I was once upbraided by a captain at the dinner table when he said, "You've got a lot of opinions for a fucking new kid."

I watched my classmates and other men receive the mentoring that I had been taught I could expect, but very little seemed available to me. I use the example that if a crew member said at the lunch table, "I'm going to pour my driveway on Saturday," the entire bunch would chime, "I'll be there, brother." Were I to say the same, I would be met with a sarcastic "Oh, have you ever even worked with concrete before?"

Though a few other women had been hired off the list (a total of twelve by the time I left), I never worked with nor saw another woman firefighter during my twenty-four-hour shifts. I delighted when the woman who delivered supplies would come by and I could get a tiny hit of female energy. But those visits were infrequent. While occasionally I would have satisfying discourse with an individual member, once that person was with a group of men, a pack mentality would overcome him and I felt a possible ally was lost.

A primitive dispatch system (now no longer in use) would broadcast *all* calls to the emergency phone line, even wrong numbers, regardless of the district from which it came. The men seemed able to sleep right through these calls, magically waking when it was for our particular station. Returning from a run, they just as mysteriously fell back into heavy slumber, belching and farting loudly as was their wont. It became increasingly difficult for me to get more than a couple of hours of sleep during the entire twenty-four-hour shift.

I eventually promoted within the ranks to engineer of the fire department. It then became my job to maintain and drive the engine, pump water at fires, and change out and service our breathing apparatuses. I received the highest test score the department had ever recorded on a promotional exam and was number one on the hiring list. I went for this position as it afforded more longevity than running in and out of toxic environments. So you see, I *was* intending to live out a full career.

As I learned more about myself, the schisms began to eat at me. I realized that, at home, I was not the same woman I was at the firehouse; I disliked who I had become. The anxieties over my metamorphosis combined with a developing and serious sleep disorder which resulted in deep depression and immunosuppression. This was not working for me.

I reflected on my once-rebellious nature and the irony that, in seeking family and belonging in a structure which would guide me and then not finding that family glow, I only wanted to rebel against authority in this paramilitary world. Something had to give. With the help of a compassionate woman doctor who prescribed time away from the firehouse and a recommendation that I assent to antidepressants, I came to see that healing my soul required leaving my job.

In the thirty-plus years since my retirement, I have flourished. For over twenty years, I had my own business as a personal fitness trainer, working almost entirely with aging women and even took on a stint bodybuilding. I thank the department for instilling my commitment to maintaining physical fitness and also for the chance to challenge their strictures and help pave the way for the women who came behind us early ones.

I survived, I prevailed, and I age contentedly in Oakland to this day.

About the Author

Lin Gentry was born, raised, and still lives in Oakland, California. Part of the boomer generation, she lived through a tumultuous fast-changing period of American history—the 1960s and '70s. Throughout her childhood years in the 1950s, she struggled with the gender expectations put upon suburban little girls and found herself in the vanguard of an emerging culture which confronted and challenged traditional values and customs, choosing to navigate a time of massive societal change through rebellion against and rejection of boundary limitations while embracing alternative cultural ways. Lin was on the front lines of this American cultural revolution which continues to influence even today's attitudes, mores, and ways of being. In this fast-paced, racy, daring, and convention-defying account of her first thirty-five years, Lin reveals her personal struggles, confrontations, successes, and failures in the midst of this cultural upheaval.